The Economic Sociology of Development

Economy and Society series

The Economic Sociology of Development

Andrew Schrank

polity

First published in 2023 by Polity Press

Polity Press
65 Bridge Street
Cambridge CB2 1UR, UK

Polity Press
111 River Street
Hoboken, NJ 07030, USA

ISBN-13: 978-1-5095-0525-8
ISBN-13: 978-1-5095-0526-5(pb)

A catalogue record for this book is available from the British Library.

Library of Congress Control Number: 2022941552

Typeset in 11 on 13pt Sabon
by Cheshire Typesetting Ltd, Cuddington, Cheshire
Printed and bound in Great Britain by TJ Books Ltd, Padstow, Cornwall

The publisher has used its best endeavours to ensure that the URLs for external websites referred to in this book are correct and active at the time of going to press. However, the publisher has no responsibility for the websites and can make no guarantee that a site will remain live or that the content is or will remain appropriate.

Every effort has been made to trace all copyright holders, but if any have been overlooked the publisher will be pleased to include any necessary credits in any subsequent reprint or edition.

For further information on Polity, visit our website:
politybooks.com

Contents

Tables and Figures

Acknowledgments

My thoughts on the economic sociology of development have been informed by conversations with a multitude of friends, students, and colleagues over the years. They include Dan Breznitz, Sam Cohn, Candelaria Garay, Nafisa Halim, Hsu Huang, Greta Krippner, Marcus Kurtz, Deepak Lamba-Nieves, Juan Pablo Luna, Gerry McDermott, Kristen McNeill, Vicky Murillo, Dietrich Rueschemeyer, Clemente Ruiz Durán, Steve Samford, Ken Shadlen, Josh Whitford, Juan Bogliaccini and his students at the Universidad Católica del Uruguay, and Chris Yenkey and the participants in his "Globalizing Organization Theory" workshop at the University of South Carolina, none of whom are responsible for my oversights or errors. Special shout-outs go to Kevan Harris, Felipe González, Aldo Madariaga, and Aeron Hunt for their encouragement; Karina Jákupsdóttir and Jonathan Skerrett for their patience; the anonymous reviewers for their feedback; Gail Ferguson and Evie Deavall for editorial feedback; and CIFAR for intellectual and material support. I dedicate this book to Mike Piore, though it will do neither his scholarship nor his friendship justice.

Preface: The Scope of this Book

What is the economic sociology of development? The answer depends first and foremost on what we mean by "development." I'll devote an entire chapter to this in the pages that follow, but for now let's just say that it's economic growth and its typical concomitants: urbanization, education, fertility and mortality decline, etc. This leads to a related question: Does the word "development" in the phrase "economic sociology of development" refer to a *process* – to be conceptualized, measured, explained, or invoked by economic sociologists – or a *place*: the so-called Global South? The answer delimits the boundaries of this book.

The question itself may seem silly. Most dictionaries define development as "the process of developing," or something similar, and make no mention of geography. So the answer – development is a *process* – would seem self-evident. But "metropolitan sociology" (Connell 2010) is decidedly parochial. It focuses almost exclusively on the metropolitan societies of Western Europe and their former settler colonies in North America and the Antipodes and assigns almost any study that takes place in the Global South to a poorly defined "sociology of development."[1] So an ethnographic study of an impoverished neighborhood in the United States is related to urban sociology, while an ethnography of a shantytown in Lima is a contribution to the sociology of development. Nor is methodology central to the assignment or assessment. One finds similar inconsistencies in the classification of survey-based and quantitative research on problems and processes like education, deviance, secularization, and family formation as well: if their data come from the Global North, they're assigned to a substantive subfield rooted in a common theory or problem; if their data come from the Global South, they're assigned to a more encompassing – but less coherent – field of "development" that's really just a residual category for any and all scholarship that takes place outside the metropole.

I balk at this division for two principal reasons. First, I think it's inimical to sociological progress. No less an authority than Emile Durkheim understood that "more advanced societies" could only be understood by way of comparison with their "less developed" counterparts (Lukes 1982: 10), and his sentiment rings no less true today than a century ago, despite his anachronistic language. And, second, I think it reproduces the broader tendency not only to define "the metropolc as a world unto itself" (Connell 2010: 76) but to give that world priority in social research and theory. When problems and processes that are analyzed on their own terms in the North are treated as mere aspects of development in the South, the "metropole/periphery division" (Connell 2010: 78) reproduces itself to the discredit and detriment of the latter.

I didn't set out to write a comprehensive survey of sociology in the Global South. I have neither the expertise to do so nor an interest in reproducing the existing divisions, and I'm therefore limiting my focus to development as a social and historical process. Where does it come from? How does it manifest itself? And how do the answers vary over time and place? Issues like education, deviance, secularization, and family formation will come up, of course, but mostly as they relate to the broader process of development and not as outcomes to be explained in their own right. The same can be said for an array of problems and processes in the Global South that deserve much more attention than they currently receive in metropolitan sociology: aging, identity, protest, and professionalization, to name but a few. Where they weigh upon the broader process of development, they'll be addressed to the best of my ability. Where they're outcomes in their own right, however, they'll be left for somebody with more time and expertise. This isn't an assessment of their importance; on the contrary, it's a recognition of my own limitations.

In short, this is neither a survey of sociology in the Global South nor a thoroughgoing evaluation of any single subfield in the periphery; it's an effort to understand the process of development by drawing upon sociological theory and methods, particularly theory and methods associated with the subfield of economic sociology (Smelser and Swedberg 2005; Krippner and Alvarez 2007; Granovetter and Swedberg 2011). I have long worried that the discipline of sociology and the subject of development have drifted too far apart, at least in the Anglo-American world where I spend the bulk of my time, and I'm writing this book in a self-conscious effort to bring them back together: to bring the issue of development back into the core of sociological theory, and to bring the core of sociological theory – particularly economic sociology – to bear on the question of development. I can't do so without drawing upon a broad array of sociological theory, and I plan to draw upon classical and contemporary theory in the pages to follow.

In doing so, moreover, I'll draw broad conceptual distinctions and leave many details and subtleties to the side. According to the late Clifford Geertz, to whom I'll return in short order, Max Weber once said that it's "only because things are so very confused in practice that we must make our distinctions clear in theory" (Geertz 1956b: 157). I have no idea whether Geertz's quote is accurate or apocryphal. But I completely agree with his sentiment. And I therefore try to invoke, introduce, and defend categories and classifications that are neither natural and self-evident nor pure social constructs but are instead subject to at least a "pragmatic definition of objectivity" (Zuckerman 2012: 232). What this means in practice is that I go to great lengths to distinguish "social facts" like marriage and money, which couldn't exist without human agreement and institutions, from "brute observational facts" like rivers and rising temperatures, "which exist whether or not there is agreement that they do" (Ruggie 1998: 856), and try to figure out whether and how the latter constrain the former. The result is a pragmatic alternative to both "pure realism," which tends to take institutions that are both malleable and controversial for granted, and "pure constructionism," which is oblivious to objective constraints on human behavior (Zuckerman 2012: 231).

Finally, I'm not taking a normative position on the desirability of development itself. Some view it as a worthy, or self-evident, goal (World Bank 2019). Others are profoundly skeptical for various reasons (Escobar 1995; Ziai 2013). But almost nobody denies the differences between the "developed" and "developing" worlds, or the "core" and "periphery" of the world-system, and I'll therefore do my best to leave the normative questions – on which I am of mixed minds – to the reader and focus my own attention on the empirical.

The book is intended for undergraduate and graduate students who are already familiar with the foundations of sociology. If read carefully, however, I think it could be understood by readers who lack a sociological background. The first chapter begins by documenting the "epistemological break" that occurred between the belle époque, when "imperial sociology" addressed the question of development in an admittedly Eurocentric fashion, and the mid-twentieth century, when "empirical sociology" in the United States in particular turned inward to address the "problems of metropolitan states" (Connell 2010: 74–5) and relegated the study of development to an interdisciplinary field populated by a broader array of social scientists. It goes on to chronicle the breakdown of interdisciplinary development studies in the decades that followed, when economists began to impose northern models and assumptions – including the full employment of all resources and self-interested behavior of individuals – on southern societies, and sociologists got distracted by an internecine struggle between adherents of modernization theory, on the one hand, and neo-Marxism, on the other. It holds that partisans of these distinct sociological perspectives contributed to their own marginalization (Viterna and Robertson 2015: 246) from the broader debates on development by embracing one, but not both, of the core economic assumptions: the full employment of all resources, in the case of modernization theorists; and self-interested behavior, in the case of neo-Marxists. And it concludes that an *economic sociology of development* would part company with both *mainstream development economics* and the traditional *sociology of development* by, first, abandoning both of these ahistorical assumptions and, second, taking actors, organizations, and institutions in the Global South – no less than in the Global North – on their own terms. Subsequent chapters bring sociological insights to bear on: the conceptualization and measurement of development (chapter 2); the structure and status order of the international economy (chapter 3); the correlates and causes of upward and downward mobility within that hierarchy in the Cold War era (chapter 4); the origins and diffusion of national development strategies since the Cold War (chapter 5); and the prospects for the economic sociology of development in the years ahead (chapter 6). In the end, I hold that development: entails more than just economic or output growth; demands sociocultural and not merely policy change; is likely to pit countries and people against each other, particularly in a world of finite resources; and is therefore no less the province of sociology – with its focus on culture, conflict, and order – than of economics and the related social sciences.

1

Introduction

Why do migrants from "developing" countries like Mexico, Morocco, and Sri Lanka take their lives in their hands in an effort to reach "developed" countries like the United States, Spain, and Australia (Feldmann and Durand 2008; Siegel 2013)? Why do Bangladeshi garment workers earn less in a month than North American consumers pay for a pair of the pants they stitch together in a few minutes (Wolf 2010)? Why does a resident of Delhi have to work for a week and a half to buy 100 kilograms of rice when his cousin in London can do so in a single day (UBS 2006: 11)? Does the prosperity of the Londoner presuppose the poverty of the Indian (Hickel, Sullivan, and Zoomkawala 2021)? And is "the number of hours it takes an unskilled male to earn enough to buy 100 kilograms of the staple food grain" (Wade 1990: 39) really a good measure of the depth of hardship, or the prospects of the poor, in today's world?

Most contemporary observers look for answers to questions like these in economics. Professional economists tend to dominate donor agencies like the World Bank and the International Monetary Fund (IMF), occupy core cabinet ministries at the national level, and hold a commanding presence in the mainstream and social media (Markoff and Montecinos 1993; Best 2018: esp. ch. 6). Their worldview is dominant in both the policy schools that train elite bureaucrats and the law schools that mold the judiciary (Popp Berman 2022: 20). And the "dismal science" is frequently portrayed as the "queen of the social sciences," much to the chagrin of sociologists – whose limited intellectual and policy influence extends to issues like aging, crime, education, and poverty that are by all accounts central to their discipline (Wolfers 2015). But for all of their power and influence, mainstream economists have left a number of questions unanswered, including the nature of development itself, whether it's a zero-sum game or a positive-sum competition, its institutional requisites, and their apparent inimitability.

This book therefore offers a sociological alternative by asking four related questions: First, what do we mean by development? Is it synonymous with economic growth, or does it convey a broader and/or more subjective notion of human potential and well-being? Second, is development gradational or relational? Is it more like a footrace, in which all countries move forward at different paces, or a football game, in which some countries win by overwhelming and enervating others? Third, whether you think development is more like a "gradational" footrace or a "relational" football game, what differentiates the winners from the losers? What's the winning formula? And, fourth, why don't all countries adopt the winning formula if it's available? What holds some back?

The classical sociology of development

These questions are hardly new to sociology. After all, the standard origin story portrays the discipline as a late nineteenth- and early twentieth-century effort to come to grips with the growth of "modernity," including industrialization, urbanization, and education, in the "western" nations of Europe, North America, and the Antipodes (Bottomore 1971; Ritzer 2011). And sociology has at times been labeled, or perhaps reduced to, the "science of industrial society" (Collin 2011: 206), one that's distinctly "modern" in origins and orientation (Greenfeld 1996a: 3). While this view has come in for considerable criticism of late (Connell 1997), three key aspects of the classical sociology of development are not in serious dispute.

First, for whatever reason, and however labeled or explained, key differences between "the West and the Rest" (Hall 1992) had taken hold by the start of World War I. Life expectancy at birth had almost doubled in the West and barely moved in the "rest" over the course of the previous two centuries (Maddison 2001: 31; see also Riley 2005). Literacy gaps between the two "regions" were similarly pronounced and relatively recent in origin (Abel and Bond 1929; Winthrop and McGivney 2015). And European sociologists were at least broadly familiar with these, and related, differences in part due to colonial contact (Connell 2010: 74). The question was less whether the differences were real or imaginary, therefore, than how to understand and interpret them (Connell 1997: 1520).

Second, early sociology highlighted the idea of "global difference" (Connell 1997: 1517) between an allegedly "civilized" metropole and a putatively "primitive" periphery. The so-called classical sociologists didn't so much ignore the non-western world as treat it with contempt. When Marx referred to "the idiocy of rural life," for example, he was expressing a common sentiment (Jepperson and Meyer 2011: 64), and the non-western world was largely rural. Urbanization was another relatively recent difference between the metropole and the periphery (Sjoberg 1955).

And, third, the most influential approaches inspired at least three different accounts of the divergence of the West and the rest that continue to animate and inform research today. The first is broadly Marxist in orientation and traces the "rise of the West" (Hall 1992: 187) to the emergence of "capitalist" labor and property markets in northwestern Europe (Brenner 1986). The second is largely Weberian in origin and assigns responsibility to the emergence of impersonal rule by expert judges and bureaucrats in Western Europe more generally (Lange 2005). And the third is associated with Durkheim and his notion of "collective consciousness" (Rueschemeyer 1994: esp. 66–7). While their influence has waxed and waned over time, the Marxist, Weberian, and Durkheimian approaches offer essential background to the material to come and merit a brief exegesis.

Capitalism and development

In their efforts to explain development outcomes, orthodox Marxists ask two questions of the direct producers – e.g., workers, cultivators, hunter-gatherers – in any given society. First, do they have access to the means of their own reproduction or survival? If they're able to grow, hunt, or find food on their own, without recourse to trade or market exchange, the answer is yes. And, second, are they subject to extra-economic coercion by non-producers? If they're forced to work for the non-producers on an involuntary basis, whether directly or indirectly, the answer is also yes. And the answers to these two questions leave us with four possible incentive systems, or "modes of production," and their corresponding outcomes, summarized in Table 1.1.

When the direct producers are free from extra-economic coercion and have access to the means of reproduction, they'll have neither an incentive to maximize wealth and investment nor the institutions they would need to do so (e.g., retail and wholesale outlets, credit markets, courts, etc.); instead, they'll feed themselves and their families and cycle between good times marked by abundance, leisure, and population growth, on the one hand, and

Table 1.1 Modes of production and their predicted consequences in the Marxist tradition

| | | Are the direct producers subject to extra-economic coercion? | |
		No	Yes
Do the direct producers have access to their means of reproduction?	No	Capitalism: surplus production, productive investment, and growth	Slavery: surplus production, unproductive investment, and stagnation
	Yes	Subsistence economy: cycles of prosperity and stagnation	Feudalism: surplus production, unproductive investment, and stagnation

4

bad times marked by scarcity, mortality, and stagnation, on the other. Shifts from good times to bad, and vice versa, will largely be driven by changing demographic, epidemiological, or meteorological circumstances. And the "subsistence economies" that result are unlikely to give rise to either rapid growth or significant inequality (Samuelson 1971: 407; see also Domar 1970).

When they're subject to extra-economic coercion, however, the direct producers will generate a surplus that will be appropriated by non-producers, like feudal landlords (or seigneurs) and slaveholders, who are compelled to compete by "investing in the means of coercion, rather than the means of production" (Brenner 1986: 42). The enserfed have access to "plots of their own," for example, but are legally obligated to devote part of their time to the lord's land and/or pay feudal dues of various sorts (Elster 1986: 86), and the enslaved are human chattel who lack the right to their land and output and devote almost all of their time to the demands of their owners.[1] The production of surplus crops by the enserfed and enslaved, and their appropriation by landlords and planters, are therefore indisputable and indispensable elements of labor-repressive agriculture. But the seigneurs and slaveholders who appropriate the surplus are by their very nature at risk of rebellion or attack and are therefore forced to allocate the surplus not to the development and deployment of new techniques and technologies but to the procurement of weapons, warriors, and watchmen. Otherwise, they risk overthrow by their subordinates or defeat by rivals who are themselves well-armed and belligerent, and the "development of the means of coercion at the expense of the development of the means of production" (Brenner 1986: 42) is the likely result.

In other words, the landlords and planters who exploit labor-repressive agriculture are compelled to compete not by investing their surplus in the "forces of production" that underpin dynamic economies but by allocating their surplus to the "forces of repression" that keep their unruly subordinates under control and their rival landholders at bay. When they emerge victorious, therefore, they retain their wealth and status but forgo the opportunity to raise productivity, for productivity gains presuppose investment in infrastructure, tools, and technology, not in arms and armies. And the resulting modes of production are thus inclined not toward growth and development but toward long-term conflict and stagnation. The demise of slavery and serfdom in the late second millennium arguably underscores this point. Both systems of labor control died violent deaths and left underdeveloped economies in their wake.

Growth is therefore most likely in capitalist societies that create an entirely different incentive structure by depriving non-producers of the means of repression and producers of the means of reproduction. Producers who are free from extra-economic coercion and lack access to the means of reproduction are both allowed and – in some sense – compelled to look for the best-paying jobs available. Otherwise, they'll starve. Non-producers who lack the ability and authority to coerce producers are left with little choice but to hire workers for a wage, on the one hand, and maximize their productivity, on the other. If they fail to do so, after all, they'll lose market share to rival producers who make and sell better products than they do for less money. And the employers who constitute the dominant class under capitalism therefore redirect their surplus not into arms and armies but into new techniques and technologies in an effort to capture market share. Marxists tend to refer to this as capitalism's "GOD imperative, for Grow or Die" (Kunkel 2011) and to debate its relative merits – ranging from raising material living standards to fostering ecological catastrophe.

This is a powerful account that has much to offer, but it raises as many questions as it answers, not least with regard to the origins of capitalism itself. We have good reason to believe that capitalism emerged in northwestern Europe in the later Middle Ages, and was subsequently disseminated to the New World, Northeast Asia, and parts beyond by means of mimicry, military conquest, and settler colonialism. And we have no less reason to believe that the "original transition from feudalism to capitalism" was less the result of some grand design than the "unintended consequence" (Brenner 1977: 78–82) of persistent conflict between serf and seigneur. While the serfs were able to gain their freedom through a combination of fight and flight, according to historian Robert Brenner, they were unable to take control of the lord's land or gain access to the means of reproduction (Brenner 1976: 51). And this left both parties on the horns of a dilemma: the lords had land but nobody to work it; and their former serfs were effectively "free to find a job" in a society that lacked a functional labor market or "free to starve if they couldn't" (Rediker 1987: 17). It was in this context, according to Brenner, that richer peasants (i.e., tenants) began to rent land from the lords, pay ex-serfs and their descendants to work it, and undertake improvements – like irrigation, fertilization, specialization, and animal husbandry – on pain of either defeat by competitors who undertook improvements of their own or eviction by landlords who wanted to maximize rents (Brenner 1977: 76; see also Brenner 1976: esp. 64). If the tenant did not maximize productivity by undertaking improvements, Brenner argued, he would fall into a vicious circle of declining profit, declining funds for reinvestment, and eventually "eviction by the landlord, who could then seek a new tenant more able to make the necessary improvements to compete on the market" (Brenner 1977: 76). In a sense, therefore, the tenants were the original subjects of the GOD imperative.

The Marxist account of the emergence of the "'three-tiered' relation of landlord/capitalist tenant/free wage labourer" (Brenner 1977: 75) is thus triply enlightening. First, it explains the dramatic growth of output in early modern England. When forced to choose between improvement and insolvency, it implies, rational tenants opted to improve their land, and thereby ushered in an agricultural revolution that not only transformed the countryside but substituted capital for human labor, facilitated urbanization, and fueled industrial growth in the cities by simultaneously freeing up resources and fostering demand for manufactured goods. Second, it explains the "grow or die" nature of capitalism more generally. Like their progenitors in early modern England, argue the Marxists, today's capitalists are forced to reinvest their profits in an effort to raise productivity and make – or exceed – the average rate of profit. Otherwise, they'll fall into debt, despair, and bankruptcy. And, finally, it offers a powerful account of both England's rise to global hegemony and its eventual supersession by the United

States and perhaps China. The basic idea is that capitalism not only motivated but facilitated England's quest for markets and raw materials and thus built a powerful feedback loop: economic growth fueled military expansion; and military expansion fueled economic growth, at least in the short run. And England's successors have followed similar trajectories: the United States in the late nineteenth and twentieth centuries, when the Civil War put paid to slavery in the South and opened the door to industrialization, growth, and global hegemony; and China today, when market reforms appear to have ushered in an era of economic dynamism.

But these accounts are nonetheless incomplete, for they're not institutionally self-contained. We're left to wonder, for example, how the key British stakeholders could trust the fragile institutions of capitalism before they had been institutionalized. Why didn't landlords simply expropriate improvements made by tenants? Why did tenants make improvements in the first place where expropriation seemed possible? What if some landlords used their residual means of coercion to dispossess others who had divested from arms and armies into fields and fertilizers? Why did landlords divest in this way, in the first place, if they couldn't see the outcome in advance? And what about the producers themselves, during the drawn-out transition from "peasant to proletarian" (Rediker 1987: 17)? How did they know they'd actually get paid for their efforts? And which, if any, jobs did they take if they couldn't be sure? Ask yourself what you would have done if you'd been in their positions during those tumultuous times. Would you have bet on promises and guarantees that had yet to be institutionalized or dug in your heels to defend what you already had?

These aren't rhetorical questions. Without some sort of institutional guarantee – whether normative, spiritual, or juridical – you wouldn't be willing to give the barber a fifty-dollar bill for a twenty-dollar haircut (Granovetter 1985: 489), let alone to sink enormous investments into irrigation systems on somebody else's land, spend a week working for somebody else in anticipation of a wage on Friday, or dispense with your retainers when their future role was uncertain. But the sources of those guarantees lie, at best, in the background of the Marxist account. It's fine to note that England had strong customary norms and a precocious legal system at the time. But this just pushes the question of transition back to the origins of those norms and systems (Sayer 1992).

The rule of law and capitalism

The development of capitalist institutions can be seen as a coordination problem. It's entirely possible that everybody, or almost everybody, would be better off under capitalism than feudalism and nonetheless be unable to anticipate that outcome or facilitate it in the absence of credible guarantees from their peers, rivals, and/or compatriots. Why should I surrender my rights under feudalism, meager though they may be, if I don't know what's coming down the road? While Marxists tend to address this problem by portraying capitalism as the unintended consequence of intentional class conflict, they leave the *resolution* of that conflict unaddressed, perhaps due to the teleological nature of their underlying worldview (Stinchcombe 1999: 52). Conflict resolution itself is a coordination problem, after all, and there's no guarantee that it will be solved, let alone solved in a dynamic capitalist fashion.[2]

Weber and his descendants viewed "large-scale coordination problems" (Lange 2005: 48) like this as a major, perhaps the major, obstacle to development. In the absence of formal institutions of coordination and conflict resolution, they argue, the prospects for development will dissolve not only in pre-capitalist societies, as in the Marxist account, but in their capitalist counterparts as well; hence, the widespread invocation of adjectives to account for the decoupling of capitalism and development in the twenty-first century. What are "political capitalism" (Ganev 2009), "patrimonial capitalism" (Mihályi and Szelényi 2017), "booty capitalism" (Auyero and Kilanski 2015: 399), and other varieties of "capitalism-with-adjectives" (Taylor 2014: 3), after all, if not the combination of *individuals who are beholden to capitalist markets* and *markets that afford them no institutional guarantees*? In political capitalism, for example, politicians and their allies manipulate markets to their own benefit and to the detriment of those who lack political connections or institutional protections.

Where would such protections come from? And what would they look like? The standard answer is the state, and involves safeguards against two distinct threats to economic activity: mistakes, like misunderstandings and miscommunication between exchange partners; and malfeasance, including crime and corruption.[3] Both threats can derail or destroy transactions that would otherwise prove satisfying to all parties concerned and conducive to economic growth. Both must therefore be avoided. And the key to their avoidance lies in public officials – like judges, regulators, and service providers of different sorts – who are recruited by exam, subject to degree requirements, well remunerated, and granted lifetime tenure.

Exams and degree requirements are both familiar and easy to understand. They're a reasonable proxy for expertise, in most societies, and experts are less likely to make mistakes than amateurs. Accountants are less likely to miscalculate your taxes; lawyers are less likely to misinterpret your contracts; and teachers are less likely to miseducate your children – at least if they themselves have been well educated. Hence the need for exams and/or degree requirements.

But why the need for good pay and life tenure? While they've frequently been portrayed as sources of public sector cohesion, or *esprit de corps*, they're no less an impediment to government malfeasance, including bias, favoritism, and outright corruption. After all, the returns to corruption are a known function of the immediate bribes and payoffs available to the official involved. When illicit payments are higher, the corrupt official makes more money. But the costs of corruption are an unknown function of the official's expected lifetime earnings multiplied by the risk of discovery and dismissal (discounted by the relevant interest rate and the opportunity cost of continued employment by the government). If corrupt officials are likely to be dismissed from high-quality, stable jobs, the costs of corruption are higher. And officials who are well paid and confident in their career prospects are, therefore, likely to find corruption less rewarding and appealing in a relative sense than officials who are poorly paid and insecure. Or, to put the matter more bluntly, you're a lot less likely to take (or demand) a bribe that puts a well-paid, secure job at risk than one that puts a poorly paid, insecure job at risk.

Ideally, therefore, public officials are dedicated professionals who are imbued with job security. While the differences between judges and bureaucrats, in particular, are well known (see, e.g., Fiss 1983), the ideal-typical judge no less than the ideal-typical bureaucrat boasts credentials and life tenure. The degree to which this is true in any given society will of course vary (Centeno 1997; Evans and Rauch 1999; Ríos-Figueroa and Staton 2014). And it's at least to some degree in tension with democratic principles since it potentially ties the hands of both voters and their elected representatives (Andersen 2018). But the broad outlines of this system are for the most part well regarded (see, e.g., Olsen 2005) and have, if anything, grown more so in light of recent global challenges like climate change and pandemic preparedness (see, e.g., Drechsler 2020).

The result, moreover, is a powerful account of both national development outcomes and international institutions. Where the rule of law is guaranteed by secure professionals, it implies, conflict recedes, coordination takes hold, public goods – ranging from roads to schools to basic norms of calculability – emerge, and the foundations of capitalist development are laid: individuals invest and hire labor; workers spend their wages and salaries on goods and services; and the result is a feedback loop marked by investment, employment, and growth. Where the state is staffed by amateurs, cronies, and partisans, however, the rule of law is tenuous and development is measured, marked by less investment and by employment of less quality and stability. And the global powers that come out on top in this struggle therefore *boast the rule of law* and *build a world in their image*. "The peripheral country is 'free' to say no," explains Michael Mann, "but the deterrents are powerful – the denial of foreign investment and perhaps of foreign trade" (Mann 2013: esp. 215–16).

Like the Marxist account, however, the Weberian alternative fails to fully address the question of institutional origins. It's one thing to say that capitalist societies are most dynamic when they're governed by expert, secure authorities who are able to impose the rule of law; it's another thing entirely to explain where those authorities come from and how they're institutionalized in the first place. We can't just build them by passing a civil service law or mandating judicial independence, note the skeptics, since it's the effectiveness of those laws and mandates that we're trying to explain in the first place. And we can't explain their varying effectiveness by invoking *other* agencies or institutions (e.g., the anti-corruption authority, the courts, foreign investors, or donors) for the same reason: it simply pushes the question of institutional origins and effectiveness one step further down the road.

The non-contractual elements of the rule of law

Existing accounts of state formation tend to be functionalist in nature. They portray the political preconditions of "rational" capitalism – as opposed to capitalism with adjectives – as products of war, revolution, or scarcity and their functional requisites. When existential crisis arrives, in other words, impersonal rule and rational capitalism emerge to solve the problem. But for every society that has responded to a major crisis by institutionalizing political authority along these lines, there are many more that have failed, only to be overrun, colonized, carved up, or condemned to ongoing poverty. There's no law of nature that says effective governments must arise where they're in demand; on the contrary, they're a rare and vulnerable breed.

What, then, underpins state formation? One answer is to follow sociological pioneer Emile Durkheim by noting that every contract, including the public sector employment contract, has a "non-contractual element," or a normative basis lying outside the contract itself. "'What governs the governor of a governed order?' is another way to render this viewpoint" (Hammond 1989: 380). And Durkheimians locate the answer in the so-called collective consciousness (Rueschemeyer 1994: 65–6), or the moral, normative, and cultural underpinnings of the society as a whole.

In fact, Dietrich Rueschemeyer has gone beyond the standard Durkheimian approach by acknowledging not only the non-contractual bases of contract but the "non-bureaucratic normative foundations" of bureaucracy as well (Rueschemeyer 2005: 147). One cannot simply pass a civil service law and expect a bureaucratic revolution, he implies. The law must be institutionalized if it is to be internalized; it must be internalized if it is to be institutionalized; and it seems to gain purchase at the ground level when it is embedded in officials who share similar backgrounds and are imbued with an *esprit de corps*. "Clearly, the development of these complementarities and their extension across different groups are incremental processes that take time" (Rueschemeyer 2005: 147), explains Rueschemeyer, and we have only the vaguest sense of how that happens (McDonnell 2020; Schrank 2020) – if it happens at all.

The Durkheimians hardly ignored the dictates of efficiency and competition (Durkheim 1982: 51). But they devoted more of their attention to shared norms, values, and cultures, and they put the professions and professionalization front and center. What is *esprit de corps*, after all, but a collective commitment to a set of norms that are grounded in "similar origins, shared education, stable career prospects and a common privileged status in society" (Rueschemeyer 2005: 145)? But this simply pushes the question back to where and when *esprit de corps* takes hold and why it takes a particular shape or drives a particular action orientation. Some suggest that it's a pure social construct (de Miranda 2020), and that efficiency considerations have nothing to do with it. But inefficient spirits do not win wars, foster innovation, raise living standards, or take the helm of the world-system. And we're thus left to try to pull all these pieces together.

Beyond single-bullet theories of development and underdevelopment

It seems clear, upon reflection, that each of the dominant sociological traditions posits a "single-bullet theory" (Bearman 2010) of development (and underdevelopment) by prioritizing a different social institution: the market, the state, and the normative under-pinnings of both market *and* state respectively. In the Marxist tradition, the key lies in the degree of "market-dependence" (Brenner 1977: 74) of the core economic actors. When people have no alternative to market competition, the story goes, they'll minimize costs, maximize profits, and foster economic growth. For Weberians, on the other hand, the key lies in impartial rule by secure experts. Without impersonal rule by capable officials, they argue, the tendency to truck, barter, and accumulate, where present, will be derailed by incompetence and corruption. And for Durkheimians the key is an "inclusive moral community" (Rueschemeyer 1994: 66), without which neither dynamic market competition nor impersonal rule is possible.

Like all single-bullet theories, however, these accounts confuse correlation with causation and seek vindication in "just-so" stories (Bearman 2010). Did market dependence, impersonal rule, and the "noncontractual bases of contract" (Rueschemeyer 1994: 65) emerge in Western Europe during the second half of the second millennium? Did growth follow? And can the case for their association be made? The answer is almost certainly yes; there's a wealth of evidence to that effect, and without it these accounts wouldn't be so influential. But there are enormous gaps between correlation and causation, and plausibility and proof, and for all of their logic and power these accounts leave as many questions as answers.

One is tempted, in this context, to move from a single-bullet theory to a multivariate account by simply *amalgamating* the three classics into a hybrid sociology of development. Market-dependent actors will maximize profit, productivity, and growth when the risks entailed by investment are minimized by impartial experts; impartial experts will actually behave themselves when they're members of a moral community imbued with *esprit de corps*; and moral communities are easier to develop and sustain in pros-perous, well-governed societies, or something like that. But the hypothetical hybrid account suffers from at least two fatal flaws.

First, and most obviously, it fails to specify how a poor society breaks into this feedback loop *de novo* when the key institutions are interdependent, and their institutionalization takes time. If you abolish feudal property relations before the institutionalization of impersonal rule, for example, you may wind up with chaos rather than capitalism. If you abolish patrimonial practices before the moral community has been established, however, you'll probably find that favor trading, bribery, and the sale of offices continue apace. And if you try to build a moral community by means of a policy mandate, you'll find yourself frustrated at best and reviled at worst – depending on the intensity and ferocity of your efforts. You can't legislate morality.

But the second problem is arguably more interesting: The hybrid account assumes, if perhaps implicitly, that the institutions of market dependence, impersonal rule, and social solidarity are complements that reinforce each other, when they may well be substitutes for, or alternatives to, each other. Take, for example, bureaucratization campaigns that are "inconsistent with government officials selling their services to the highest bidder" (Block 2018: 29). Aren't they effectively substituting the state for the market, just as the privatization of public services is a move in the contrary direction (cf. Harris 2013)? Or consider the abandonment of pork-barrel politics, which tend to reward and reinforce community and family networks, for "meritocratic" alternatives, which are by their very nature impersonal (Evans and Rauch 1999). Doesn't this pit impersonal rule against social solidarity? Or, to take one last example, a move from community or market provision to publicly provided reproductive services or eldercare, which almost certainly substitutes the welfare state for social solidarity and/or market dependence.

The point is not simply that the institutional underpinnings of development are as likely to be substitutes as complements, though this is *a* key point, or that development is therefore more like a "combination lock than a padlock" (Wade 1992: 312), though this also rings true. It's that the institutional underpinnings of development are themselves social constructs, and that their contributions and assessment depend in part on concepts and categories that are contextually specific and culturally mediated. When we say that people are market dependent, for example, we mean that they depend on markets to achieve material living standards that are themselves dictated, at least in part, by their cultures (Arrighi 1970) – just as "the definition of impersonal" (Schuyler 1964: 17) and "demands of solidarity" (Spillman and Strand 2013: 88) depend in large part on country and context (see, e.g., McNeill and Pierotti 2021).

Ideas like these are by now commonplace in economic sociology, where a large body of scholarship addresses "more or less conscious efforts to categorize, normalize, and naturalize behaviors and rules that are not natural in any way, whether in the name of economic principles (e.g., efficiency, productivity) or more social ones (e.g., justice, social responsibility)" (Fourcade and Healy 2007: 300). But they have been slow to trickle into the sociology of development due to an "epistemological break" (Connell 1997: 1535), or shift in sociological focus, that took hold in the middle of the twentieth century. Whereas classical sociology addressed differences *between* the West and the rest, albeit in a Eurocentric fashion, the "new sociology" addressed differences and disorder "*within the metropole*" (Connell 1997: 1535), and thereby relegated the question of development to the periphery of the discipline – and/or to "rural sociology" departments in agricultural schools that focused on the problems of agrarian societies. In some ways this was salutary. Peripheral societies and their study were in large part insulated from the worst tendencies of western sociology and "assigned" to history and anthropology.[4] In other ways, however, it was costly, for it simultaneously isolated the periphery from real advances in sociology and ceded territory to inferior alternatives in both the outer reaches of sociology and cognate disciplines. What it was not, however, was unusual, for in the postwar era the non-western world was treated as *sui generis* throughout the northern social sciences and relegated to an interdisciplinary field of development studies that merits additional consideration.

Interdisciplinary development studies in the mid-twentieth century

Interdisciplinary development studies assigned different problems to different disciplines in an effort to build a coherent perspective on post-colonial and/or poor countries. Wages and prices were the realm of economics, to be sure, but the preferences and reactions that drove their evolution and permitted their interpretation were to be studied, rather than simply invoked, as were their institutional foundations and human consequences. This left ample opportunity for political scientists, sociologists, anthropologists, historians, and the like to get in on the act. When he grew frustrated with his own field of economics, for example, Bert Hoselitz began to explore the "non-economic barriers" (Hoselitz 1952) to growth in the early 1950s, and founded a journal dedicated in large part to their study: *Economic Development and Cultural Change (EDCC)*.

Hoselitz was by no means alone at the time. In the 1950s and 1960s, development was seen as an almost inherently interdisciplinary field, in part because mainstream (or "neoclassical") economics made two assumptions that were considered ill-suited to so-called backward or underdeveloped (see, e.g., Myint 1954–5; Leibenstein 1957) societies: first, self-interested behavior on the part of the individual; and second, the full employment of all resources in the economy as a whole. If both assumptions held, of course, individuals would be forced – by dint of necessity – to make trade-offs when allocating their resources and would be inclined – by dint of rationality – to do so in a manner that left them better off than the next available alternative. Self-interested individuals would only give up one thing, in a world of scarce resources and voluntary trade, if they thought whatever they'd get in exchange was even better, and the thing they gave up would necessarily go on to benefit someone else. The result was a sort of Panglossian perspective in which "everything was for the best in the best of all possible worlds" (cf. Solow 1980: 2; Klein 1989: 548). Individuals were little more than self-regarding automatons,

Table 1.2 Maximum output per day in Fredonia and Oceania in units

	Foodstuffs	Manufactured goods
Fredonia	0.5	2.5
Oceania	I	3

who made whatever trade-offs came closest to fulfilling their needs and desires given their resources and opportunities, and countries and communities were little more than aggregations of individuals.

Perhaps the best example of this Panglossian perspective is the theory of "comparative advantage," which has always loomed large in discussions of economic development. In a simple treatment, derived in part from the early nineteenth-century work of David Ricardo, we'll assume a universe in which two countries, Fredonia and Oceania, live off foodstuffs and manufactured goods alone and need a minimum of one unit of food per week to survive. Imagine that the Fredonians can produce a maximum of half a unit of foodstuffs *or* 2.5 units of manufactured goods per day, and the Oceanians can produce a full unit of foodstuffs *or* three units of manufactured goods per day – that is, if they dedicate all of their available resources to one commodity or the other (Table 1.2).

What this means, in practice, is that in the absence of trade, Fredonia has to spend the first two days of the week just meeting its basic food needs, leaving no resources for manufacturing, whereas Oceania can meet its food needs on the first day of the week and produce three units of manufactured goods on the second. If the two countries decide to allocate their resources in this way, moreover, their combined (or *global*) output at the end of two days will be two units of food and three units of manufactured goods.

Nor does such an allocation seem unlikely, at least not at first glance. Both countries have mouths to feed, after all, and Oceania is more productive in both products: twice as productive in foodstuffs, and 20 percent more productive ($3/2.5 = 1.2$) in manufactured goods. Why should the more productive Oceanians waste their time trading with the less productive Fredonians? Why should the less productive Fredonians risk an import surge from

Table 1.3 Consequences of specialization in Fredonia and Oceania

	Foodstuffs	Manufactured goods
Fredonia	0	5
Oceania	2	0

more productive Oceania? One might easily anticipate the pursuit of self-sufficiency in both countries, perhaps as a result of competitive market forces in Oceania and tariffs designed to protect fragile producers in Fredonia.

But Ricardo and his offspring point out that for every three units of manufactures they produce, the Oceanians have to give up a whole week's supply of food – whereas the Fredonians have to forgo a mere 0.6 units of food ($[3^*.5]/2.5 = 0.6$) to produce three units of manufactures – and that it therefore makes sense for the Oceanians to specialize in food, where they have not only an absolute but a relative (or *comparative*) advantage, and trade for manufactures, where the comparative – if not absolute – advantage belongs to Fredonia. If, for example, both countries allocated the first two days of the week entirely to the product in which they had a *comparative* advantage, and traded for the good they'd stopped producing, global production at the end of two days would look like the payoff matrix in Table 1.3.

Their combined output has grown from two units of food and three units of manufactured goods to two units of food and five units of manufactured goods, and both countries can therefore dedicate themselves to specialization going forward, meaning everyone will be better off. Consider the difference, for example, between a week in which both countries pursue self-sufficiency and a week in which they embrace specialization and trade. In the first week, both countries fulfill their food needs first before moving onto manufactures, and produce a joint total of two units of food over three days (two days in Fredonia and one day in Oceania) and 19.5 units of manufactured goods: 7.5 units over the three remaining days in Fredonia ($2.5 \times 3 = 7.5$) and 12 units over the four remaining days in Oceania ($3 \times 4 = 12$). In the second week, Oceania fulfills both the food needs of both countries in the first two days (2 × 2 = 2) and goes on to add nine units of manufactured goods (3 × 3 = 9) to Fredonia's 12.5 units of manufactured goods (5 × 2.5 = 12.5) for a global total of 21.5 units of manufactured goods over the rest of the week.

The key point is not the precise product mix that results but the difference between *absolute* and *comparative* advantage. Whereas the former accrues to the country that produces a good or service at the lowest *overall* cost, the latter accrues to the country that does so at the lowest *opportunity cost,* where "opportunity cost" refers to the value of the next best use of the resources dedicated to a given activity in the first place. So the opportunity cost of a unit of food production in Oceania is three units of manufactured goods, whereas it is five units of manufactured goods in Fredonia, and the opportunity cost of a unit of manufactured goods in Oceania is one-third of a unit of foodstuffs, whereas in Fredonia it's one-fifth, or 20 percent, of a unit of foodstuffs. In *relative* terms, therefore, Oceania forgoes more food to make manufactured goods and Fredonia forgoes more manufactured goods to make food, and it thus makes sense for each country to dedicate itself to the activity in which it has a relative, or *comparative*, advantage and to import the rival product from its neighbor – differences in their overall levels of development or productivity notwithstanding. *In this scenario, resources are fully employed, specialization and trade are in everybody's self-interest, and voluntary exchange redounds to their mutual benefit.*

The so-called law of comparative advantage has an undeniable appeal, and it has been used to justify everything from basketball star Michael Jordan's decision to abandon his dreams of adding baseball to his repertoire in the 1990s (Buckingham 2015: 17–20) to the household division of labor. "If you are much, much better at the laundry and only a little better at cleaning the toilet," explains economist Emily Oster, "you should do the laundry and have your spouse get out the scrub brush" (Oster 2012). Otherwise, you'll forgo the opportunity to make the *most* of your skills in the laundry room in an effort to yield a *slight* improvement in the bathroom. But the law of comparative advantage has been particularly prominent in development economics, where it has been used to defend free trade and condemn government intervention more generally. If relatively poor countries like Fredonia would just let the market work its magic, the literature implies, they would make the most of their admittedly scarce resources by letting their people specialize in whatever they do best – perhaps even jump-starting a bit of growth in the process.

In fact, the most optimistic accounts portrayed the pursuit of comparative advantage in a world of free trade and capital flows as an all but sufficient basis for growth and development. First, they argued, poor countries would specialize in the export of primary products – like food and minerals – and labor-intensive goods and services and, in so doing, foster wage acceleration at home, as employment growth soaked up the labor surplus, and deceleration in rich countries, as unskilled workers lost their bargaining power vis-à-vis both their employers at home and their counterparts overseas. And second, they added, rich countries would respond to diminishing returns on investment by exporting capital to poor countries and, in so doing, transfer new techniques and technology to the latter (Sandilands 2015: 75). Over time, therefore, poor countries would be caught in a virtuous circle of wage and productivity growth that would foster the cross-national convergence of per capita income – unless they opted to forgo their comparative advantages by imposing barriers to trade and foreign direct investment (FDI).

The limits to this Panglossian perspective are by now well known, not least of all among economists themselves. The problem is not only – or even primarily – that poor countries *do* forgo their comparative advantages, though impediments to imports and investment are not at all uncommon, but that the gains from trade and FDI are often smaller in practice than in theory; are not necessarily allocated to the poorest trading partners, let alone to their poorest citizens, when they do emerge; and are not necessarily dynamic in nature – meaning that a shift from self-sufficiency to specialization and trade that generates an *initial* boost in output will not necessarily increase the *rate* of growth over time (Yellen 1998: 25). The analytical problem is not only that "the degree of trade liberalization is hard to define," according to economist

Mehrene Larudee, but that it's hard to distinguish "the long-term effect of liberalization" itself (Larudee 1998: 275) from short-run fluctuations in factors like demand, investment, and inflation. So reasonable minds can differ, and the debate is still unresolved, despite the fact that more than 160 countries have joined the World Trade Organization (WTO) in an effort to "ensure that trade flows as smoothly, predictably, and freely as possible" (World Trade Organization 2021: 1).

Proponents of free trade and investment have reason to believe that they'll foster growth and equity, to be sure, but their critics have no less reason to believe the opposite. Some point out, for example, that the very poorest countries have a comparative advantage in commodities produced by child labor, and that by exploiting their advantage – and their children – they actually derail schooling that would prove more conducive to growth in the long run, and more humane in the here and now (Gordon 1996). Others worry that developing countries will pursue comparative advantages in noxious industries or products to the detriment of their people as well as their environments (Hall 2009). But in the mid-twentieth century, doubts about open markets were, in a sense, rooted in more fundamental reservations about the assumptions of self-interested behavior and fully employed resources that are at the heart of the mainstream model. Skeptics wondered not only whether egotism was really inherent in human nature but whether it was a realistic assumption in poor countries in particular. Hoselitz, for example, believed that "traditional values" posed a "formidable" obstacle to development (Hoselitz 1952: 9). His fellow economist, W. W. Rostow, agreed that the "take-off into self-sustained growth" would require a "major change in political and social structure and, even, in effective cultural values" (Rostow 1956: 27), given that the latter were not particularly "acquisitive" in "traditional societies." And Hoselitz, Rostow, and many of their contemporaries joined forces with sociologist Talcott Parsons to develop "a uniform evolutionary vision of social, political, and economic development" (Margavio and Mann 1989: 110), inspired by classical sociology that came to be known as modernization theory.

Orthodox modernization theorists held that the western path from "tradition" to "modernity" was natural, inevitable, and appropriate to all countries and contexts, including the many former colonies that had gained their independence in the aftermath of World War II. The key questions concerned not *whether* these newly sovereign nation-states should or would experience development – marked by social, political, and economic concomitants like urbanization, industrialization, and democratization – but *when* and *how* they would do so. And the answers typically emphasized the diffusion and dissemination of "modern" norms and values – i.e., rationality and self-interest – by means of trade, foreign investment, migration, and cultural exchange. "If they'd just interact with rich countries," modernization theorists seemed to be saying, "poor countries would absorb their values, adopt their habits, and follow their growth and development trajectories in due course."

Taken to their logical conclusion, however, doubts about rationality and self-interest in "traditional" societies fueled doubts about full employment itself. This was best illustrated, perhaps, by the great St Lucian economist Arthur Lewis in a 1954 article entitled "Economic Development with Unlimited Supplies of Labour." According to Lewis, who would eventually win the Nobel Memorial Prize in Economic Sciences for his argument, much of the non-western world was characterized not by full employment at all but by populations that were so large relative to their capital and natural resources that the marginal productivity of their labor was "negligible, zero, or even negative" (Lewis 1954: 402), meaning that rational investors could in principle create "new industries or new employment opportunities" (1954: 406) for them without drawing valuable resources away from other uses. If Fredonia has many more workers than jobs, in other words, it need not give up *any* food to produce manufactures; it can do so with workers who would otherwise be underemployed.

In short, Lewis drew a distinction between the *neoclassical* assumption of full employment and the *classical* assumption of an unlimited supply of labor at near-subsistence wages, holding that the latter was more applicable to poor countries than the former

(Toye 2009: 223). The obvious question, therefore, was why nobody had taken advantage of those underemployed workers, and their presumed willingness to work for rock-bottom wages, by putting them to work in factories, farms, or mines. And the less obvious answer lay in the distinction Lewis drew between "a capitalist and a non-capitalist sector, where 'capitalist' is defined in the classical sense as a man [sic] who hires labor and resells its output for a profit" (Lewis 1968: 2). So housekeepers are part of the capitalist sector when they work in hotels, where they contribute to the accumulation of profits that are reinvested over time, but not when they work in private homes, where they are little more than a luxury or marker of social status. And underdevelopment is more common to societies in which luxury and status considerations take pride of place over profit than vice versa.

In fact, the root cause of underdevelopment, according to Lewis, is that the dominant classes in traditional societies *do not* "think in terms of investing capital productively" (Lewis 1954: 420), or pursuing profit, but instead follow a "code of ethical behavior" (1954: 406) that treats employment of the poor as a sign of status and standing. "Social prestige requires people to have servants," he argues, "and the grand seigneur may have to keep a whole army of retainers who are really little more than a burden upon his purse." Nor is the problem limited to domestic service; on the contrary, Lewis explains, it is found in every sector of the economy, meaning that traditional societies are marked not by full employment and scarcity but by veritable armies of underemployed tenant farmers, traders, day laborers, and domestic workers who, in practice, add little or no value to their enterprises or economies.

The irony of their underemployment, however, is that it constitutes an opportunity as well as a problem, for it allows investors and entrepreneurs to create productive capital out of human labor at virtually no cost. "Food cannot be grown without land," Lewis explains, "but roads, viaducts, irrigation canals, and buildings can be created by human labor with hardly any capital to speak of – witness the Pyramids, or the marvelous railway tunnels built in the mid-nineteenth century almost with bare hands" (Lewis 1954: 421). If similar projects are not being pursued today, Lewis implies, it is not for lack of capital but for lack of *capitalists*, and he therefore directs his attention to "the sociological problem of the emergence of a capitalist class, that is to say a group of men [sic] who think in terms of investing capital productively" (Lewis 1954: 420).

Lewis labels this a "sociological problem" because it concerns not the optimal allocation of resources (e.g., foodstuffs or manufactured goods) but what constitutes rationality in the first place. Do I want to maximize wealth or status? Power or income? Kin or their individual prospects? And his prognosis would eventually prove prescient, for the two sources of productive investment he would identify – foreign investors and state-owned enterprises – would in time take root in poor countries, and they will command a good deal of attention in the chapters that follow. But the origins of capitalism and capitalists were by no means the only sociological questions of interest to Lewis, whose approach has been labeled "economic sociology" (Bottomore 1962: 316; Wisman 1986: 170) rather than economics per se. He was similarly intrigued by the "social attitudes" that were in part responsible for prevailing wages in economies marked by unlimited supplies of labor (Lewis 1968: 4), and the "social, political, and religious rules" that influenced fertility, migration, savings, and entrepreneurship in poor countries more generally, and he therefore warned his fellow economists not to rush in "with economic answers beyond the limits within which they apply" (Lewis 1984: 8).

For a while, they heeded his warning, and interdisciplinary development studies not only flourished but began to reshape our understanding of the industrial countries as well. For instance, Albert Hirschman pointed out that "unlimited supplies of labor," which were supposed to be limited to poor countries, were at times found in their wealthy counterparts, "owing in large part to massive immigration" from the Global South, and that "sociological" accounts of labor market dynamics in the United States arguably owed much to the Lewis model (Hirschman 1981: 9–10; see, e.g., Piore 1973). Latin Americanists developed no less "sociological" accounts of inflation – rooted in the notion of preemptive price increases driven by inflationary expectations – that eventually gained ground in the North, "usually without due credit being given" to their southern roots (Hirschman 1981: 12; see also Hirschman 1980). Alexander Gerschenkron portrayed large-scale factories, foreign investors, investment banks, and public enterprises as potential substitutes for entrepreneurship and, in so doing, explained not only their prevalence in Central and Eastern Europe, where "entrepreneurial deficiencies" were the norm, but their paucity in the West, where the prospects for entrepreneurship were much better (Gerschenkron 1966: 256). And Ronald Dore came up with the concept of the "diploma disease," or the use of formal degrees and credentials as proxies for substantive skills and abilities, in an effort to explain the gap between the qualifications and the capabilities of professionals in late developing countries, only to find that the disease "eventually takes hold in earlier developers as well" (Whittaker 2001: 13; see also Dore 1976) – leading to the simultaneous expansion of higher education and contraction of genuine learning.

In other words, the mid-twentieth century saw a productive dialogue not only between economics and cognate disciplines but between North and South, or rich and poor parts of the world, to the benefit of the social sciences as a whole. Ideas that were born in one discipline or region fueled debates and filled gaps in the others, and participants therefore began to view themselves – and their efforts – as part of a common project with a coherent goal: improving the lot of the world's poor, however defined and classified.

As soon as their efforts began to pay off, however, they fell victim to a brutal assault by a "curious alliance" (Dore 1975: 205; see also Hirschman 1981: 15) of neoclassical economists, who doubted the importance of "non-economic" factors like norms, values, and institutions, and neo-Marxists, who doubted the very possibility of capitalist development and put their faith in "socialist" alternatives in the late 1960s and 1970s. "Because the adherents of neoclassical economics and those of various neo-Marxist schools live in quite separate worlds," argued Hirschman (Hirschman 1981: 15), "they were not even aware of acting in unison." But their shared faith in material self-interest, and contempt for alternative drivers of human behavior, would nonetheless win the day and, in so doing, prove fatal to the interdisciplinary dialogue that had proven so productive in the postwar era.

The consequences are by now well known. Whether or not they really admired authoritarian countries like North Korea that tried to pursue self-sufficiency (Chirot and Ragin 1982: 99; cf. Wallerstein 1981–2; Gough 1982), and the answer is neither obvious nor – in all likelihood – uniform, neo-Marxists openly derided the goal of national development on the grounds that it was at best illusory (Arrighi 1990) and at worst likely to prove zero-sum in a capitalist world. "Catching up implies competition," argued Immanuel Wallerstein by way of explanation, "and competition means that one country's development will come at somebody else's expense" (Wallerstein 1988: 2022; see also Arrighi and Drangel 1986). So poor countries would be better off trying to "transform the system as a whole" by building a "socialist world-government" than seeking "relative advantage" by pursuing their own development (Wallerstein 1976: 466; see also Arrighi 1991: 64).[5]

The problem with this logic was threefold. First, it's not *ex ante* obvious that one country's gain means another country's loss – let alone zero-sum loss. The logic of comparative advantage implies positive-sum gains. Most observers believe that globalization has been accompanied by a net *decrease* in "global interpersonal inequality" (Lakner and Milanovic 2016; see also Therborn 2012; Milanovic 2015; Ram 2015) – despite widespread *increases* in within-country inequality – over the course of the last quarter of a century or so. Gains and losses must always be specified in light of a counterfactual, and the choice of counterfactual is inevitably controversial. And the case for a zero-sum world is even harder to make when the definition of "development" is expanded to include things like literacy, life expectancy, and the like – for the latter have gone up almost inexorably, if not necessarily rapidly, in poor as well as rich countries for the better part of the last half-millennium.[6] Second, even if national development was a zero-sum game, in which the individual "units" shift places but the overall "quantity and/or quality of economic activity takes

27

a constant form" (Schwartz 2007: 118), it would still be worthy of study. We'd want to know *which* units grew or declined, and how and why, for practical as well as normative reasons. Is growth compatible with values like equity, sustainability, and democracy? Might they even be complementary? And how would one know? And, finally, by leaving the individual units to others, while they devoted their own energies to the study of systems-level causes and constraints (Schwartz 2007: 119), sociologists ceded the field of national development to neoclassical economists. And the economists took advantage of the opportunity not only to apply the assumptions of self-interest and full employment to poor countries – when they had previously been applied almost exclusively to the rich (Toye 2009) – but to take them to their optimistic, if at times implicit (Boianovsky 2010: 245), conclusion: that the rate of capital investment would be inversely related to the level of capital formation in a world of diminishing returns, and that capital would therefore flow from rich countries to poor countries as a matter of course. "Since the marginal product of capital is higher in capital-scarce countries than in capital-rich countries," explains economist Jeffrey Sachs, "and since the technologically lagging countries can import the technologies of the richer countries, the poorer countries are expected to grow faster than the rich countries" (Sachs 2000: 30) over time.

The birth of the Washington Consensus and the rise of "DIY sociology"

The result was a "Washington Consensus" (Williamson 1990; Babb 2013) in favor of policies that would allow poor countries to take advantage of their alleged good fortune by: opening their markets to more competitive foreign products; eliminating taxes and regulations that served to impede foreign investment; selling state-owned enterprises (SOEs) to more efficient foreign owners; and shifting spending priorities "toward education and health (especially to benefit the disadvantaged) and infrastructure investment," all of which were considered more "productive" than traditional spending priorities by policymakers and donor agencies like the World Bank that were housed in the US capital (Williamson 1990: 3). John Williamson, who christened the alleged Consensus in 1989, argued that it marked the end of the "intellectual apartheid" that assumed that people in the Global South behaved differently from their northern counterparts (Williamson 2009: 9) and relegated their study to distinct subfields and disciplines.

By the end of the Cold War, therefore, the study of development had come full circle. The neoclassical assumptions of rationality and full employment were no longer considered alien or ill suited to the developing world. Instead, they formed the basis of a consensus that: first, put paid to both modernization theory, which accepted full employment – albeit not always in a "capitalist" sector – and rejected universal rationality, and neo-Marxism, which accepted universal rationality and rejected full employment; and in so doing, second, purged sociology from the development policy debate and brought the periphery back into the core of economics (Naím 2000: 91).

What the Washington Consensus failed to consider, however, were the social and institutional underpinnings of growth and development: the fact that the best-designed policies are all but inconsequential if they are ignored or unenforced; that the rule of law is unlikely to be built by means of a policy imperative alone; that even the most entrepreneurial individuals will fail to take advantage of opportunities if they lack the knowledge, confidence, and resources needed to do so; and that the very meanings of terms like "status," "self-interested," and "unemployed" are themselves socially constructed, at least in part.

By the end of the twentieth century, therefore, poor countries and their people were in a bind. On the one hand, they had embraced the Washington Consensus with a vengeance, in some cases going above and beyond the demands of the donor agencies and the WTO. Markets had been opened. SOEs had been privatized. Taxes had been cut. And regulations had been rolled back in an effort to generate investment and growth. On the other hand, they had experienced little of the promised payoff. Growth rates in the "neoliberal" 1980s and 1990s were lower, on average, than in the decidedly illiberal 1960s and 1970s. "Between 1994 and 1999 alone," adds Moises Naím, "10 middle-income developing countries experienced major financial crises" (Naím 2000: 94). And by the dawn of the new millennium, therefore, the alleged consensus had given way to conflict and confusion in both donor and developing countries (Naím 2000).

How did economists respond to the apparent failure of their predictions? Some argued that free-market reforms had "gone too far" (Weisbrot 1999: 18), and called for their abandonment or moderation. Others argued that they had not gone "far enough" (Zettelmeyer 2006: 1), and called for their reinforcement or hastening. And a number of the most prominent voices in the room turned to "do-it-yourself sociology" (de Sardan 2005: 28) by invoking information, institutions, and social norms by way of explanation. The real barrier to late development, they implied, is that it requires a combination of "bureaucratic competence and ruthless dedication to national economic success that is relatively rare and may be impossible to sustain" (Romer 1993: 88).

The retreat to DIY sociology was common among practitioners as well as scholars. Consider, for example, the apparent underperformance of irrigation projects in developing countries. "Ex-post evaluations repeatedly show how sociologically ill-informed and ill-conceived is much irrigation policy," explained economist Ian Carruthers in the early 1990s, when irrigation investment consumed an enormous share of World Bank rural development lending and delivered highly variable returns in different contexts. When farmers joined forces to operate and maintain irrigation systems, he argued, they were able to reconcile the often-conflicting goals of development and conservation. When they shirked their collective commitments, however, the systems declined before their time. And despite widespread awareness of the problem, DIY sociology was not only the norm in the donor community at the time but was typically "applied too late, as a negative vision with 20/20 hindsight, and not at the initial or policy review process" (Carruthers 1990: 292).

Indeed, Michael Cernea, who was one of the few sociologists at the World Bank in the 1990s, held that irrigation initiatives offered a particularly "good test" (Cernea 1993a: 13) of the organizational intensity of development projects, insofar as they depend upon cooperation and collective action, and traced their failures in large part to their insensitivity to institutions and social capital. When donors designed irrigation systems without regard to their users, Cernea argued, they contributed to their premature deterioration or collapse. When they encouraged farmers to join forces in the "management and maintenance of such systems" (Cernea 1993b: 22), however, they contributed to a "culture of maintenance" that combated inefficiency and prolonged the life of the system (Cernea 1993b: 22).

Before extending Cernea's comments beyond the realm of irrigation, we should take a moment to define three related – and potentially "chaotic" (Dale 2002: 7; Smart 2008: 11) – sociological concepts that have already made brief appearances and will reappear in the chapters to come: social capital, institutionalization, and institutions. First, I follow the great French sociologist Pierre Bourdieu, who defined social capital as "resources which are linked to possession of a durable network of more or less institutionalized relationships of mutual acquaintance or recognition" (Bourdieu 1986: 242). When you take advantage of resources you've acquired from people you know and trust, explains Alejandro Portes, you're exploiting your social capital (Portes 1998: 4). Second, I follow Lynne Zucker in defining institutionalization as "a phenomenological process by which certain social relationships and actions come to be taken for granted" (Zucker 1983: 2). When the major actors, parties, and interest groups treat contested elections as "the only game in town" (Linz 1990: 158), for example, procedural democracy has been institutionalized. And, finally, I follow a "collective consensus that institutions represent the more enduring features of social life, that they tend to be reproduced and that they serve to structure and organize social action" (Mohr and Friedland 2008: 421; cf. Swedberg 2005: esp. 422), whether formally or informally.[7]

Irrigation projects are not alone in their need for institutions and social capital. Cernea added forestry, education, and infrastructure projects to the list, and underscored the importance of sociological knowledge *whenever* projects affected indigenous peoples. "The applied social scientist who responsibly takes on the challenge of social engineering," he argued, "provides an important service: he or she replaces the amateurish, do-it-yourself brand of social engineering of the nonsocial scientist with the state-of-the-art tools of understanding offered by a field of professional expertise" (Cernea 1991: 30). But Cernea simultaneously bemoaned the "staff/skill mix" (Cernea 1993c: 4) at agencies like the Bank, which was heavily skewed toward engineers, economists, and accountants at the time, and went on to highlight the "absence of socio-cultural expertise" (Cernea 1993c: 7) among their managers in particular. "Although such managers 'decide' all the time on matters of a social and cultural nature," he argued, "they are not expected . . . to have themselves trained cultural skills, or at least to include among themselves sociological experts" (Cernea 1993c: 7). It's not surprising, therefore, that the donor community's professed sensitivity to the rights of indigenous, marginalized, and impoverished people was often perceived as little more than window dressing.[8]

Given their fondness for specialization, however, an obvious question presents itself. Why didn't the economists who ran and advised these donor organizations focus on their own comparative advantages and outsource the sociology to the specialists? Surely future Nobel Prize winners like Paul Krugman and Paul Romer, both of whom characterized their own answers as "amateur sociology" at one point or another (Krugman 1991: 95; Romer 1993: 88; see also Killick 1993: 57; Lewis 2004: 47; Pritchett 2009: 28; Subramanian 2014: 1; Surowiecki 2015: 35; *Economist* 2020: 59), could have found collaborators among the professionals, or hired them on a fee-for-service basis. And the answers tend to fall into two different camps: demand-side accounts that blame the economists for their alleged arrogance and insularity, and supply-side accounts that blame sociologists for their own shortcomings. After all, for the better part of the past half-century, the sociology of development had been dominated by two approaches – modernization theory and neo-Marxism – that were arguably no less reductionist than neoclassical economics. Factors that loomed large in the sociology of developed market economies – ranging from norms, values, and networks (Portes 1997, 2006), on the one hand, to commensuration, classification, and valuation (Espeland and Stevens 1998; Fourcade and Healy 2007), on the other – were largely ignored in the Global South, where power politics and self-interest dominated the literature, and sociologists thus forswore their own comparative advantage in a failed effort to take on mainstream economists on their own terrain.

What's needed, by way of contrast, is an approach to development that treats self-interest as a variable to be explained, rather than an assumption to be invoked (Stinchcombe 1986: 5–6), and explores the "deep structure of moral categories" (Stinchcombe 1986: 145), like employment and unemployment. Take, for example, the late Arthur Stinchcombe's juxtaposition of the antebellum United States, where "most blacks were legally prohibited from selling their labor, and children were allowed and even encouraged to sell theirs" (Stinchcombe 1986: 156), and the late twentieth-century United States, where the opposite was closer to the truth. It suggests that the very notions of employment and unemployment – not to mention rationality and self-interest, or race (ASA 2003: 7) and childhood (Zelizer 1985) – vary over time and space and shape the flow of capital.[9]

It's no coincidence that Stinchcombe was a sociologist. Insofar as he treats both self-interest and full employment as variables, rather than assumptions, his approach is emblematic of a "new economic sociology" that emerged in the mid-1980s – with the publication of a "manifesto" by Mark Granovetter (Granovetter 1985; Swedberg 1997: 161; Convert and Heilbron 2007: 40) – and has gained more purchase in the Global North than the Global South (Schrank 2015). What's central to the new economic sociology, according to Granovetter, is a belief that economic behavior is "embedded in social relations" (Granovetter 1985: 482), no less in rich countries than in poor ones, and that both the "oversocialized" accounts of human behavior in modernization theory and the "undersocialized" accounts found in the utilitarian tradition were wrongheaded (Granovetter 1992: 4–5). People are neither the docile automatons of Parsonian theory nor the atomized utility maximizers of neoclassical (or Marxist) economics, Granovetter argued, but are instead products of both "the contingencies associated with historical background, social structure and collective action, and the constraints imposed by already existing institutions" (Granovetter 1992: 5).

In some sense, therefore, the new economic sociology took the relatively catholic approach pioneered by the most sophisticated practitioners of interdisciplinary development studies back into the heart of the discipline and in so doing tried to bridge the gap between metropolitan and peripheral scholarship. In fact, Granovetter drew ideas and inspiration from "premarket" as well as market societies and held that the break between the two was far less sharp than most observers realized (Granovetter 1985: 482; see also Granovetter 1995). But the new economic sociology nonetheless gained more traction in the North, where development was taken for granted, than in the South, where underdevelopment was the presumed norm and incumbent theories held sway (see, e.g., Arrighi 2001). And the *economic sociology of development* has therefore been slow to crystallize if not entirely stillborn.

Table 1.4 contrasts the economic sociology of development to the three aforementioned alternatives: mainstream economics, which takes full employment and self-interest for granted and anticipates the decline of international inequality due to the pursuit of comparative advantage; modernization theory, which assumes full employment but forgoes self-interest and predicts the decline of international inequality due to the diffusion of northern norms

Table 1.4 Four approaches to understanding development

| | | Self-interest | |
		Assumption	*Variable*
Full-employment	*Assumption*	Mainstream economics: predicts cross-national convergence	Modernization theory: predicts cross-national convergence
	Variable	Neo-Marxism: predicts cross-national divergence	New economic sociology: agnostic regarding cross-national patterns

and values; and neo-Marxism, which assumes self-interested behavior but rejects full employment and predicts the growth of international inequality in a world of zero-sum competition. *By way of contrast, the economic sociology of development abandons both the full-employment and self-interest assumptions in an effort to explain divergent life chances and living standards over time and space. It's agnostic with regard to long-term patterns of international inequality and focused more on "middle range" (Merton 1949) questions and concepts.*

This book tries to advance the sociology of development not sequentially, by reviewing in the early chapters and renewing in those that follow, but synthetically, by bringing the insights of the new economic sociology to bear on five issues that are particularly salient to the Global South: the conceptualization and measurement of development; the structure and status hierarchy of the international system; the correlates and causes of upward and downward mobility within that system; the origins and diffusion of development policies themselves; and the prospects for socio-economic change in the years ahead. In effect, I try to bring the Global South back into the mainstream of economic sociology and to bring economic sociology back into debates over the Global South. I have divided the rest of the book into five chapters, each designed to address a particular question.

Chapter 2 asks what we mean by "development" and answers by way of reference to the "sociology of quantification" (Espeland and Stevens 2008). It begins by noting that economists tend to equate development with the production of more and better commodities, and to use growth in gross domestic product (GDP) per capita as an indicator of the process, before addressing criticisms of the narrow, "commodity-centered," approach and introducing an alternative indicator designed to capture a broader notion: the Human Development Index (HDI) devised by economist Mahbub ul Haq and grounded in his fellow economist Amartya Sen's distinction "between commodities and capabilities, between our economic wealth and our ability to live as we would like" (Sen 1999: 13). It goes on to distinguish between "gradational" and "relational" notions of inequality more generally (Wright 1980:

201, fn. 10; London 2018: 49). And it concludes by classifying existing approaches into the four derived categories – broadly or narrowly gradational, and broadly or narrowly relational – and making the case for a "broadly relational" understanding of development that takes culture and context into account.

Chapter 3 asks how sociologists positioned themselves in debates dominated by economists in the first place and uses the answer to conduct a *tour d'horizon* of late twentieth-century development theory. It notes that postwar growth theory assumed both the self-interested behavior of rational individuals and the full employment of their resources; doubted that either assumption applied to the non-western world; and thus opened the door to sociologists, anthropologists, and others who treated "noneconomic factors," like attitudes, values, and institutions, "as variables, with causal relationships flowing to as well as from them" (Hagen 1960: 623; see also Hagen 1966). But the resultant conflict between modernization theorists, who expected the diffusion of western values to issue in the development of peripheral societies, and neo-Marxists, who expressed no less faith in the persistence of peripheral poverty, produced more heat than light (Portes 1997; Centeno and Cohen 2012). And the chapter therefore concludes by invoking the debate over stratification and mobility *within* capitalist societies in an effort to reconcile – and eventually transcend – the two perspectives, highlighting the limits imposed by finite nonrenewable resources in particular.

Chapter 4 asks what drove the growth of commodities, in some countries, and capabilities, in others, and pays particularly careful attention to the roles of public officials and the public sector more generally. While efforts to bring "the state back into development sociology" (Schrank 2015: 231; see also Kim 2007: 37) in the late twentieth century have typically been treated as *alternatives* to modernization and neo-Marxism, they're more accurately portrayed as the hybrid offspring of *both* approaches – with roots running through Gerschenkron's account of late development. It goes on to array late developing societies along two dimensions: the degree to which they transformed or accommodated their traditional rural elites; and the extent to which they developed or repressed price-setting (or capitalist) markets. And it uses the resultant fourfold typology to assess four different types of states in the Global South: *patrimonial states*, where the authorities accommodated the rural elite, blocked the growth of capitalist labor markets, and fostered the underdevelopment of both capabilities and commodities; *distributive states*, where the authorities transformed the rural elite, blocked the growth of capitalist labor markets, and fostered the growth of capabilities but not commodities; *populist states*, where the authorities accommodated the rural elite, built an urban labor market, and fostered uneven growth of both capabilities and commodities; and *developmental states*, where the authorities transformed the rural elite, built an urban labor market, and fostered the growth and development of capabilities and commodities.

Chapter 5 asks why seemingly illiberal development policies and their champions were, to one degree or another, defanged or discredited in the 1990s and answers the question by way of reference to the sociological literature on diffusion, convergence, and isomorphism. While economists tend to assume that institutions – like central banks, tax authorities, and regulatory agencies – take on similar shapes and/or adopt similar strategies in light of market competition, and thus incline toward efficiency, sociologists hold that they're no less responsive to pressures from powerful organizations, the values and norms of their managers, or uncertainties that lead them to imitate peer institutions (DiMaggio and Powell 1983), and that these were the key drivers of policy convergence in the late twentieth century (see, e.g., Markoff and Montecinos 1993; Henisz, Zelner, and Guillén 2005; Kogut and Macpherson 2011; Babb 2013; Pinheiro, Chwieroth, and Hicks 2015). The result is an account that emphasizes the potentially non-rational bases of free-market reform and liberalization – and their variegated, and often disastrous, consequences – but is nonetheless unable to explain their reversal in the twenty-first century or the origin of new alternatives. In an effort to fill the resultant gap, therefore, I draw upon recent work that links the sociology of classification and valuation to work on individual and organizational behavior with a recognition that "culture requires agents

– whether individuals, organizations, or the state – to bear it" (Gong and Jang 1998: 89).

Chapter 6 concludes by asking how the study of development would look if sociologists had as much influence as economists (cf. Zuckerman 2010). It asks what sociologists have – and have not – learned in the era of "grand theory" discussed in chapter 3 and the era of "middle range" theory discussed in chapters 4 and 5 (Merton 1949). It moves on to discuss four more or less unique contributions being made by sociologists today: reflections on development concepts and indicators; quantitative analyses of social and political networks; social and political demography; and ethnographies of communities and organizations. And it asks how one might take the lessons thereby learned and aggregate them into a broader sociological understanding of development in the years to come. After all, the new economic sociology promises to take historical and cultural context seriously, but its goal is still to find "general principles, correct for all times and places" (Granovetter 1992: 5). There is a difference between historically sensitive and historicist, and the trick is to find the sweet spot.

2

What Do We Mean by "Development?"

What do we mean by "development?" Dictionaries tend to define the word by way of reference to "growth," "advancement," or "improvement," and their readers tend to treat it as a goal to be pursued. Most people prefer development to the alternative, especially when the alternatives include antonyms like "stagnation" or "decay."

When applied to a society or country, however, the dictionary definition generates as many questions as answers. Growth of what? Advancement toward what goal? Improvement by whose standards? Some argue that the answers to these questions are inherently subjective, making the very study of development a fool's errand. Others worry that by ranking countries on a "universal scale of development" that privileges their own countries – and penalizes the Global South – analysts from the Global North are reproducing western notions of "the good life" that are not only subjective but biased against non-western values (Ziai 2013: 128). So-called developed countries are not in fact richer, they argue, but have simply designed and defended performance criteria that highlight their own advantages and preferences. And Mark Granovetter goes further, noting that the "rank ordering of societies" (Granovetter 1979: 489) in terms of development or adaptive capacity would be fruitless *even if* the individual members of each society had *identical* preferences (Granovetter 1979: 497–8), as it would merely move the problem of interpersonal comparison to the societal level and leave the problem of "predictability" unaddressed. "Did Imperial Germany have high adaptive capacity?" Granovetter asks rhetorically (Granovetter 1979: 501). "A contemporary observer might have thought so; subsequent events would have rendered this judgment dubious."

There is much to be said for this position, and it cannot be dismissed out of hand. Social scientists ignore the normative underpinnings of "development" to their peril, and global challenges like pandemics, cyberterrorism, and climate change threaten rich as well as – or perhaps more than – poor countries (see, e.g., Moore 2020; Cohn 2021). But the migrants we encountered at the beginning of chapter 1 are risking their lives traveling from developing to developed countries defined in conventional terms, and the reforms discussed at the end of the chapter failed according to equally conventional metrics, and we'd therefore do well to understand those terms and metrics before turning to their critics.

In this chapter, therefore, I discuss the two leading approaches to thinking about development: as the production of "commodities," or material wealth, measured by gross domestic product (GDP) per capita; and as the enhancement of "capabilities," or freedom (Sen 1999), measured by an indicator of "human development" produced by the United Nations Development Programme (UNDP). I'll discuss their respective advantages and disadvantages, their tendency to "remake the world" (Espeland 1997: 1115) in their image, their "degree of redundancy" (Cahill 2005: 1) in both statistical and theoretical terms, and their inability to capture cross-national differences in interpersonal inequality. Finally, I'll note that the factors that loom largest in sociological accounts of development and underdevelopment, including the *relationships* between countries, communities, and people, are captured neither by GDP per capita nor by the Human Development Index (HDI) and thus require more imaginative theories and measures. In effect, I'll argue that development is a "social fact" (Ritzer 2011: 79; see also Gong and Jang 1998: 89) that is manifest or made evident in indicators like – but not limited to – GDP per capita and the HDI.

The traditional approach to development: the production of commodities

Historians and social scientists have traditionally thought of development as the production of material wealth: more food, more factories, and more fun – at least insofar as the latter is provided by modern-day services (e.g., movies, television, theme parks, and the like) and facilitated by the production of labor-saving technologies, like the vacuum cleaner, that free up people's time to enjoy them. By this logic, moreover, the most developed societies in the world are found in the North Atlantic region, Northeast Asia, and the Antipodes, where industrial and service employment predominate, and the most commonly used measure of their development is gross domestic product per capita.

What's GDP? It's an estimate of the market value of all the goods and services produced in a given country in a given time period – typically a calendar year. When we divide GDP by the country's population, moreover, we get an estimate of the average income per person, or living standard, in the country. Some prefer gross national product (GNP), which measures the value of the goods and services produced not within a country but by the citizens of the country, wherever they're located, and thus attributes foreign direct investment to the country of origin rather than the country of destination. So, for example, US-owned auto plants in Mexico are assigned to US GNP and Mexican GDP. Others prefer GDP per worker, which leaves the non-working population (e.g., children, students, pensioners, the unemployed) out of the denominator, and thus tracks conventional notions of productivity better than GDP per capita. In practice, however, the choice of numerator or denominator doesn't matter much; all three indicators are highly correlated, and unless you're particularly interested in countries that are highly dependent on FDI (e.g., Ireland; see O'Hearn 2001: 176), or have highly skewed age distributions (e.g., Japan; see Katz 1998: ch. 4), they tend to paint similar portraits and have similar advantages and disadvantages. Since GDP per capita tends to be the standard international

Table 2.1 GDP per capita in the 10 largest countries in the world, 2018

Country	Population, millions	GDP, trillions 2010 US dollars	GDP per capita
China	1,392.73	10.797	7,753
India	1,352.62	2.842	2,101
United States	326.688	17.856	54,579
Indonesia	267.663	1.147	4,285
Pakistan	212.215	0.254	1,198
Brazil	209.469	2.310	11,026
Nigeria	195.875	0.470	2,396
Bangladesh	161.356	0.194	1,203
Russian Federation	144.478	1.722	11,729
Japan	126.529	6.190	48,920
World	*7,594.27*	*82.71*	*10,404*

Source: Data from World Bank, World Development Indicators, May 3, 2020.

metric, moreover, it's the one I'll use as the default in the rest of this book.

Table 2.1 includes data on the population in millions, GDP in trillions of 2010 US dollars, and GDP per capita in 2010 US dollars in the 10 most populous countries in the world, as well as data on the global population, gross world product, and gross world product per capita.

As you can see, GDP per capita ranges from a high of almost US$55,000 per year in the United States, which we typically think of as a developed country, to a low of approximately US$1,200 per year in Bangladesh and Pakistan, which we typically think of as developing countries. What this means in practice, of course, is that your life chances – in material terms – are largely dictated by the country in which you're born, a fact that gives the study of development enormous real-world importance and goes a long way toward explaining why migrants tend to go from poorer to richer countries and not vice versa (Martin 2013; Milanovic 2015).

It's perhaps worth noting, as an aside, both that population and GDP are positively – albeit imperfectly – correlated across countries and that global population is highly skewed toward a small number of very large countries. The ten countries in Table

2.1 therefore produce approximately half the world's output and play host to well over half of its population. Are they representative of the world's 200 or so countries in terms of income, if not population? In 2018, the richest country in the world, in terms of per capita income, was the city-state of Monaco at US$195,880, followed by tiny Luxembourg at US$110,742 and Norway – with more than 5 million people – at US$92,078. Peru and Thailand were in the middle of the distribution, with per capita incomes of approximately US$6,400. And Burundi brought up the rear with a per capita GDP of just over US$200 per year – well below Bangladesh and Pakistan. It would therefore seem that worldwide the mean GDP per capita in Table 2.1, US$10,404, is dragged upward by a small number of very wealthy countries, the typical country is far poorer, and the very poorest countries are destitute. Well over half a billion people are currently living in 25 countries that are poorer, in terms of GDP per capita, than India and Bangladesh. Approximately half of them work in agriculture, in contrast to less than 5 percent of the labor force in the rich countries of the North Atlantic and Northeast Asia, and yet they grow much less food.

It's no surprise that GDP per capita is commonly used as a proxy for development. It's conceptually simple and parsimonious, and it's made available annually by the World Bank, an international donor organization that has recently responded to competition from rival sources of development finance (e.g., regional development banks, commercial lenders, the Chinese government) by repositioning itself as a "knowledge bank" (Broad 2007). Per capita GDP is not, however, a perfect indicator of development, and critics have expressed doubts about: what it includes, or coverage; how it's calculated, or measurement; and whether it really captures the essence of development, or meaning. I'll address each question in turn.

Coverage

Insofar as they're used to measure development, or progress, data on GDP suffer two distinct coverage problems: what they include, and what they exclude. They include not only goods and services that are generally considered valuable, like electric vehicles, composters, and life-saving operations, but the destructive products that make their development necessary. Firearms, fossil fuels, and McMansions in the suburbs offer three obvious examples.[1]

The problem is not only what GDP figures include, however, but what they exclude: goods and services that are not bought and sold and/or registered by the authorities. So, for example, consider three identical – but hypothetical – plumbing repairs: one undertaken by a homeowner for her own benefit; a second undertaken by a licensed plumber who charges US$200 and pays the requisite taxes; and a third undertaken "off the books" by an unlicensed plumber who charges US$200 and keeps all the money. They're equally valuable to the homeowner, but only the second is incorporated into GDP – and there's something odd about an indicator of development that treats the same product differently depending on who provides it and how.

The problem's not simply the inconsistent treatment and tracking of different goods and services, however, but their inconsistent (or uneven) treatment and tracking by country. If the share of undesirable and/or unregistered activity was more or less evenly distributed by country, we wouldn't worry that much. GDP per capita would offer an inefficient measure of development but not a biased one. But the fact is that GDP per capita is biased: Some countries have huge arms industries, large numbers of noxious factories, and/or inefficient transport systems; others produce, utilize, and export energy-efficient mass transit systems. Some countries register the bulk of their economic activity; others register almost none of it. And so on. By way of illustration, hydrocarbons make up a disproportionate share of Nigeria's GDP, and almost all of the country's exports, and the World Bank's fraternal twin donor organization, the International Monetary Fund (IMF), estimates that more than half of Nigerian GDP goes unrecorded (Davies 2020).

Nor are the biases predictable. Most analysts agree that the underground, or informal, economy looms larger in poorer countries on average (Davies 2020), and that GDP figures thereby underestimate the incomes of the world's poor. If people in poor countries tend to grow their own food, make and wash their own clothes, undertake their own repairs, and/or hide their activities from the authorities, after all, they'll look poorer than they live *ceteris paribus* – at least when compared to people in rich countries who tend to buy food, clothing, and consumer services from registered enterprises. But there's an ongoing debate as to whether pollution and deforestation are greater in rich countries or poor countries or start low in poor countries, reach their peaks "at intermediate levels of development" (Ehrhardt-Martinez, Crenshaw, and Jenkins 2002: 227), and decline in rich countries with service economies and/or post-materialist values (Dasgupta, Laplante, Wang, and Wheeler 2002; Marquart-Pyatt 2004; Fairbrother 2013). And dangerous products and processes – like armaments, poisons, and Ponzi schemes – are produced in rich and poor countries alike, making GDP a decidedly imperfect measure of development.

Measurement

A related critique concerns the units in which GDP is measured. Given that different countries use different currencies, the choice isn't at all obvious. Do we measure GDP in dollars, pesos, shillings, or rupees? Which ones? Why? Reasonable minds can offer different answers.

One approach, reflected in Table 2.1, simply converts the relevant currencies to US dollars, the world's "reserve currency," at prevailing market rates and compares them, a relatively straightforward exercise. But residents of developing countries buy most of their goods and services in their local currencies, and foreign exchange transactions arguably confound the real prices they pay with currency shocks. So, for example, if a Mexican peso is worth 5 cents on Monday, and 4 cents on Tuesday due to a sudden devaluation, the real incomes of most Mexican consumers will not have fallen by 20 percent because most Mexican consumers don't buy most of their goods and services in dollars; much of what they buy is made locally of local inputs – and all the more so after a currency adjustment that makes their pesos less valuable vis-à-vis the dollar.

A simple foreign exchange conversion will thus underestimate the incomes of consumers in poorer, or peripheral, countries like Mexico, who don't undertake such conversions before buying most of their goods and services. The problem is compounded, moreover, by the prevalence of non-traded goods and services in the purchasing profiles of the peripheral poor. In a classic example, a haircut tends to cost less in poor countries than in rich ones, meaning a shilling goes further in Nairobi than it would in New York at prevailing exchange rates, *ceteris paribus*, and efforts to compare average incomes that fail to take such differences into account therefore tend to underestimate incomes in poor countries and overestimate incomes in rich countries and, by extension, cross-country inequality.

By way of solution, the International Comparison Program (ICP) established by the United Nations and the University of Pennsylvania in 1968 endeavors to facilitate cross-country comparisons by documenting the prices of hundreds of products in approximately 200 participating countries and using the results to estimate the rates at which Country A's currency would have to be converted to Country B's currency to buy an equivalent basket of goods and services there. Because many goods and services are less costly in poor countries than in rich ones, the resultant "purchasing power parity" (PPP) exchange rates tend to temper the gap between the Global North and the Global South. For instance, the United States is approximately five times richer than Brazil in Table 2.1, using market exchange rates, but "only" about four times richer using PPP dollars in 2018, when per capita GDP was US$55,719 in the United States and US$14,283 at PPP.

But the results of the ICP are not uncontroversial, and skeptics still prefer market exchange rates for several reasons. First, not all countries participate in the ICP survey, and several countries, including China, have participated sporadically, meaning that PPP estimates are based on data of highly uneven quality (Wade 2012). Second, not all goods and services are cheaper in poor countries, and some of the exceptions are particularly important. Oil tends to be traded in US dollars, for example, and debts tend to be serviced in foreign currencies as well – meaning PPP exchange rates arguably overestimate the incomes of highly indebted countries and oil importers (Wade 2004). And, finally, allegedly equivalent baskets of goods and services aren't necessarily equivalent. Might haircuts in New York be better, and not simply more expensive, than those in Nairobi? And how would one know?

In a lighthearted effort to address these problems, the wags at the *Economist* went looking for a product that's identical all over the world and settled on the McDonald's Big Mac (*Economist* 2018). Despite adjustments for religious customs and dietary laws in a few countries, it's basically the same wherever it's sold: two all-beef patties, special sauce, lettuce, cheese, pickles, onions on a sesame seed bun. Add some low-cost labor and *voilà*: a uniform price benchmark!

Since 1986, therefore, the magazine has published a "Big Mac Index" that illustrates both the principle of purchasing power parity and the cost of living in dollar terms in different cities and countries around the world. If the price I pay for a Big Mac in Nairobi, once I convert my US dollars into Kenyan shillings, is the same as the price I pay in New York, the Big Mac Index equals 0, and implies equivalent costs of living. If the price is higher, the Big Mac Index indicates a higher cost of living in dollar terms, and an overvalued currency, in Nairobi; and if it's lower, the index suggests the opposite: a lower cost of living in dollar terms and an undervalued currency.[2]

Figure 2.1 compares the relative prices of Big Macs in dollars and the broader basket of goods and services used by the ICP in 17 countries and suggests that the choice of benchmark – Big Macs or the broader basket – makes a difference.

Most countries have lower price levels than the United States, whether in Big Macs or the broader basket, and developing country price levels are invariably – and for the most part substantially – lower. But the degree of difference depends on the price benchmark. For instance, the Chinese yuan is undervalued by just over 25 percent, according to the ICP, but by almost 40 percent in Big Macs, whereas the Brazilian real is undervalued by more than 30 percent, according to the ICP, and close to parity in Big Macs.

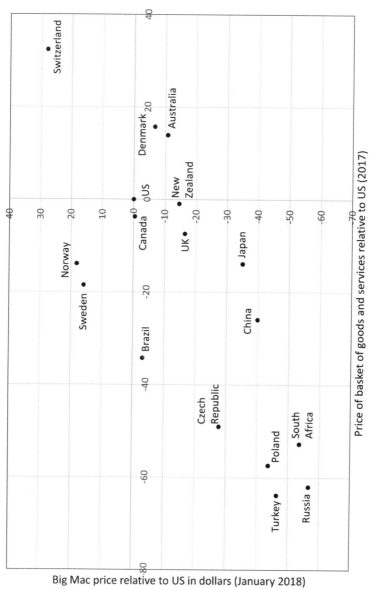

Figure 2.1 Price indexes of Big Macs and broader baskets of goods and services.

Source: Compiled with data from the *Economist* (2018) and ICP (2020); calculations by author.

To make matters worse, moreover, the two indices yield inconsistent – and not simply different – results for the Australian dollar and Danish kroner, which are undervalued at PPP and overvalued in Big Macs, and the Norwegian krone and Swedish krona, where the opposite pattern holds. And the Swiss franc is overvalued in both units.

One needn't make too much of these differences. On average, the two price indexes are correlated with each other across countries and time periods, developing countries have lower prices no matter which benchmark is used, and the Big Mac Index represents a narrow, if uniform, range of commodities in any event: a small number of food products and some unskilled human labor. But the comparison does suggest that the choice of benchmark matters both analytically and substantively.[3] Developing countries can't repay their lenders in "purchasing power parities." Cheap Big Macs are in all likelihood cold comfort to Danes who want balanced diets. And insofar as "development" implies something like "a move toward the good life," therefore, the real problem is that notions of the good life vary markedly over time and space; that is, they're not commensurable.

Meaning

It would seem likely that the real gap between rich and poor country incomes lies somewhere between the one portrayed by the market and PPP rates. But it's huge either way: a factor of four is less than a factor of five, to return to our Brazilian example, but it's still a big factor, at least when people's livelihoods and life chances are at stake. But the limits to GDP per capita, whether measured at PPP or market rates, are compounded when one looks under the hood at the distribution of income within countries, where incomes also tend to be skewed. After all, the typical Brazilian doesn't earn US$14,283 a year at PPP, because Brazil's GDP per capita is dragged upward by a small number of very wealthy families and a much larger "middle class" that's still small in relative terms. Brazil's median (or "typical") household income is actually one-tenth the US median (Nunes 2016: 3).

Consequently, the same GDP per capita can mean different things in different countries.

Consider, for example, two hypothetical countries with 10 residents each and per capita incomes of $10,000. In the first country, all 10 residents have incomes of $1,000, whereas in the second country one resident has an income of US$8,200 and the remaining nine have incomes of $200 each. From the exterior, the two countries look equally "developed" in terms of GDP per capita, but from inside they have radically different living standards and offer their residents distinct life chances.

Chile and Uruguay offer a stark, if less pronounced, real-world example. In 2017, they were the 63rd and 64th wealthiest countries in the world in terms of GDP per capita, at US$14,749 and US$14,437 respectively, but the top 10 percent of the population claimed a full 36 percent of the income in Chile and an outsized – but much lower – 29 percent in Uruguay. (To give a sense of proportion, the top 10 percent claimed about 23 percent of the income earned that year in the Nordic countries, which are often portrayed as the most equitable in the world.) Meanwhile, Romania and Brazil, ranked 72nd and 73rd richest overall at approximately US$11,000 per capita, diverged even more sharply in distributional terms – for the top 10 percent captured 25 percent of the income in Romania and a full 40 percent of the income in Brazil (World Bank 2020). It's hard to believe that the poor share similar life chances in these and similar pairings.

Beyond the traditional approach: development as freedom

Life chances are central to the leading alternative conceptualization of development: the "capabilities" approach originally formulated by economist Amartya Sen. According to Sen, the mark of a developed society is not material wealth per se but the maximization – or at least augmentation – of human freedom, including not only the "negative" freedoms of speech, press, association, and the like (i.e., freedom from repression and arbitrary authority) but "positive" rights to health, education, nutrition, and security, which at one point he labeled "freedom to achieve a valuable functioning" (Sen 1988: 280). In Sen's formulation, in other words, development is multifaceted and necessitates not only the production of material goods and services but their translation into "basic human capabilities" including, by way of illustration, "the ability to meet one's nutritional requirements, the wherewithal to be clothed and sheltered, the power to participate in the social life of the community" (Sen 1979: 218), and so on.

In an attempt both to *operationalize* and *popularize* this notion of development, Sen worked with economist Mahbub ul Haq to develop a composite Human Development Index under the sponsorship of the United Nations Development Programme (UNDP). The original HDI incorporated data on average life expectancy, which provided a proxy for the nutrition and health status of the population, literacy and school enrollment levels, which tried to tap education and skill formation, and GNP per capita, which offered an indicator of overall living standards (Somers 2007). The precise formula by which these indicators are collected and aggregated into an index that ranges from a theoretical minimum of 0 to a theoretical maximum of 1 need not detain us here (see UNDP 2019 for more information; and Anand 2018 for a discussion of recent methodological adjustments). The key point is that taken together, according to Sen, they provide a "crude index" of human capabilities and "broaden public interest in the other variables that are plentifully analyzed in the *Human Development Reports*" (Sen 1999: 4–5) published annually by the UNDP.

Furthermore, this is precisely what has happened. "Over the years, the reports have kept the HDI and the disaggregated data," according to philosopher Martha Nussbaum, "but they have also added other suggestive aggregations" (Nussbaum 2011: 60). For instance, the Gender Development Index adjusts the HDI for countries, like Japan, that display marked gaps between men and women in life expectancy, education, and earnings. The Gender Empowerment Index "measures not women's attainments in longevity and education but their access to managerial and political positions" (Nussbaum 2011: 60). And "inequality-adjusted HDI"

(IHDI) purports to take not just the average level but the distribution of health, education, and income into account. But the HDI is still the UNDP's "flagship" (Sen 1999: 4) indicator, and it thus merits particularly close attention.

A key difference between the HDI and GDP per capita is that the former is self-consciously multidimensional. The only way to increase GDP is to make (or track) more (or more expensive) goods and services, whereas HDI can be improved by increasing per capita income, boosting education, and/or raising life expectancy. But this distinction is arguably semantic. One might argue that "goods" and "services," including education and health care, are *different* dimensions of output that are arbitrarily treated as one by the producers and consumers of GDP data; that both can be further subdivided on demand (e.g., agricultural versus industrial goods; consumer versus producer services, etc.); and that GDP incorporates information on price as well as volume. And a social constructionist might go further, arguing that GDP figures aren't unidimensional because goods and services (or their prices and volumes) are *inherently* part of a single dimension but that we *think* of goods and services as components of a single dimension *because* they've been folded into GDP; that is, that concepts are naturalized, and in a sense made, by the indicators and not vice versa. "How constructed an object or relation appears is a function of how successful groups have been in securing its durability and legitimacy," according to Wendy Espeland and Mitchell Stevens, "in making it seem inevitable" (Espeland and Stevens 2008: 419). My point is less to question the – to my mind convincing – constructionist approach, therefore, than to note that the HDI is *intrinsically* and *self-evidently* broader in scope and possibility than GDP or GNP, not least of all because it includes an indicator of the latter.

By way of illustration, Norway and Australia had the highest reported HDIs in the 2015 report, at 0.944 and 0.935 respectively. But they got there in very different ways. Norway outperformed Australia by more than 50 percent in GNP per capita (US$66,584 versus US$43,246), but lagged Australia by approximately five years of expected schooling and one year of life expectancy at birth. Their almost indistinguishable overall performance thus masks multiple paths toward human development: some emphasizing material wealth, others prioritizing education, health care, and the like.[4]

This is true not only at the top of the scale, moreover, but down below. In a classic article entitled "Routes to Low Mortality in Poor Countries," demographer John Caldwell identified a number of countries that had dramatically over- or underperformed their respective incomes in terms of infant and child mortality and, largely by extension, life expectancy at birth. The overperformers included both liberal market economies like Costa Rica and Sri Lanka, that evinced deep commitments to education, empowerment, and the education and empowerment of women in particular, and state socialist societies like Cuba and China, where "education, health services, and improving the position of women were central ideological aims" (Caldwell 1986: 207–8) but their translation into human development was very different. We'll return to Caldwell's findings, and the broader relationship between gender relations and human development, in chapter 4. In the meantime, however, I'll explore some of the limits of the HDI in terms of coverage, measurement, and meaning.

Coverage

You may recall that GDP and GNP purport to capture all goods and services produced in or by a given country in a given year, but actually capture only those goods and services that are observed and tracked by government, leaving out goods and services produced by families and individuals for their own consumption and/or off-the-books in an effort to avoid regulation or taxation. Insofar as the HDI includes *direct* indicators of health and education, it mitigates this "coverage" problem. Gains in life expectancy and literacy are incorporated into the index whether they're the products of public or private efforts: hospitals and schools, for example, or farms and families. Since health, education, and income fail to capture all aspects of human development, however, the HDI is incomplete.

53

The most obvious oversights are civil and political liberties, or "negative freedoms" (Qizilbash 1996), which Sen admits are necessary – if by no means sufficient – to human capabilities. To stick with his example, it's hard to fully "participate in the social life of the community" (Sen 1979: 218) if one lacks freedom of speech and association, and Sen is perhaps best known for his finding that there's never been a famine in a political democracy (Sen 1999: 16), something he attributes in large part to the fact that democracies tend to respond to major crises – especially when a free press and opposition parties "sound the alarm" (Massing 2003). But the HDI nonetheless ignores political inputs and focuses on social and economic outputs.

Why does the HDI omit civil and political liberties? The problem is not, as many assume, that these concepts are too fuzzy to be measured or quantified. Scales of democracy and human rights exist (Giebler, Ruth, and Tanneberg 2018). Proponents of the capabilities approach admit that some capabilities need not be measured "on a quantitative scale" but can instead be evaluated in terms of an "acceptable threshold" (Nussbaum 2011: 62). And candidate thresholds are readily available (see, e.g., Alvarez et al. 1996). The real problem is political: the HDI is compiled by the United Nations (UN), and autocratic member states would oppose an index that punished them for their politics. Inasmuch as this reminds us that indicators are socially constructed and subject to political controversy, it's of theoretical as well as practical import. In particular, it speaks to broader debates between "realists" and "social constructionists" that will loom large in chapter 5 (Zuckerman 2012).

Measurement

Oversights are not the only problem. Components of the index are also problematic. Insofar as it includes GNP, for instance, the HDI suffers all of GNP's problems, including concerns about pricing and exchange rates. And it suffers additional problems that stem from the inclusion of education and life expectancy. School quality varies enormously across countries (see, e.g., Heyneman and Loxley 1983; Lee and Barro 2001; Baker, Goesling, and Letendre 2002), for example, and the aforementioned Norwegian students tend to do as well as their Australian counterparts on international tests of math and reading proficiency – which are themselves controversial – despite spending less time in school (Schleicher 2019). But the HDI makes no effort to take the quality – as opposed to quantity – of education into account. And the quality of life is no less variable. In some places, people are prone to live not only long but healthy and happy lives; elsewhere they live less healthy, if perhaps long, lives – especially given that life expectancy faces a ceiling effect. (People can't live forever, and average life expectancy currently tapers off in the eighties.) While indicators of quality-adjusted life years exist, and in a sense acknowledge the dilemma, they have not been incorporated into the HDI – in part, perhaps, because they are controversial as well as complicated.

Meaning

We've already seen that national data on average personal income mask enormous internal inequality, and, insofar as they're responsible for one-third of the HDI, the same problem holds. If a small share of the population captures an outsized share of the country's income, human development may be exaggerated. (Conversely, the HDI may underestimate human development in more equitable countries.) But the same goes for health and education: If they're distributed unequally across the population, human development may be exaggerated – and the inequities are compounded, from a normative, substantive, and policy perspective, when they're tied to individual identities or inherited characteristics like sex, gender, race, or ethnicity. (Consider, for example, the fact that white male life expectancy in the United States is about six years longer than black male life expectancy.) While the "inequality-adjusted HDI" (IHDI) tries to address these concerns, it is subject to conceptual and practical limitations that lead at least one sympathetic critic to recommend dropping it "from the armory of UNDP's human development measures" (Anand 2018: 39) entirely. Others disagree with his recommendation, of course, which just reminds us that these indicators are social constructs.

Reactivity in Rwanda: the social construction of development indicators

When Mahbub ul Haq first pitched the idea of a human development indicator, Amartya Sen expressed profound skepticism about trying "to catch, in one simple number, a complex reality about human development and deprivation" (Sen 1999: 4). Haq argued that, insofar as it would draw attention to "the social aspects of human lives" (Sen 1999: 5), the indicator's vulgarity was an asset rather than a liability. He hoped that the HDI would constitute "an improvement on, or at least a helpful supplement to, the GNP, but also that it would serve to broaden public interest in the other variables that are plentifully analyzed in the *Human Development Reports*" (Sen 1999: 5). Over time, Sen came to agree with him, and they undertook a successful effort to defend and propagate the HDI.

Consider, for example, the East African country of Rwanda. In the aftermath of a horrific genocide in 1994, President Paul Kagame announced an ambitious plan to boost the former European colony's HDI by the year 2020 (Ansoms 2009: 291; see also Beswick 2010: 230), and in so doing demonstrated both the success of Haq's campaign to legitimate the HDI and the "reactivity" of social indicators more generally. "Although definitions of reactivity vary across approaches," explain Wendy Espeland and Michael Sauder, "the basic idea is the same: individuals alter their behavior in reaction to being evaluated, observed, or measured" (Espeland and Sauder 2007: 6). While performance indicators don't guarantee reactivity (Fourcade 2011: 1724), they are an all but necessary component of the phenomenon. If the HDI didn't exist, for example, Kagame wouldn't have been able to target it.

Whether that targeting has been successful or not is another story. On the one hand, Rwanda's HDI has increased continuously since 1994, when at 0.189 it was the world's lowest, to

2018, by which point it had surged past 30 countries – including all four of its neighbors – to reach 0.536, an all-time high by far for the landlocked country. On the other hand, there are competing accounts and interpretations of Rwanda's gains. Some argue that Kagame has manipulated data and/or pressured the UNDP in an effort to make good on his commitment to raise the country's HDI (Ansoms et al. 2017; Ingelaere 2010: 47–8; Reyntjens 2011: 21–2; Congressional Research Service 2018: 8; Takeuchi 2019: fn. 4). Others hold that he is a brutal dictator and that the gains to health, education, and income, if real, have occurred at a cost in terms of substantive freedoms that are no less central to human development (Ansoms 2009; Himbara 2015; Dawson 2018; Hasselskog 2018; cf. Harrison 2017; Jones and Murray 2018; Weitz 2019).[5] And many have bemoaned the distributional costs of the alleged gains, noting that they have accrued disproportionately to urban dwellers and political insiders – leaving peasants and rural minorities far behind (Ansoms 2009; Beetz 2017; Dawson 2018; Bearak 2019).

I'm not trying to take a position in these debates, which are particularly incendiary in the current Rwandan context, but using them to "show how quantitative authority is accomplished and mobilized, how it gets built into institutions, circulates, and creates enduring structures that shape and constrain cognition" (Espeland and Stevens 2008: 419). What's not controversial, after all, is that Kagame and his supporters have used Rwanda's human development indicators to justify and defend their rule (Butty 2015; Rwakakamba 2016). They do this explicitly and self-consciously – whether justifiably or not.

Conventional development indicators are no less readily put to "political use" (Block and Burns 1986: 768), however, and Kagame and his allies have invoked their GDP growth performance toward similar ends (Beswick 2010: 230; World Bank 2011: 1; Ansoms and Rostagno 2012: 430). The point therefore is neither to discredit the HDI in particular nor to cast doubt upon development indicators *tout court*. On balance, they're probably credible, if not necessarily precise, in part because their mere availability need not guarantee their influence or efficacy (Stinchcombe 1997: 17–18;

Fourcade 2011: 1724–5); if they're not simultaneously *believable*, on average and over time, they're unlikely to prove influential – which is perhaps why international organizations tend to police the data integrity of their members (Webber 2013), albeit imperfectly (IMF 2016), and countries like North Korea refuse to join organizations like the World Bank that demand at least a minimal degree of openness, transparency, and data sharing among their members (Morrow 2006: 42). We'll return to these issues in our discussion of institutional change in chapter 5.

But the bottom line is that development indicators don't speak for themselves. They need to be interrogated. And when they're being interrogated, the interrogator will in all likelihood find that they provide an incomplete – if by no means worthless – guide to the international distribution of income and wealth, poverty and affluence, opportunity and constraint, etc., in part due to their uneven coverage, imperfect measures, ambiguous meanings, and – perhaps most important of all – reactivity.

Are GDP per capita and the HDI redundant?

Ongoing disputes between proponents of the traditional, commodity-centered approach and their critics shouldn't blind us to a simple reality: in practice, human development and per capita income are positively correlated. Figure 2.2 includes data on income and literacy for 150 countries in an effort to unpack the different dimensions of human development, with incomes per capita presented in terms of their natural logarithms for ease of exposition, and makes the relationship abundantly clear: more literate countries tend to be wealthier countries and vice versa.

Relatively prosperous countries, like Trinidad (US$16,784), therefore tend to approach the theoretical maximum of 100% literacy. Desperately poor countries like Guinea (US$750) tend to have extremely low rates of literacy (25%). And the Congo's literacy rate of 79% is almost exactly what you'd expect of a country with a per capita income of US$3,106.

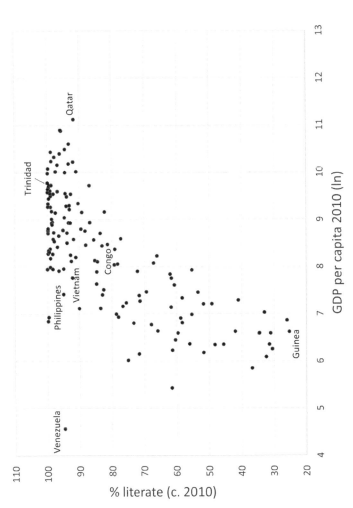

Figure 2.2 Literacy by GDP per capita for 150 countries.

Source: Data from World Bank (2021). GDP per capita presented in terms of natural logs. So, for example, Congo's GDP per capita in 2010 US dollars is about $3,106, or the antilog of 8.041201. The rank correlation between the two variables is 0.7 (p < 0.001).

Some have therefore asked whether human development indicators are "redundant" (Cahill 2005) in the presence of income data or add value to traditional measures of output (Kelley 1991). But less than half of the 150 countries in Figure 2.2 are found in the same income and literacy quintile. More than 15% are separated by *more* than a single quintile (i.e., 30 ranks). Only half the overall variation in literacy can be explained by income. And income and literacy sometimes move in the opposite direction. Qatar is one of the richest countries in the world (US$67,443), for example, and fails to reach median literacy of 92%. The Philippines and Vietnam exceed 95% literacy, despite falling well below the median income of US$6,136. And Venezuelan literacy rates have reached a comparable level (95%), despite an income decline from almost US$16,000 in the late 1970s – when literacy was 10 points lower – to about US$14,000 today.

The role of literacy is particularly important in sociology, moreover, for sociologists have long held that primarily literate societies are "fundamentally different from those made up primarily of illiterates" (Stinchcombe 1965: 150; Gellner 1987: 15–16). They're capable of carrying out large-scale trade with the help of formal record-keeping, operating railroads that require strict timetables, disseminating ideas and innovations to decentralized populations, employing clocks to coordinate precise schedules, and synchronizing the efforts of geographically diffuse people more generally. Formal organizations demand written rules, records, and procedures, and literacy and schooling are therefore indispensable to the survival and growth of institutions like research universities, regulatory agencies, stock markets, trade unions, and the multidivisional enterprise. While literacy has frequently been portrayed as a mere by-product of capitalism (Anderson 1983; Gellner 1983; cf. Eisenstein 1979; Leed 1982), or part of a broader "bundle of developments – urbanization, industrialization, income growth – due to the legacy of modernization theory" (Darden and Grzymala-Busse 2006: esp. 90), there's ample reason to believe that it's a "stand-alone skill" (UNESCO 2017: 39–40) with independent consequences. And radical governments have therefore made self-conscious efforts to combat illiteracy in religious, nationalist, and socialist contexts (Bhola 1984; Arnove and Graff 1987; Kowalewski and Saindon 1992; Cheng and Manning 2003). We'll return to these issues in chapter 4 in particular, when we discuss distributive regimes.

From cross-national inequality to interpersonal inequality in global context

You may be asking yourself about the global distribution of *personal* income, as opposed to the distribution of income, wealth, health, or knowledge among countries. Would our sense for who was better or worse off change markedly if we looked at individual-level data rather than country averages? In order to address this issue, economist Branko Milanovic has gone beneath the national-level data by aggregating the results of hundreds of household surveys conducted in the late twentieth and early twenty-first centuries. His findings are fascinating, but in no way inconsistent with the portrait painted by Figure 2.2. On the one hand, he finds that a disproportionate share of world income accrues to people in the "old rich" countries of Europe, North America, Japan, and the Antipodes, including not only their upper classes but their middle and lower-middle classes as well. The Global South lags behind, and sub-Saharan Africa lags far behind. On the other hand, he finds that recent income *gains* have been captured almost entirely by "global plutocrats," who also tend to be found in the old rich countries, and a "global middle class" (Milanovic 2016: 19) that's concentrated disproportionately in Asia. Most people in Latin America and the "transition countries" of Eastern Europe and Central Asia, and "poor people or lower middle classes in rich countries" (Milanovic 2014) have experienced stagnation or downward mobility.

Skeptics might therefore conclude that data from a single year, like those in Figure 2.2, obscure more than they reveal, including "the diverging economic trajectories of people in the old rich world versus those in resurgent Asia" (Milanovic 2016: 20). And they'd have a point: The diverging trajectories of the Atlantic and

Asian worlds were among the biggest stories of the late twentieth century, and they've been largely attributed to globalization
(Milanovic 2016). But "trajectory" and "fate" aren't synonyms.
Milanovic worries that Asia's rise will be undermined by populism, protectionism, and pandemics that are in part produced
by globalization itself (Bevins 2016; Milanovic 2020). And recent
events add further cause for concern (Erlanger 2020; James 2020;
Johnson and Papageorgiou 2020; and Roberts 2020).

What is middle about the "global" middle class?

Milanovic treats people whose household incomes fall between the
fortieth and sixtieth percentiles of the global income distribution
as members of a "global middle class," and notes that in "nine out
of ten cases" they're found in China, India, and Southeast Asia
(Milanovic 2016: 18–19). While they're still "relatively poor" by
western standards, and shouldn't be accorded "the same middle-
class status (in terms of income and education) that we tend to
associate with the middle classes in rich countries" (Milanovic
2016: 19), they're the most "obvious beneficiaries of globalization" (Milanovic 2016: 19), and therefore boasted per capita
incomes of US$1,000–2,000 per year at PPP in the early twenty-
first century. By way of contrast, the "lower-middle classes of the
rich world" had annual incomes of about US$5,000–10,000 after
taxes (Milanovic 2016: 29).

For all their merits, however, Milanovic acknowledges at least
two limits to his data. First, they're drawn from household surveys
that are conducted irregularly and imperfectly and tend to under-
count both the very poor – who are hard to find – and the very
rich – who are hard to recruit – in particular. And, second, they're
measured in purchasing power parities that are themselves subject
to criticism (Milanovic 2016: 15–17).

Others have discussed both the arbitrary and inconsistent
nature of income-based definitions of middle-class status and the
merits of consumption-based alternatives (Dadush and Ali 2012:
5). In the early 1980s, for example, sociologist Nathan Keyfitz

held that passenger car ownership signaled not only employment at a wage or salary that would provide for material comfort as well as basic needs but participation in a "worldwide middle-class culture" (Keyfitz 1982: 651) that's both a product and indicator of development. "Like any culture," he explained, "this one exists in people's heads, but its expression depends on material artifacts" (Keyfitz 1982: 651; see also Vasconcellos 1997) including passenger cars that offer both a strict criterion for middle-class membership and broadly reliable data. Keyfitz therefore treated development as a social fact and used data on passenger car ownership to estimate a global middle class of approximately 500 million people in the late 1970s, and others have gone further. For example, Uri Dadush and his colleagues have developed a "car index" that places the middle classes of the largest 35 developing countries at approximately 1.5 billion people today, and holds that they're growing much more rapidly than Milanovic surmised (Arbouch and Dadush 2019: 10–12; see also Dadush and Ali 2012; Islam 2014; Lutz 2014; Tannenberg 2014).

It's by no means clear that they can keep growing at that pace, however, especially if their expansion entails evermore fossil fuel consumption, urban sprawl, and environmental degradation (Balbo 2014: 275; Drabble et al. 2015: 18). Motor vehicles are the single largest contributor to climate change and a key source of particulate pollution, particularly in developing countries (NASA 2010; Taylor 2020). And no less an authority than Dadush recognizes the ecological limits to the growth of the global middle class (Dadush 2014: 28; see also Harris 2016: 129).

The point is less to endorse his car index, therefore, than to rescue a broader sociological point from a mass of statistical data. Economic development is in large part, if not entirely, a product of class, culture, and their constant interaction. When Lewis asserted that development demands a group of actors who "think in terms of investing capital productively" (Lewis 1954: 420), therefore, he was talking less about their incomes than their roles and mentalities. Where do they get their money? And what do they do with it? And when he worried that the middle classes would rather "buy big American cars" (Lewis 1954: 429) with their incomes than pursue the necessary capital formation, he was ruling out one potential candidate, just as he ruled out landlords who would engage in "prodigal consumption" (Lewis 1954: 419), peasants who would "pay off debt" to the lords (Lewis 1954: 429), and merchants who would speculate in scarce commodities along the way. "There is really only one class that is pretty certain to reinvest its profits productively," Lewis argued, "and that is the class of industrialists" (Lewis 1954: 429), ennobled as they are by both their "passion" for profit and their competitive need to rule over "bigger and better factories."

The nature of international inequality

Was Lewis right? We'll address that question in the chapters that follow. But in the short run his simultaneous confidence in the industrialists and contempt for their rivals serves as a useful reminder that incomes, indexes, and indicators like the ones we've discussed in this chapter for the most part *reflect* economic development; some reactivity notwithstanding, they probably don't cause it (Islam 2014). International inequality is ultimately, as Lewis knew, a *sociological* problem, and sociologists have long been divided over the idea of inequality itself. Some believe that it is *gradational* in nature, and that different people and communities simply have access to different levels, or grades, of key assets: income, wealth, status, etc. Others – including Marxists – believe that it is *relational* in nature, and that the better-endowed have achieved their assets in large part by taking advantage of their disadvantaged counterparts. If this is the case, moreover, the differential endowments of individuals and groups are less the returns to their distinct investments, let alone rewards and punishments for their respective behaviors, than predictable products of underlying relations of domination between, for example, lords and serfs, slaveholders and slaves, employers and workers, or for that matter colonizers and the colonized (Wright 1980: 201, fn.10; London 2018: 49).[6]

In fact, Marxists have drawn explicit parallels between class inequality within countries and cross-national inequality among countries. For instance, John Roemer imagines two broadly similar trading partners that are endowed with different ratios of capital to labor: Country A has more capital, in relative terms; Country B has more labor, in relative terms; and when the residents of A import goods from B they are in effect getting the better of the deal by exchanging the "dead labor" in their capital for the "living labor" of B's workforce, or consuming the embodied fruits of the "surplus" labor found in B, just as employers are inevitably getting the better of the deal when they hire workers cheap and sell the fruits of their labor dear (Roemer 1982: 281). What trade economists have come to call "unequal exchange" is therefore nothing more than a global manifestation of "capitalist exploitation" writ large (Roemer 1982: 300; see also Carling 1991: 114–17).

Roemer's point is not simply that different countries will be in different "classes," however, or that the country classes will inevitably come into conflict with each other over their respective gains and losses. It's that insofar as the different class positions – e.g., export enclave versus high-tech hub, debtor versus creditor, country of origin versus point of departure, etc. – are products of distinct capital-to-labor ratios that are at best arbitrary, and at worst the legacy of "robbery and plunder" (Roemer 1988: 9) that occurred long ago, the system itself is morally bankrupt.[7] Why should Alix have to work five times longer than David to earn enough money for a Big Mac? Or move to David's country to gain an opportunity? Because her country was robbed and plundered by his country more than a century ago?

Of course, the extent to which capital–labor ratios and their entailments are in fact the products of robbery and plunder is subject to dispute, albeit perhaps less so in the post-colonial environment. But the key point is that the relational account has normative as well as empirical implications. It says that consumers in the Global North are in effect consuming a disproportionate and unwarranted share of global output, especially when compared to a *hypothetical* counterfactual "in which each country is endowed with its per capita share of international capital" (Roemer 1982: 300). In the real world, of course, that counterfactual is unavailable, and poor countries have little choice but to endure the current system. But that doesn't make the current system fair, let alone indisputably so, or gainsay the value of a relational approach.

The case for a relational approach is, if anything, more powerful in a world on the brink of ecological collapse. The theory of "ecological unequal exchange" holds that rich countries not only consume more than their fair share of the world's goods and services but displace the environmental costs of their consumption onto poor countries that lack the power to resist (Bunker 1985; Martinez-Alier 1995; Rice 2007). For instance, Mexico's northern border has been portrayed as a "pollution haven" that attracts "dirty" industries from the United States in an effort to generate jobs and growth (James 2019; see also Giljum and Eisenmenger 2004; Berry, Kaul, and Lee 2021). And Roemer and his associates are particularly sensitive to the distributional implications of human-induced climate change (Llavador, Roemer, and Silvestre 2015). While the ratio of greenhouse gas emissions to output (i.e., "GHG intensity") is more than 50 percent higher in the Global South, they argue, the level of *emissions per capita* is more than three times higher in the Global North (Llavador et al. 2015: 219). Climate justice therefore demands both an overall slowdown in the global growth rate – to protect future generations from the effects of climate change – and a *relative* increase in the growth rate in the South to foster distributive justice and – in all likelihood – cooperation. The problems of emissions and development are "inextricably intertwined, on this account, and it is hopelessly naive to suppose that one problem can be addressed in isolation from the other" (Llavador et al. 2015: 29).

A classification of development concepts

The discussion so far lends itself to four different understandings of development arrayed along two key dimensions. The first dimension, discussed at the outset of the chapter, differentiates commodity- and capability-centered approaches: Does development demand material wealth alone or the broader fulfillment of culturally mediated human potential? The second dimension,

Table 2.2 A typology of development concepts

		Conceptualization of inequality	
		Gradational	*Relational*
Concept of development	*Commodities*	Mainstream economics: development material; countries independent	Neo-Marxist: development material; countries interdependent
	Capabilities	Modernization: development social; countries independent	New economic sociology: development social; countries interdependent

discussed in the previous section, distinguishes gradational from relational notions: Is development a characteristic of individual countries, comprehensible in isolation, or a systemic product of the relationships among countries, in need of a more holistic perspective? The answers to these two questions produce the different perspectives on the conceptualization and, by extension, measurement of development in Table 2.2.

The most common approach is found in the northwest quadrant: a gradational and commodity-centered notion of development. This is the default perspective of both mainstream economists, perhaps in part because it accords with their baseline assumption of material self-interest, and international financial institutions like the World Bank and the International Monetary Fund, which collect, maintain, and propagate data on GDP per capita.

The southwest quadrant may come as a surprise to some since modernization has frequently been portrayed as a "conservative" theory and the capabilities approach has typically been invoked as a "critical" alternative. But modernization theorists got their start with a broad notion of development (or modernity) before standardized GDP data were available (Rostow 1956: 26), and expressed ambivalence about national accounts data when they appeared. No less an authority than Rostow, for example, placed "welfare" next to "output" among his chief concerns, worried that data on national accounts would prove a distraction if treated in isolation (Rostow 1956: 26, 1957: 520; 1963: esp. xix–xx), and he came under attack for his "imprecise" (Habakkuk 1961: 602) definition of the term "modern" in particular. But his successors would nonetheless invoke even broader definitions of modernization (Feldman and Hurn 1966: 378–9) and eventually treat the HDI as a broadly comprehensive indicator of the process (Welzel and Inglehart 2001: 11; Marsh 2008: esp. 818–19).

Neo-Marxists, on the other hand, hewed pretty close to mainstream measures of development itself but viewed it in relational terms. In their classic study of "the stratification of the world-economy," for example, Giovanni Arrighi and Jessica Drangel wanted to understand "differences in command over world economic resources rather than . . . differences in actual standards of living" (Arrighi and Drangel 1986: 31), and therefore focused on cross-national and longitudinal variation in GNP per capita. And, in a posthumous tribute to Arrighi's earlier work on the Calabrian case, Beverly Silver draws a sharp distinction between "catching-up development" of the sort studied in the earlier article and "popular welfare," proxied by things like "health indicators" (Silver 2019: 573).

In short, the two perspectives that assume material self-interest on the part of the individual treat material output as the key indicator of development, while the perspective that takes on a broader notion of human motivation and behavior takes on a broader notion of development. In that sense, there is a certain consistency to the table and argument. But the southeastern quadrant is novel because, to my knowledge, nobody has made an explicit case for a *broadly relational* notion of development, i.e., one that takes non-pecuniary goals and values seriously and recognizes human interdependence.[8]

The resultant oversight offers an opportunity for economic sociology. Even scholars who are wary of the notion of exploitation, for example, are likely to recognize the interconnectedness of today's world, the fact that what happens in one country almost inevitably affects what happens in others, and the fact that these effects are *patterned*. Rich countries in the Global North tend to be the growth poles, creditors, and host countries; poor countries in the Global South tend to be the export enclaves, debtors, and countries of origin. Whether consumers in the Boston Banana Republic are exploiting Bangladeshi workers or not, therefore, they're certainly consuming more than their proportionate share of the world's finite resources, and it's therefore impossible to fully understand either group in purely gradational terms. This is true, moreover, regardless of one's normative assessment of the inequalities involved.

Conclusion

In this chapter, I've tried to do four things. First, I've tried to describe and distinguish two different ways of thinking about development – the commodities and capabilities approaches – and their most common indicators: GDP per capita and the HDI. Second, I've discussed their relative advantages and disadvantages, including – but not limited to – their potential for reactivity, redundancy, and insensitivity to interpersonal income differences. Third, I've acknowledged that both indicators ultimately capture a social fact that "exists in people's heads" (Keyfitz 1982: 651; see also Horowitz 1964: 353; Harms 1981: 404–6; Gong and Jang 1998: 89) but is manifest, in part, by their possessions, livelihoods, and living standards. And, finally, I've drawn a distinction between gradational and relational understandings of development and made the case for a *broadly relational* approach in economic sociology, particularly in a world of finite resources in the midst of a global ecological crisis. Chapter 3 builds on this typology by digging deeper into the distinction between "broad but gradational" modernization theory and "narrow but relational" neo-Marxism and defends the broadly relational alternative on empirical and theoretical, and not merely conceptual, grounds.

Before moving onto these issues, however, I'd ask you to consider life expectancy data, which tend to be drawn from census and/or vital statistics (e.g., birth and death registration). Life expectancy figures are almost certainly more accurate and accessible than data on either: GDP (or GNP) per capita (Maddison

2001: 169), which not only incorporate census data and vital statistics into their denominators but add more complex data into their numerators; or the HDI, which incorporates life expectancy, output, and education data. And life expectancy has no less a claim to proxy for human well-being. What most of us want out of life is more time, for better or for worse (Abbott 2005: 420), and with more time we could produce more goods and services in any event. But life expectancy is at best a second-tier indicator of well-being in both national and cross-national contexts. Chief executives are judged on the rates of growth they achieve, or fail to achieve, and driven from office during recessions. Why is this the case? And what would the world look like if life expectancy, and not GDP per capita, was the dominant measure of progress? Would policymakers and people pursue different priorities and/or allocate their resources differently? Toward what end? Answers to questions like these will allow us to denaturalize the current order and produce a more productive economic sociology of development in the years ahead.

3

Is International Inequality Gradational or Relational?

Why do living standards in the Global South lag their northern counterparts? The answer is by no means obvious. While historians have reconsidered the label "Dark Ages," and for the most part abandoned the term, they've done so less by comparing Europe to non-western regions than by raising doubts about the degree of "change and continuity" (Nelson 2007: 197) within Medieval Europe itself. Most historians agree that the "rise of the West" (McNeil 1963) is a relatively recent phenomenon, and that European living standards were no higher – and in some cases lower – than their non-western counterparts at the end of the first millennium (McNeil 1990: 6–7; Landes 1998: 98; Goldstone 2000: 180–1; Pamuk and Shatzmiller 2014: 223). And neoclassical growth theories have little to say about their initial divergence – let alone the subsequent "catch-up" of latecomers like the United States, Japan, and Korea (Chang 2002).

This shouldn't be surprising. Postwar growth theories purported to explain the *persistence* of "growth at full employment" (Toye 2009: 222), not the *origins* of growth itself, and their architects were quick to recognize not only their demanding assumptions but their limited generality (Boianovsky 2018). While the best-known growth theorists tailored and/or applied their models to the European countries and the "neo-Europes" (Crosby 1986) they had settled by means of genocide in the New World and the Antipodes (see, e.g., Seers 1963; Myint 1965; as well as Solow 2001: 283), the study of development in the rest of the world was seen as an inherently interdisciplinary endeavor – one that required input from myriad experts and fields. When Brazilian economist Celso Furtado published his classic piece on capital formation and development, therefore, he invoked the contributions of anthropologists, sociologists, and historians – in addition to economists – and disdained the idea that his subject matter belonged to a single discipline or perspective (Furtado 1953; see also Boianovsky 2010).

Many of the sociologists in question were modernization theorists. They rejected the self-interest assumption distilled into Table 1.4, embraced a broad notion of development like the one in the lower row of Table 2.2, and anticipated growth in the global periphery in large part due to the diffusion of western values – including asceticism and acquisitiveness in particular. While Furtado had doubts about their apparent optimism (Furtado 1969: 60; see also Boianovsky 2010), he expressed similar concerns about mainstream economics, and therefore remained committed to an interdisciplinary approach that would "break the barriers between the economic, the social, and the political" (Furtado 1976: 12; my translation) well into the 1970s (Furtado 1979: 33).

By the 1970s, however, the interdisciplinary approach he favored had already fallen victim to a tacit alliance of mainstream economists, who wanted to expand the realm of self-interest, and neo-Marxists, who viewed identities, relationships, norms, and values as little more than by-products of material motivations and resources and attacked "almost everything for which people said they were willing to make sacrifices" (Olson 1965: 104), including religion, nation, culture, and community, as masks for what was ultimately self-serving behavior. While the economists for the most part embraced the logic of diminishing returns, and anticipated the convergence of rich and poor countries in a world of full employment, mobile capital, and self-interested utility maximization, the neo-Marxists believed that the rich would build on their first-mover advantages by exploiting the poor and therefore had no less faith in persistent underdevelopment. If the global labor supply is really "unlimited," they argued, and the most desperate, defenseless, and vulnerable sources of labor are really confined to the Global South, convergence is much less likely than the ongoing exploitation of poor workers in (or from) poor countries by rich employers in (or from) rich countries and the corresponding repro- duction of international inequality. Just as the wealth of capitalists presupposed the poverty of workers *within* countries, according to this version of Marxism, the wealth of global capital presupposed the poverty of workers who tend to originate or be concentrated in poor countries – where they serve as a "global reserve army of labor" (Szreter 2018: 764) – and development is therefore a "rela- tional" rather than a "gradational" process; that is, more like a football game, in which one side vanquishes the other, than a foot- race, in which everybody crosses the finish line at different times.

In short, the disputes between Marxism and the mainstream derived less from different attitudes toward human motivation than from different perspectives on global markets. Where main- stream economists believed that full employment would give rise to diminishing returns in the North and a shift in economic activ- ity to the South, Marxists believed that rich countries would build on their head starts by exploiting underemployed resources in the South and keeping the valuable activity at home. But the two groups agreed on the power of material self-interest, and for the most part put paid to the study of non-material factors in development.

My goal in this chapter is to document, explain, and assess the evolution of development theory in the postwar era. I'll begin in the 1950s, when modernization theorists asked why diminishing returns had not opened the door to growth in the non-western econ- omies, traced the answer to their "traditional" cultures and values, and predicted that the breakdown of the latter would bring about the acceleration of the former. Economic development demands cultural transformation, they argued, and would follow the intro- duction of "modern" attitudes and values from external sources. I'll go on to discuss the mirror image of modernization theory pre- sented by neo-Marxists, who believed that people in poor countries were no less acquisitive or materialistic than their western counter- parts but were exploited by the latter – who captured increasing, rather than diminishing, returns to trade and investment over time.

Underdevelopment follows imperialism and neo-colonialism, they argued, and would prove enduring in the absence of revolutionary change. I'll pay particularly careful attention to Clifford Geertz and Giovanni Arrighi who, to my mind, offered the most sophisticated and influential defenses of modernization and neo-Marxism respectively. And I'll try to reconcile their rival perspectives by drawing parallels between the late twentieth-century debate over the origins and implications of *international* inequality and the ongoing debate over inequality and social mobility *within* the advanced industrial countries, concluding that we'll need insights from both perspectives if we're to understand development and underdevelopment in the twenty-first century.

Modernization theory

Economic growth demands investment. Investment presupposes savings. And Lewis therefore held that the principal problem in development theory was "the process by which a community is converted from being a 5 per cent to a 12 percent saver – with all the changes in attitudes, in institutions and in techniques which accompany this conversion" (Lewis 1955: 226). Why would people save for a tomorrow they might never live to see and enjoy? Especially when the legal and institutional foundations of saving and investment were at best unreliable and underdeveloped?

The best-known answer derives from Max Weber and his "Protestant Ethic" (Weber 1930). According to Weber, the Protestant Reformation gave birth to the notion of predestination. Members of the Puritan faiths, and Calvinists in particular, believed that their fates were foreordained by God; that is, their fates were determined before their births. They were either among the elect, who were "called" to eternal salvation, or the damned, who would burn forever in Hell. And the Puritans therefore came to view an industrious, ascetic life as a sign – but not a means – of their eventual salvation.

In other words, the Puritans viewed hard work, savings, and accumulation not as a means toward wealth in this world but as a sign of salvation in the next, and the arrival of ascetic Protestantism thus broke "the link between production and consumption" (DeLong 1989: 234) that inhibited growth in traditional societies. Where members of traditional societies produced in order to consume, and enjoyed the fruits of their labor, Puritans consumed – as little as possible – in order to produce as much as possible, and in so doing fueled a fundamental transformation of the economy and society.[1]

The Weberian approach thus divides the world into "modern" societies, marked by savings, investment, and growth, and "traditional" societies, marked by stagnation and stasis. While formal institutions that expand people's time horizons – like schools, banks, bureaucracies, law, and contract – are indispensable to growth in the former, they're not simply transferable to the latter; on the contrary, they'll be wasted and worthless in the absence of acquisitive goals among the population and appropriate behavior by government officials. This is what we mean when we say that institutions are culturally mediated. Merely adopting a limited liability law won't foster entrepreneurship if potential entrepreneurs don't trust the government to uphold the law – or to stay in power long enough to enforce its provisions (Stinchcombe 2003: 423). And limited liability is by no means the only example. The Global South is littered with property titles that protect no property, currencies that have been devalued to the point of abandonment, civil service laws that are "aspirational" (UNDP 2007: 6), and courts that have earned the confidence of neither plaintiffs nor defendants, to mention just a few examples.

Schools arguably provide the most important example of all, insofar as they both presuppose and produce the prudence and foresight that allegedly underpin modern society. Industrial societies presuppose literacy, numeracy, and record-keeping, after all, and schools tend to propagate both these skills and their value. But parents who rely upon child and family labor are unlikely to entrust their children to unproven schools that are run by unpredictable regimes, and traditional societies are therefore marked by high rates of illiteracy, innumeracy, absenteeism, and the like.

75

What do these traditional societies look like? According to modernization theorists, they're marked by high fertility, high mortality, and – contrary to the Lewis model – not by labor surplus but by labor scarcity. For instance, Wilbert Moore drew a distinction between the overall *size* of the labor force and "its attitudes toward disciplined, rationalized endeavor," noting that the latter were no less "crucial determinants of industrial development" and subject to "infinite variation" (Moore 1948: 44–5). Alexander Gerschenkron argued that "industrial labor, in the sense of a stable, reliable, and disciplined group that has cut the umbilical cord connecting it with the land and has become suitable for utilization in factories, is not abundant but extremely scarce in a backward country" (Gerschenkron 1962: 9). And Clifford Geertz described the Javanese peasants he studied in post-colonial Indonesia as "addicted to labor – the more they use the more they need" (Geertz 1963: 101; see also 32) – and invoked the notion of a "ratchet effect," arguing that they'd find it easy to add workers to their sophisticated irrigation and cultivation systems but difficult to withdraw them without putting their social and physical infrastructure at risk. Population growth in traditional society was therefore accompanied by "shared poverty" (Geertz 1956a: 141) – rather than the simultaneous concentration of land in the hands of the rich and dispossession or expropriation of the poor – as peasants divided "the economic pie into a steadily increasing number of minute pieces" (Geertz 1963: 97) in an effort to preserve their way of life. Efforts to transfer labor from the countryside to the city in keeping with the principle of comparative advantage would therefore prove fruitless if peasants said no, disastrous if they said yes, or more likely both – if enough left to undercut the traditional social structure and enough stayed to suffer the consequences.

The foundations of Javanese peasant society had deteriorated by the late twentieth century, according to sociologist Nathan Keyfitz, but enough had survived to justify the continued use of the term "shared poverty" (Keyfitz 1985: 705, 1995: 32; see also Storm 2015: 691). What were those foundations? Geertz had argued that the sharing of poverty was a product less of the innate humanism of Javanese peasants than a culturally embedded approach to collective problem solving. The rural Javanese economy presupposed a complicated system of land and labor exchange "among both kith and kin" (Geertz 1956a: 140), he argued, as well as an explicitly defined – albeit adaptable – array of rights and responsibilities that all but obliterated the hoary distinction between the cultural and the material (Geertz 1984); hence, his "attack on both neoclassical and Marxist explanations of economic change in Third World countries" from the standpoint of *"cultural* ecology" (Geertz 1991: 8; my emphasis).

Geertz is best known as an anthropologist. But he completed his PhD in the Department of Social Relations at Harvard under the mentorship of Talcott Parsons, and his early work on the Indonesian peasantry is best understood in that context (Gilman 2002: 6). Under the leadership of Parsons, and with ties to Walt Rostow at nearby MIT, the Department of Social Relations has been described as "the fountainhead for modernization theory in sociology" (Gilman 2002: 5), and Geertz played a key role in their collective effort to develop "the sociological equivalent of the Newtonian system" (Geertz 1995: 100). Like Rostow, for instance, he challenged the "pure Arthur Lewis" (Rostow 1970: 198; see also Rostow 1982) model of development by denaturalizing the notion of employment and unemployment and asking whether labor could really be withdrawn at no cost from rural communities like the one he encountered in Java. Geertz argued:

> If a unit of labor is added to a productive process without adding anything to production, it is possible that the process may nevertheless alter its structure, after a period, in order to assimilate this new "redundant" labor, that a withdrawal of it again will now cause a fall in output, at least until the system "re-adapts," which may be quite a while if the process is more "used" to expanding than contracting its labor element. (Geertz 1956b: 114)

He would go on to invoke the addiction analogy, once again, by noting that the added pleasure a heroin addict gets from a larger dose "may be almost infinitesimal," but the additional pain he would suffer if denied access to the drug could prove "overwhelming" (Geertz 1956b: 114). And later scholars would build on his critique by acknowledging the social construction of employment and unemployment more generally and developing "more flexible and culturally relevant measures of labor utilization" (Collins 1987: 24).[2]

The key point, however, is that modernization theorists like Geertz held that traditional societies were trapped in a low-level equilibrium: Unable to deploy "modern" technology, in light of both their penury and their culture of keeping everyone employed (Geertz 1956b: 36), they had no choice but to deepen their commitment to labor-intensive, low-productivity, and "ultimately self-defeating" (Geertz 1963: 80) productive systems like wet-rice agriculture. Whereas take-off in Rostow's model therefore entailed the investment, industrialization, and income growth familiar to residents of rich countries (Rostow 1956), take-off in traditional society, according to Geertz, combined population growth and material privation (Geertz 1963: 69–70). More people meant more baroque adaptations that simultaneously required even more people and reproduced their poverty.

What this means in practice, of course, is that development will not flow smoothly – or perhaps at all – from the reallocation of labor anticipated by Lewis. Recall that Lewis viewed labor as the abundant factor of production in poor countries and capital as the constraint. If poor countries could produce or attract capitalists to exploit their cheap labor, therefore, they would experience the employment, income, and productivity growth anticipated by the theory of comparative advantage; that is, shared prosperity rather than shared poverty. But Geertz's model suggests that, in traditional societies like Java, labor is not necessarily more readily available than capital; on the contrary, peasants may be loath to abandon their friends, families, and communities no matter how high the money wage, especially in the presence of labor-intensive agricultural systems and the absence of a functioning labor market.[3]

Modernization theory is frequently portrayed as naively optimistic. On careful inspection, however, it is both more pessimistic and more deterministic than the Lewis model. Where Lewis believed that traditional societies were awash in underemployed labor just waiting to be unleashed and exploited by savvy capital-ists, to everyone's benefit, the most sophisticated modernization theorists thought traditional societies were damned either way: if their most productive members left their communities in order to take jobs offered by savvy capitalists in the cities, for example, they'd condemn their friends and family members back home to hunger and hardship; if they stayed home to maintain the terraces and irrigation canals, however, they'd be condemned to shared poverty forevermore. "Discussions of capital transfers mean little in the absence of some sort of discussion of through what kind of man [sic] the transfer is to be mediated, what sort of institutions might regulate its distribution, what sort of cultural traditions determine its mode of employment," argued Geertz, "and these are all partially historical questions" (Geertz 1956b: 108).

By way of illustration, Geertz traced the transformation of Javanese culture – later corroborated by Keyfitz – in part to the "adoption of culture patterns external to the system" (Geertz 1956a: 140; see also Keyfitz 1985: 698), and to the early twentieth-century arrival of pious "Muslim modernists" (Geertz 1956a: 144) in particular. Unlike their more traditional and less pious neighbors, Geertz argued, the modernists prioritized reli-gious education, the pilgrimage to Mecca, and the diligence and frugality that would make both financially possible. Just as the Puritans invoked by Weber consumed in order to produce, there-fore, the Muslim modernists treated "individual effort, thrift, and simplicity" (Geertz 1956a: 145) – all of which militated against cooperative endeavors and mutual aid – as ends in themselves, despite the fact that their traditional neighbors viewed them as greedy misers, and in so doing set in motion a process of class dif-ferentiation involving the growth of small-scale sugar plantations in the countryside and urban commerce "capitalized with rural wealth" (Geertz 1956a: 145–6).

Muslim modernists were by no means the only source of new ideas and institutions. Geertz also discussed the role of Dutch colonialism and the "demonstration effect" (Geertz 1963: 114) that allegedly motivated and facilitated modernization in the colo-nies more generally (Rostow 1960: 26–7) – in part by introducing

European ideas, institutions, and values and in part by fanning the flames of nationalism and rebellion. "Without the affront to human and national dignity caused by the intrusion of more advanced powers," argued Geertz's associate Rostow, "the rate of modernization of traditional societies over the past century-and-a-half would have been much slower than, in fact, it has been" (Rostow 1959: 5–6).

But Geertz held that modernization in Java had nonetheless been constrained by three contingent factors and one cultural. First, the Dutch colonial authorities imposed a series of burdensome regulations designed to protect the traditional village from disruption in the early twentieth century. Second, the Great Depression depressed global sugar prices and, with them, the growth of the plantation complex. And, finally, the departure of the Dutch turned elite "interests away from the economic field toward the political" on the assumption that "if your party gets elected, the rest is easy" (Geertz 1956a: 149). But no less – and arguably more – important, according to Geertz, were traditional values like modesty, mutual aid, and self-restraint that left the budding entrepreneurs unwilling to adopt primogeniture, resist community demands for charity or support, or "exploit the available labor without regard for the traditional norms and prescriptions regulating its employment and remuneration" (Geertz 1956a: 149). While the Muslim modernists had turned away from traditional Javanese values, Geertz argued, they had "not turned so very far" (Geertz 1956a: 149).

My point in rehearsing this sequence of events is not to pass judgment on Geertz's account of the transformation of Javanese society, let alone the transformation of peasant societies more generally. His critics and defenders are both legion and I have nothing to add to their efforts (Gilman 2002; White 2007; Hauser-Schäublin 2015). It is simply to use him to illustrate three common aspects of modernization theory: first, a portrait of traditional society "trapped" in a low-level equilibrium by both *diminishing returns* to labor and *sociocultural* as well as *material* impediments to its redeployment; second, the invocation of *external* sources of transformation, where and when it occurs; and, third, the recognition that the transformation itself will entail *hardship*, whatever the long-term consequences. Geertz is quite clear on this latter point: The question is not whether the demise of traditional society will entail hardship; it's whether the hardship will usher in development, as in Japan, or more poverty, as in Java (Geertz 1963: 143).

Modernization theory is therefore neither as naive nor as optimistic as its critics suggest (Gilman 2002). Insofar as it implies that there is "no free lunch" offered by underemployed labor, foreign capital, patriotic politicians, or any other source, in fact, it offers a more depressing portrait than the one painted by Lewis and his associates. Even Rostow, whose work constituted a self-conscious defense of modernization as a process, and not merely a theory, acknowledged both the role of foreign conquest in the transformation of traditional society (Rostow 1960: 6) and the possibility of an "aborted" take-off nonetheless (Rostow 1963: xix, 1970: 163).

The neo-Marxist alternative

Modernization theory is not nearly as depressing, however, as the neo-Marxist alternative by which it was deposed in the late 1960s and 1970s. Whereas modernization theorists believed that the so-called laws of economics militated in favor of development, and traditional cultures were to blame for its delay, neo-Marxists believed that cultures were largely malleable, but that the laws of economics themselves militated toward international inequality. People in poor countries were no less acquisitive than their rich-country counterparts, the neo-Marxists believed; they simply had fewer opportunities to produce or acquire valuable things, in large part due to the legacy of European colonialism, and there was no reason to believe this would change (Valenzuela and Valenzuela 1978: 545).

By way of contrast, Marx himself has been portrayed as a modernization theorist *avant la lettre* (Wallerstein 1997a: 25), and for predictable reasons. His portrait of modernity is "surprisingly similar" (Avineri 1969: 176) to the one put forward by twentieth-century modernization theorists, not to mention Weber.

He ultimately portrayed "European colonial expansion as the only guarantee for modernization and change" (Avineri 1969: 181) in the non-western world. And his well-known declaration that "the country that is more developed industrially only shows, to the less developed, the image of its own future" (Bendix 1967: 308; Palma 1978: 889) could easily have been written by Rostow, and came in for harsh criticism by "neo-Marxists" who believed that twentieth-century capitalism offered "a less hospitable environment for economic development than did nineteenth-century capitalism" (Mandle 1980: 868; see also Foster-Carter 1978).

The problem, according to the neo-Marxists, was that European imperialism had indeed undermined the foundations of traditional societies like Java – including their solidarity and cohesion – but had not opened the door to their industrialization. On the contrary, it had augmented international inequality by relegating their descendants to the production and export of low-value primary products (i.e., bulk commodities and unprocessed raw materials) and the importation of high-value manufactured goods from the former colonial powers – a possibility introduced, but not fully explored, by Marx himself (Palma 1978: 887).

Consider, for example, the "deterioration in the terms of trade" (Prebisch 1959: 258; Singer 1961: 395) predicted by the economists Raúl Prebisch and Hans Singer in the postwar era. According to the "Prebisch–Singer" thesis, as it came to be known, the pursuit of comparative advantage will not prove beneficial to developing countries because the income elasticity of demand for the primary products they export *to* rich countries (i.e., additional demand for their products attendant upon a given change in the buyer's income *ceteris paribus*) is lower than the income elasticity of demand for the manufactured goods they import *from* rich countries for at least two reasons: first, because foodstuffs, fibers, forest products, and minerals are vulnerable to the development of alternative sources of supply, conservation, and new technologies in rich countries; and, second, because there's a biological ceiling on human food consumption – but no such ceiling on the human desire for manufactured goods – that guarantees differential elasticities of demand.

Table 3.1 Prebisch on the terms of trade between center and periphery

Center	Income growth	Income elasticity of demand	Import growth
Center	3%	0.8	2.4%
Periphery	3%	1.3	3.9%

What these differential elasticities mean in plain English, of course, is that for every additional dollar earned in rich countries, *ceteris paribus*, less will be spent on imports from poor countries, whereas for every additional dollar earned in poor countries, more will be spent on imports from rich countries – yielding a trade imbalance over time. Prebisch offers the following illustration. Imagine a world of two countries: a rich, or "center," country that has a comparative advantage in the production and export of manufactured goods, with an income elasticity of demand of 1.3; and a poor, or "peripheral," country that has a comparative advantage in the production and export of primary products, with an income elasticity of demand of 0.80. If both of their economies grow at 3% per year, and they have identical rates of population growth, the rate of import growth in the center will be 2.4% (3% × 0.8) per year and the rate of import growth in the periphery will be 3.9% (3% × 1.3) per year (Table 3.1), leaving the peripheral country with a growing trade deficit.

Nor will productivity gains in the primary product sector solve the problem. On the contrary, they will aggravate international inequality by allowing peripheral producers to lay off workers in an effort to cut costs, lower their prices in an effort to lure customers, and thereby transfer the fruits of their productivity improvements from producers in the periphery to consumers in the center (Prebisch 1959).

In fact, Singer drew upon similar ideas to challenge the very notion of diminishing returns discussed in chapter 1. While primary products would indeed confront diminishing returns, he argued, due to the emergence of scarcity, substitutes, and conservation, manufactured goods would be governed by increasing returns (Shaw 2002: 51; Ho 2012: 883), particularly insofar as they drew upon education, skilled labor, and human brainpower.

"Investment in education not only is highly productive," Singer argued, "but yields increasing returns in so far as cooperating teams of skilled and educated people are worth more than the sums of the individuals of which they are composed" (Singer 1961: 390).

Over time, therefore, peripheral countries will either have to radically reduce their consumption of the high-technology goods that constitute the very essence of modernity – that is, to suffer austerity – or abandon their comparative advantage in primary production by pursuing industrialization and innovation (Prebisch 1959: 254). Where industrialization appeared relatively straight-forward in the Lewis model, however, and a likely outcome in the best-known versions of modernization theory, it seemed a near impossibility to the neo-Marxists; instead, they drew upon the work of Prebisch, Singer, and their associates to formulate theories of unequal exchange that posited declining commodity prices in the periphery, rising incomes in the center, and the growth of international inequality over time (Frank 1976; Love 1980).

The impediments to development within the system lay not, however, in attitudinal barriers to wage labor and industry, according to the radicals, but in the structure of the world economy itself. While neo-Marxists recognized the distinct features of traditional society, including both the limited development of land, labor, and commodity markets and the widespread collaboration of families and friends, they held that colonial and post-colonial powers, first, had introduced commercialization, competition, and conflict; and, second, had thereby engendered a "global proletariat" (Jonas and Dixon 1979: 6) of hundreds of millions of suddenly landless, unskilled peasants who'd be willing to work at almost any price (Feder 1976: 533; M. Davis 2004: 18; Therborn 2014: 8). If the unlimited supplies of labor assumed by Lewis were not the original condition of the Global South, therefore, they'd apparently become commonplace by the late twentieth century, in large part due to imperialism.

They had not, however, animated the industrial development anticipated by Lewis. On the contrary, they'd begun to reproduce themselves in cities, and by the early twenty-first century their numbers included not only the unemployed but the under-employed and the marginalized as well (Arrighi 2009: 77). One well-regarded study placed the number of informal workers in the Global South at approximately two billion, with almost half of the total concentrated in the non-farm labor force (Jütting and de Laiglesia 2009: 2). And the gap between jobs and jobless on a world scale is expected to grow larger before it grows smaller (Benanav 2019: 700).

In short, neo-Marxists assume that rational investors will repro-duce international inequality by keeping capital and skill-intensive activities in rich countries and relegating their land- and labor-intensive counterparts to the Global South, and therefore make two predictions that directly contravene modernization theory: first, that peripheral countries are unlikely to move to the center, given the global distribution of human and physical capital; and, second, that if upward mobility occurs, the peripheral country's rise will entail a center country's decline, given the process of unequal exchange. Development and underdevelopment are there-fore "two sides of the same coin" (Sánchez 2003: 32; Amin 2017: 14).

Perhaps the most consistent and compelling neo-Marxist account of international inequality lies in the work of Giovanni Arrighi, which offers a particularly apposite contrast to the mod-ernization theory espoused by Geertz. Where Geertz was mentored by a sociologist in the United States and gained fame as an anthro-pologist in Southeast Asia, Arrighi was trained as an economist in Italy and came to sociology through the study of Africa – where he taught, in Rhodesia and Tanzania, in the 1960s – and an appointment at the State University of New York at Binghamton, where he joined Immanuel Wallerstein and others to build the neo-Marxist "world-system perspective" (see, e.g., Arrighi, Hopkins, and Wallerstein 1983; Arrighi 2009) on international inequality.

The world-system perspective holds that the "core" of the capi-talist world economy "exploits" the periphery through a process of unequal exchange not unlike the one described by Prebisch and Singer (Hopkins and Wallerstein 1977: 114–15) but that it's assisted, in a sense, by a middle-income "semi-periphery" (Arrighi

1991: 46) that – like the middle classes *within* capitalist societies (Chirot 1980: 539; Breen and Rottman 1998: 4) – serves to
legitimate and stabilize the system as a whole. In that sense, the
international class or status order is like the domestic status order
writ large. "Politically," explains Arrighi:

> a system polarized in a small distinct high-status and high-income
> sector, on the one side, and a large, relatively autonomous, low-status,
> low-income sector, on the other side, would lead quite rapidly to
> acute and disintegrating struggles. The major political means by which
> such crises are averted is the creation of 'middle' sectors, which tend
> to think of themselves primarily as better off than the lower sectors
> rather than worse off than the upper sector. (Arrighi 1990: 31)[4]

Arrighi and Geertz are among the most sophisticated representatives of neo-Marxism and modernization theory respectively,
and despite their disciplinary, regional, and theoretical differences,
their portraits of "traditional society" in sub-Saharan Africa and
Southeast Asia are superficially similar. Like their Southeast Asian
counterparts, for example, Arrighi's peasants were guaranteed
access to the inputs they needed – including land – through a
series of customary rights and obligations including "obligatory
gift- and counter-gift-giving between persons who stand in some
socially defined relationships to one another, and/or by obligatory payments or labour services to some socially organised centre
which re-allocates portions of what it receives" (Arrighi and Saul
1968: 144). Market transactions were very much the exception to
the rule, in his view, and technology was "rudimentary" by contemporary western standards – albeit sufficient to guarantee the
individual's "security of subsistence" (Arrighi and Saul 1968: 144).
And, finally, Arrighi was no less sensitive to the social construction
of categories like "unemployed," "productive," "leisure," and
"necessary" than Geertz and his fellow modernization theorists.
Whereas Lewis and his associates viewed indigenous African men
as underemployed, for instance, Arrighi noted that they

> were not only in charge of development works, hunting and the care
> of cattle. They also helped the women in cultivating the land, espe-

cially at planting and harvesting time, and were in charge of a number of non-agricultural productive activities (weaving, net-making, iron-working, etc.) which must have absorbed a non-negligible amount of labour-time until they were supplanted by the importation of capitalist manufactures. (Arrighi 1970: 201, 2002: 25)

The very notion of "disguised unemployment" is, of course, meaningless in this context (Arrighi 1970: 202), and Arrighi therefore condemned the ahistorical application of the Lewis thesis to Africa – just as Geertz had condemned ahistorical assumptions of "capital transfers" in Indonesia (Geertz 1956b: 108).

Where Arrighi and Geertz parted company, however, was in their discussion of the *dynamics* and *downfall* of pre-industrial society. By way of synopsis, Geertz held that the interaction of modern and traditional productive arrangements can either advance or impede development, and "that the most important set of variables determining the difference between the two outcomes – the developmental and the anti-developmental – is broadly cultural and social rather than narrowly economic" (Geertz 1956c: 434). Where traditional values prioritized modesty and cooperation, he argued, individual peasants and their families would rather divide "the economic pie into smaller and smaller pieces" than tolerate dramatic growth in inequality (Geertz 1956a: 141) – and when they relocated to cities in the twentieth century they brought the "share-the-poverty syndrome" (Geertz 1963: 146) along with them. By way of contrast, Arrighi held that traditional values were no match for the colonial powers, who actively created the "unlimited supplies of labor" imagined by Lewis in societies that "were structurally incapable of absorbing them" (Arrighi 1970: 226; Silver 2019: 574), and thereby produced a persistent gap between the low-wage periphery and the high-wage core.[5]

On both accounts, the result is "dualism," or the parallel and inequitable growth of a capital-intensive "modern" sector and a labor-intensive "traditional" one in the Global South (Geertz 1963: 101; Arrighi and Saul 1969: 158; Arrighi, Aschoff, and Scully 2010: 426), but their diagnoses are antithetical to each other. For Geertz, the problem is that the traditional society refused to embrace the modern; for Arrighi, the problem is that it had no alternative.

Arrighi first began to address colonialism when he took a position in Rhodesia in the early 1960s (Arrighi 2009). In search of land and labor, he found, the British had imposed taxes designed to force indigenous Africans into the money economy, expropriated their land, and divided the society into a series "of non-competing racial groups" in a process that was coercive and violent (Arrighi 1966: 41; see also Arrighi 1970). In fact, the "color bar" that emerged in Rhodesia bore a striking resemblance to similar institutions that had been established in settler colonies throughout the world, and it played a similar part in the production and preservation of European privilege (Coulter 1935; Malinowski 1943; Drake 1951; Burawoy 1974; Greenberg 1980). Whether formal or informal, enforced by law, custom, or agreement, institutions like these prevent indigenous workers from acquiring, exercising, and/or obtaining due reward for their skills, and thereby leave them little choice but to take second-rate jobs for third-rate wages (Hooker 1965: 3, fn. 1). "Roughly speaking," in the words of one more or less contemporary observer, "the African's ceiling is the European's floor" (Gussman 1953: 139).

Over time, therefore, African peasants began to display "greater responsiveness to wage employment opportunities" (Arrighi 1970: 205) in the absence of *direct* coercion, according to Arrighi, in part due to the elimination of viable alternatives and in part due to the transformation of their needs. Just as terms like "productive" and "leisure" are socially constructed, he argued, terms like "necessities and subsistence are not to be understood in an exclusively physiological sense: people get used to what they consume and 'discretionary' consumption items can, with the mere passage of time, become necessities" (Arrighi 1970: 211). Arrighi gave the examples of foodstuffs, like sugar, salt, and jam; agricultural equipment, ranging from hoes and picks to wagons and ploughs; and services, including education and transportation; and he went on to discuss a "cumulative" and "irreversible" process of proletarianization in Southern Africa: European expropriation and population growth fostered land shortages, driving peasants into marginal areas that necessitated costly investments in equipment and transportation; soil quality and economic returns declined accordingly, driving peasants into the growing wage-labor market; and wages therefore declined, augmenting "the African worker's interest in the security afforded by membership of a rural-based kinship group" (Arrighi 1970: 218) that no longer provided much security. Mid-twentieth-century Rhodesia therefore bore at least some resemblance to mid-twentieth-century Java: torn between a traditional society that was no longer viable and a "modern" society that was barely tolerable.

Of course, Rhodesia and Southern Africa were distinct insofar as they were colonized in large part by European settlers on their own behalfs rather than by their governments on behalf of agricultural and mineral interests (Arrighi 1966: 36; Arrighi and Saul 1969: 154), and Arrighi would eventually highlight the differences, as well as the similarities, between the two models when addressing Africa north of the Zambezi and south of the Sahara, where capital-intensive firms had kicked off a "spiral" (Arrighi 1970: 125) of wage increases and mechanization in the mining and plantation sectors in particular: low aggregate labor costs allowed capital-intensive employers to appease their workers with short-run wage concessions; and short-run wage concessions gave capital-intensive employers a reason to double down on capital-intensive techniques and technologies, to the detriment of the labor force as a whole, over time.

The eventual story in the tropics, therefore, was the emergence of a small "labor aristocracy" (Arrighi and Saul 1969; Arrighi 1970) – made up largely of better-educated Africans – using capital-intensive methods to produce primary products for northern corporations and consumers – and a mass of underemployed "semi-proletarians" who would find neither good jobs in the cities, security in the countryside, nor allies among post-colonial bureaucrats and labor aristocrats who owed their very existence to international capital (Arrighi 1970: 141–2). The parallels not only with the "bifurcated" economies found in the "New States" discussed by Geertz (Geertz 1977: 259) but with the "older" societies of Latin America, where different terms captured similar dynamics

(Arrighi and Zhang 2011: 31), were striking. And Arrighi would go on to decry the growth and exploitation of a "global reserve army" (Arrighi 2009: 77) of unemployed, underemployed, and marginalized labor in the periphery as a whole.

By the late twentieth century, in short, traditional societies were dead and their peripheral successors were being impoverished not only by means of the process of unequal exchange discussed by Prebisch, Singer, and their successors (Arrighi 1970: 106) but through the voluntary transfer of their most valuable human and financial resources – via emigration, capital flight, and profit repatriation – to central economies in which they'd yield the largest, most stable returns (Arrighi 1990: 13; 2002: 11). The problem was not the absence of "modern" values like rationality, individualism, and self-interest, however, but their *presence* in a world of desperate workers and increasing, rather than decreasing, returns to human, physical, and financial capital. In essence, Arrighi believed, the international economy is subject to the "Matthew effect," as the rich get richer and the poor get poorer, and not the law of diminishing returns at the heart of mainstream economics.

Toward a resolution?

Modernization theorists and neo-Marxists part company over the relative weight of culture and colonialism in producing underdevelopment. But they're no less divided over the consequences of "national development" were it to occur. While modernization theorists viewed development as a worthy goal open to all comers, at least in principle, neo-Marxists worry that developing countries are "running fast to stay in the same place" (Silver 2019: 573; Arrighi and Drangel 1986: 60).

Who is correct? Are developing countries living up to their name, or forever condemned to remain on the margins, or periphery, of the world economy? The answer depends in part upon one's preferred indicators and predicted patterns of development. Modernization theory fell out of favor in the late twentieth century, in part for good reason, but its proponents can point toward almost universal increases in life expectancy, decreases in fertility, and growth in urbanization, education, income, and the "world culture" (Meyer et al. 1997) by which they're allegedly accompanied to defend their approach. Words like "backward" and "modern" may well offend contemporary sensibilities, but insofar as they viewed the "literacy – of more than a small esoteric group – as the single most important criterion for transition from 'primitive' to more advanced societies" (Parsons 1970: 515), the modernization theorists weren't entirely wrong. More than half the world's adults couldn't read in 1950; by 2000, illiterates were a distinct minority (Patrinos and Psacharopoulos 2011: 5). By way of contrast, neo-Marxists can invoke both the persistence – and, by some metrics, growth – of international inequality and the reconsideration of the diminishing returns assumption within mainstream economics itself (Romer 1986) to defend their position – and take comfort in the corresponding legitimation, if by no means hegemony, of their own arguments (see, e.g., Acemoglu, Johnson, and Robinson 2005: 550–1). But none of this will resolve a debate that is driven less by different understandings of development than by different understandings of inequality and, perhaps more importantly, mobility.

Mainstream economists and modernization theorists defend their positions by pointing not only toward *global* increases in literacy, life expectancy, and income but at the upward mobility of *individual* nation-states in the course of the twentieth century. If countries like South Korea and Ireland can jump from the periphery to the center by dint of effort, skill, and luck, they ask, can't any country do so, and isn't it misleading to portray peripheral countries as victims of an unfair world-system, let alone condemned to underdevelopment? The neo-Marxists have responded by invoking an analogy from the animal kingdom first introduced by the late R. H. Tawney in discussions of inequality *within* capitalist societies. The mere fact that the most diligent and/or fortunate tadpoles will "shed their tails, distend their mouths and stomachs, hop nimbly on to dry land, and croak," argued Tawney, does nothing to console the tadpoles left behind, let alone to moderate the "social evils" that pervade the system as a whole (Tawney 1929: 108–9).[6]

Neo-Marxists have described "developmental ideology" as the "global version" of Tawney's tadpole philosophy (Wallerstein 1974a: 9; Arrighi 1990: 36), or a mask for an unjust world-system. "States pursuing national wealth in a capitalist world-economy face an 'adding-up' problem similar to, and in many ways more serious than, the one faced by individuals," argued Arrighi. "Opportunities for economic advance, as they present themselves serially to one state after another, do not constitute equivalent opportunities for economic advance by all states," he continued. "Economic development in this sense is an illusion" (Arrighi 1991: 58; see also 61–5 on the tadpole philosophy more generally).

The neo-Marxists are definitely onto something. Our country of origin has a bigger effect on our life chances, on average, than our assigned gender, race, or class (Sangiovanni 2011: 581), and is no less arbitrary. So the world-system is inherently unfair. And there's no inherent reason to believe it would be fairer with more mobility. On the contrary, it's entirely possible that one country's upward mobility is offset by another country's downward movement – or worse. For instance, Arrighi worries that core states will respond to successful challenges by closing ranks and defending their privileges, "and thereby deepen and widen the gulf for those who are left behind" (Arrighi 1990: 18). And the interdependent, or *relational*, nature of development and underdevelopment are all the more apparent in a world of climate change, ozone depletion, pollution, and the like – where externalities, or spillover effects, ensure that your fate in your country depends on my behavior in my country.

One need not consider the system fair, however, to consider mobility prospects important. Biologists have extensively studied the origins of success and survival among tadpoles, after all, despite their full awareness that most tadpoles will die (see, e.g., Newman 1987; Morey 1998), and they would never dismiss frogs – or confuse their terms – by labeling them an illusion; instead, they would ask which tadpoles become frogs under which circumstances, why, and what might be learned from the answers.

Similarly, sociologists are well aware of the limits to social mobility: not everybody can be a chief executive officer, elite surgeon, or award-winning chef; somebody has to operate the machinery, clean the floors, and pick the tomatoes – whether they want to or not. But sociologists still have good reason to study at least two different types of mobility among individuals: first, "exchange mobility," which occurs when people move up or down in a theoretically fixed class or occupational structure; and, second, "structural mobility," which occurs when there's a shift in the class or occupational structure itself – e.g., when the number of farmers declined markedly and the number of factory workers grew in late nineteenth- and early twentieth-century Europe and North America (Beckfield 2020: 23).

Why study upward and downward movement if the positions themselves are fixed? Consider a world in which we didn't study exchange mobility but instead derided it as a mere mask for an inherently inequitable and unjust system. Individuals and families would have no idea how to improve their life chances. Policymakers wouldn't know which regulations and social programs were more likely to foster or constrain opportunity. And organizations like unions, parties, and social movements wouldn't know whom to organize, how, or toward what end, among other things. It's easy to say that mainstream politics and modest reforms are mere distractions from the broader campaign for a more equitable society, but in the short run they make an enormous difference in people's lives – and set the stage for the broader campaign – and they're all but unintelligible without an understanding of social mobility.

By the same token, the neo-Marxists can encourage policymakers and activists in the Global South "to seek to transform the system as a whole rather than profit from it" (Arrighi 1991: 64), but they've yet to present any empirical evidence that "developmentalism" is an *alternative* to "human solidarity and equality" (Arrighi 1991: 63), rather than their *complement*, or perhaps is simply *unrelated*, and they're unlikely to find converts to their cause in any event. People on the periphery of the world-system are no less, and perhaps more, interested in material well-being than their counterparts in the core, and their political representatives, rulers, and champions will have a hard time resisting their demands; hence, the power of the "development ideology" the neo-Marxists decry.

There is a second reason to study national development, however, despite its apparent infrequency. Specifically, in their efforts to improve their relative standing, or to pursue the cross-national equivalent of exchange mobility, *peripheral* policymakers and their people can in principle improve *global* living standards or contribute to the cross-national equivalent of structural mobility. Nor is this far-fetched. Just as dirty, dangerous, and ill-paid jobs have gradually and unevenly given way to better jobs – if not necessarily "good" or "clean" jobs in an objective or ecological sense – *within* countries, as individuals and organizations have pursued education, training, automation, and the like, bad world-system positions have been improved over time, as policymakers have pushed national development. Consider, by way of illustration, the fact that at the dawn of the modern world-system, Wallerstein's periphery specialized in the export of primary products that "favored the use of slavery and coerced cash-crop labor as the modes of labor control" (Wallerstein 1974b: 401), whereas today's periphery is marked mostly by wage labor – a mode of labor control that was unique to the core in the long sixteenth century. Isn't this, in some sense, a case of structural mobility on a world scale induced by industrialization at the national level, particularly insofar as all but the worst-off wage laborers live longer, healthier lives than all but the best-off slaves and serfs? While the neo-Marxists have – at times implicitly – answered in the affirmative, they've gone on to invoke the ecological costs of any material improvements that have been made (Arrighi 1991: 41; Wallerstein 2004: 278; Wackernagel et al. 2004: 265). "Sure," they seem to be saying, "a few countries have industrialized. But the ecological costs are overwhelming, and their experiences are therefore inimitable."

In fact, the most pessimistic neo-Marxists bemoan the growth of "ecological unequal exchange" (Rice 2007; Shandra, Leckband, and London 2009; Jorgenson 2016) that is, in some sense, akin to the unequal exchange identified by Prebisch and Singer in the mid-twentieth century. The rich countries monopolize the "clean" industries and activities, in this perspective, and offshore their "dirty" counterparts to the Global South. Perhaps unsurprisingly, however, they've been challenged by advocates of "ecological modernization theory" (Mol, Spaargaren, and Sonnenfeld 2014), who not only expect growth to facilitate the development of clean technology, the diffusion of green values, and the passage of protective legislation but hold that modernization is therefore "necessary for societies to achieve ecological sustainability" (Pellow and Nyseth-Brehm 2013: 232).

My point is less to take a position in this debate, which is both complicated and contentious, than to note that it's unlikely to be resolved in the absence of insight into *national* development (Buttel 2003: 336; Fairbrother 2016: esp. 380). Will developing countries grow by burning fossil fuels or developing sustainable alternatives? Will the global middle class demand green products and policies or dirtier, cheaper alternatives? Is the "willingness to pay" for pollution control positively related to income and, if so, to what degree? Only by answering questions like these can we discern the relationship between economic development and environmental protection, and we're unlikely to answer these questions in the absence of careful, case-based evidence (Jorgenson and Clark 2012: 9).

Conclusion

In this chapter, I've tried to do three things. First, I've tried to discuss modernization theory and its role in bringing the study of development into twentieth-century sociology. Second, I've discussed neo-Marxist alternatives and their challenge to both modernization theory and mainstream economics. And, finally, I've tried to reconcile the two perspectives by noting their distinct levels of analysis: modernization theory is operating at the "unit level," trying to understand why different countries develop at different paces and/or occupy different positions in the international system at different points in time; whereas neo-Marxism is operating at the "systems level," trying to understand the persistence of the "core–periphery income divide" (Schwartz 2007: 115) in the world as a whole. Chapter 4 will delve deeper into the unit level by asking why different "units," or countries, prospered or stagnated by different metrics in the second half of the twentieth century.

But, in the meantime, I'd ask you to reconsider the debate on the systems level by asking yourself two related questions. First, is the struggle for development more like a footrace, in which everybody crosses the finish line at different times, or a football game, in which one country's victory is another's defeat? And, second, does the answer depend on (or perhaps influence) your preferred indicator of development? Modernization theorists tend to think of development as a race, and insofar as they use a broad notion of development there's a good deal of support for their gradational view. Literacy and life expectancy are converging toward their literal or ostensible ceilings in poor as well as rich countries, for example, and middle-class culture is for better or worse gaining ground. However, neo-Marxists tend to think of development as a football game, and insofar as they reduce development to GDP per capita can find support for their relational view. Convergence in income has been neither as rapid nor as consistent as convergence in literacy and life expectancy in the postwar era and, insofar as it has occurred, it's taking an enormous toll on the world's environment and habitability.

What if we used the broadly relational notion of development advanced in the prior chapter? Would development look more like a footrace or a football game? I suspect it would look like a football game, especially in a world of finite resources, since continued growth in the rich countries would leave fewer resources for the poor countries. But the answer will depend in large part on patterns of growth at the national level, which will be addressed in part in chapter 4.

4

Explaining National Mobility in the Cold War Era

Between 1965 and 1990, real per capita incomes in the so-called high-performing Asian economies (HPAEs) of Hong Kong, Indonesia, Malaysia, Singapore, South Korea, Taiwan, and Thailand grew at approximately 4 percent per year, on average, or more than twice as fast as real incomes in the developing countries of Africa, Latin America, the Middle East, and South Asia (Campos and Root 1996). The most successful HPAEs, South Korea and Taiwan, grew faster still – at an average of 6 percent per year (Ito 1994: 276). And observers therefore began to discuss an "East Asian miracle" (World Bank 1993).

The principal paragons of *human* development, however, are not the HPAEs but poorer countries that have translated *slower* growth into *comparable* levels of health and education. Consider, for example, Costa Rica and Chile, where growth rates lagged the HPAEs but life expectancy nonetheless kept pace in the late twentieth century (McGuire 2001); the larger group of "superior health achievers" studied by John Caldwell (Caldwell 1986: 174), only one of which was found among the HPAEs; or the revolutionary communist countries, including Cuba and Vietnam, that Caldwell believed "should be included among the superior health achievers" (1986: 175) but that he nonetheless omitted due to a lack of complete data. While people in the HPAEs are healthy and well educated, to be sure, they're neither healthier nor better educated than their incomes would predict; on the contrary, they tend to confirm the widely held belief that "wealthier is healthier"

(Pritchett and Summers 1996), not to mention better educated, whereas the superior health achievers suggest that health doesn't necessarily demand wealth in the first place.

The late twentieth-century growth of income in East Asia and life expectancy in countries like Costa Rica and Cuba posed a challenge to both neo-Marxism and modernization theory. While neo-Marxists had anticipated stagnation, inequality, and crisis in Asia, and dismissed talk of a miracle as "propaganda" (Frank 1984: 800; see also Fröbel, Heinrichs, and Kreye 1978; Hettne 1983), modernization theorists had anticipated *more* growth *beyond* Asia and the *convergence* of growth and human development. If modernity is a "package deal" (Berger, Berger, and Kellner 1973; Woolcock 2011; El Amine 2016), after all, literacy, life expectancy, and income should be highly intercorrelated not only with each other but with industrialization, urbanization, capitalism, and liberal democracy (Rowden 1998/9: 165; Darden and Grzymala-Busse 2006: 112), whereas the actual correlations are relatively modest and decidedly uneven.[1]

By the late twentieth century, therefore, modernization theorists and neo-Marxists were beginning to address these anomalies by asking how international pressures interact with local politics to shape development outcomes, paying particularly careful attention to the peripheral state. Modernization theorists traced peripheral stagnation to the misdeeds of incompetent, corrupt, or venal officials who frittered away the "advantages of backwardness" (Gerschenkron 1962: 51; Bendix 1967: 332; Smith 1979: 278–9) including the availability of foreign capital, technology, and experience. Neo-Marxists treated the occasional success story as evidence that under exceptional conditions capable and committed states could turn the lemons of imperialism and unequal exchange into the lemonade of growth and human development (see, e.g., Eckstein 1982; de Brun and Elling 1987; Chibber 2002; Shin and Hytrek 2002). And the grand theories that dominated chapter 3 thereby gave way to an ever-growing array of "states with adjectives" (Leander 2005: 134) – failed, predatory, protective, developmental, warlord, and quasi-, among others – designed to account for their anomalies.

This chapter is designed to bring order to the literature on states and development by, first, distinguishing industrial from pre-industrial societies in general (Gellner 1983); second, discussing the development strategies adopted by low-income countries in the twentieth century and their respective consequences; and, third, attributing their consequences in large part to the interaction of two variables: the accommodation or transformation of the rural elite by political authorities; and the development or underdevelopment of price-setting (or capitalist) markets, and particularly labor markets, in the course of industrialization. While the transformation of the rural elite and the development of capitalist markets are frequently viewed as two sides of the same coin, I argue, they need not hang together, and by considering them separately we can develop a parsimonious typology of states and development outcomes that has the dual advantage of incorporating both capitalist and non-capitalist cases, on the one hand, and distinguishing growth and human development, on the other: Where the authorities accommodate the rural elite and impede the growth of capitalist labor markets, I contend, *patrimonial* states continue to pose an obstacle to both growth and human development. Where the authorities transform the rural elite but impede the growth of capitalist markets, however, *distributive* states wind up putting human development first, albeit for ambivalent reasons. Where the authorities accommodate the rural elite and build an urban labor market, by way of contrast, *populist* regimes leave ambiguous legacies on unstable foundations. And where the authorities transform the rural elite and build an urban labor market, instead, *developmental* states jump-start growth, which itself boosts human development. Obviously, these are blunt categories that leave much to be explained, but I conclude the chapter with thoughts on the origins of the different authority types and economies and dig deeper into both in chapter 5.

From agrarian to industrial society

The late Ernest Gellner divided world history into three broad stages: a pre-agrarian stage marked by limited specialization, spatial reach, and centralized authority; agrarian societies characterized by a more expansive division of labor into specialized roles including – but not limited to – military and political authorities; and an industrial stage distinguished by a role structure that's not only more expansive but less stable than the division of labor found in agrarian society. Industrialization both presupposes and produces economic growth, Gellner argued, and "is thereby committed to the need for innovation and hence to a changing occupational structure" (Gellner 1983: 32).

One need not accept Gellner's use of the world "stage," or his implicit teleology, to accept his overarching portrait, at least in broad outline. It would be foolhardy to ignore the family resemblances among the pastoral and hunter-gatherer societies that fall into his "pre-agrarian" camp, caste, millet, and feudal economies that make up his "agrarian" category, and free-market and centrally planned economies that form his "industrial" family, just as it would be foolhardy to ignore their myriad differences. Where rival typologies highlighted the many *differences* between "capitalist" and "communist" countries during the Cold War, for example, Gellner's typology highlights their key similarities (Gellner 1982: 269). First, the authority structures of pre-industrial – and in particular agrarian – societies are almost entirely personal, whereas industrialization is a necessary – if by no means sufficient – condition for impersonal rule (Gellner 1983: 102). Second, pre-industrial society leaves inequality on the surface, whereas industrial society buries it beneath a myth of equality, whether capitalist or socialist (Offe and Wiesenthal 1980; Gellner 1983; Eisenstadt 1992). And, third, pre-industrial societies tend to empower warriors and watchmen, whereas industrial societies tend to empower civilian professionals. "At the base of the modern social order stands not the executioner but the professor," Gellner argued. "The monopoly of legitimate education is now more important, more central than is the monopoly of legitimate violence" (Gellner 1983: 34) emphasized by Max Weber a century ago – in part because schools indoctrinate and socialize the very officers and foot soldiers who themselves monopolize the threat of force. If one cannot prevent a *coup d'etat* by passing "an article in the constitution," as Guillermo O'Donnell later argued, one must instead stop it by building schools and socializing the citizenry and soldiers (Przeworski 2004: 529).

Of course, Gellner was quick to acknowledge both the contested origins of European industrialization and the unique nature of the original transition. "No imitative industrialization can be treated as an event *of the same kind* as the original industrialization," he argued, "simply in virtue of the fact that all the others were indeed imitative, were performed in the light of the established knowledge that the thing could be done" (Gellner 1982: 268). But he also believed that industrial societies – whether capitalist or not – had more similarities than differences when viewed in long-term historical perspective, and he therefore welcomed the apparent shift of scholarly attention from the "origins of capitalism" to the "origins of industrialism" in the late twentieth century (Gellner 1982: 269).

After all, the so-called latecomers were united less by their desire to build capitalism than by their desire to build industry (Kautsky 1997; Wallerstein 1997b). Most of them set out to foster the local manufacture of durable and non-durable consumer goods (e.g., appliances, apparel, footwear, etc.) either by abolishing private property and building command economies, in the former communist countries of Eurasia, or by embracing a policy package known as import-substituting industrialization (ISI) in the non-communist countries of the so-called Third World. In other words, the command economies abandoned or bypassed price-setting markets in favor of central planning, whereas ISI simply imposed limits on their operation. While the former communist countries have long since been absorbed into either the European Union, legally, or the Global South (Öniş and Kutlay 2010: 109), conceptually, they should be evaluated on their own terms, for their industrialization occurred amidst distinct conditions that go a long way toward explaining their fate, according to Shmuel Eisenstadt, including social mobilization and educational expansion (Eisenstadt 1992: 33). "A pretense of equality, even if very shabby, evolved," he explained. "With respect to the middle and lower groups, it was not only pretense" (1992: 33). I will therefore begin the discussion of late industrialization in the command economies of early twentieth-century Eurasia before moving south geographically and forward historically into a discussion of ISI.

Industrialization via central planning

The best-known command economies are the Soviet Union, the People's Republic of China, and their fellow communist societies, where revolutionary parties took power in predominantly rural contexts only to find themselves on the horns of a dilemma. Illiteracy inhibited nation-building and state formation by limiting not only the supply of expert administrators but the extent to which their subjects could understand and carry out their orders and recommendations; and bureaucratic underdevelopment posed an obstacle to education and schooling by limiting not only the supply of teachers but the broader underpinnings of their success. If the modern state really is "more jealous of its near-monopoly of education than it is of its monopoly of legitimate violence" (Gellner 1975: 209), as Gellner argued, then the *initial monopolization of education* – hindered, as it is, by a lack of teachers, students, and resources that are themselves the *products* of formal schools – is arguably the *fundamental dilemma of late development*.

The point is not to equate "illiteracy with ignorance or literacy with wisdom" (Fordham 1983: 21), moreover, but to recognize that, *for better or for worse*, literacy and numeracy provide the foundation of a different *kind* of economy and society. In their absence, explained Arthur Stinchcombe, people cannot read and write checks and contracts; calculate interest payments, profits, or bills of exchange; administer the law, extract taxes, or conduct large-scale trade over longer and longer distances; develop, codify, and disseminate knowledge to more and more people; or know and defend their rights. Literacy not only fosters the growth of new organizations, including firms and political organizations, but increases their "staying power" (Stinchcombe 1965: 150; see also Stinchcombe 1974: esp. 105–6). While patrimonial authorities have therefore tried to limit the spread of education to their most loyal allies, like kith and kin, they've faced little opposition from their illiterate subjects – and, in particular, peasants, pastoralists, and nomads – who lack not only the means but the inclination to redirect their resources and children from traditional household enterprises to schools that are entirely alien to them. "To refuse or to abandon writing and literacy," explains James C. Scott, "is one strategy among many for remaining out of reach of the state" (Scott 2009: 229).[2]

Take, for example, the Soviet Union. When the Communist Party took power in the fall of 1917, illiteracy was by far the norm, especially in the countryside, and posed a threat to both human resource development and political indoctrination (Lauglo 1988; Clark 1993).[3] No less an authority than Lenin had already declared literacy a prerequisite to "mass participation in control and accounting" (Wright 1974–5: 87–8), and he therefore inaugurated a nationwide campaign to "liquidate" illiteracy almost immediately upon taking power (Kenez 1982; Clark 1993). If the communists, who'd already transformed their party from a "voluntary association into an administrative apparatus" (Stinchcombe 1968: v; see also Selznick 1952), could educate and indoctrinate the population, he believed, the dilemma of late development might well be surmounted in short order. If they could not educate the population, however, they'd stand no chance.[4]

Peasants, however, saw things differently (Kline 1958: 17–18; Clark 1993: esp. 62–3). From their perspective, after all, Lenin's intentions were hardly benign. Why should they have welcomed "control and accounting," including not just the loss of their children to schools they didn't know but the surrender of their autonomy to an authority they didn't trust? The answers weren't obvious, and the results of the literacy campaign were therefore anything but a foregone conclusion. In the end, however, the campaign proved successful, and illiteracy fell from well over half the Soviet population to approximately 10 percent in a generation (Kline 1958: 21; McLean 2021: 58; see also Kenez 1982).

Similar campaigns have been undertaken in the rest of the socialist world, where revolutionary parties have endeavored to build states capable of carrying out their agendas, and they've typically achieved similar results (Sen 1981; Arnove and Graff 1987; McLean 2021). The Chinese doubled the country's literacy rate – from about 40 percent to 80 percent of the population – between the early 1960s and the early 1990s, and all but eliminated illiteracy in the younger age cohorts (Dreze and Loh 1995: esp. 2876). More than a quarter of a million volunteers known as *brigadistas* "reduced illiteracy from 23.6 percent to 3.9 percent" (Benson 2016: 199) in Cuba in 1961 alone. And Nicaraguan *brigadistas* claim to have reduced illiteracy from approximately 40 percent to 13 percent in a mere five months in 1980 (Baracco 2004: 345).

Literacy campaigns are nonetheless designed to assimilate as well as educate, and they've therefore provoked opposition not only from rural dwellers but from members of ethnolinguistic, racial, and religious minorities and their advocates. For instance, the Soviet campaign has been portrayed as the prelude to a de facto Russification process that would eventually put entire languages and cultures at risk (Kirkwood 1991; Krouglov 2021). China dispatches hundreds of thousands of indigenous children to boarding schools in an indoctrination campaign that echoes long-abandoned – and universally condemned – practices pioneered in the United States, Canada, and Australia (Qin 2020; see also Postiglione and Jiao 2009; Grose 2010). And the Cuban literacy campaign has been condemned for simultaneously portraying white revolutionaries as "heroes of racial equality" (Benson 2016: 213), Afro-Cubans as "indigents in need of government aid" (Benson 2016: 221), and racism itself as "a legacy of the colonial past aggravated by US intervention and eliminated by the revolution" (Benson 2016: 222), despite – or perhaps in an effort to obscure – persistent racial discrimination.

We needn't endorse these campaigns or their tactics, however, to acknowledge their administrative distinction: By repurposing revolutionary cadres, like the illiteracy *likvidators* in the Soviet Union and the Cuban *brigadistas*, they taught people to read and write, for good or for ill, and in so doing helped address the "mutual dependency" (McLean 2021: 57) of education and state formation that marked the fundamental dilemma of late development. If the professor is the modern-day version of the executioner, to return to Gellner's evocative metaphor, we shouldn't be surprised to find her committing sins in the name of state formation – or rule out the possibility that the most prolific sinners are the more successful state builders. Contemporary Chinese efforts to assimilate and indoctrinate minority youth provide a particularly distressing example (cf. Leibold 2019; Qin 2020).

Where revolutionary governments were less successful, however, was in the realm of industrialization itself. The Soviets manufactured the weaponry they would need to beat back the German assault in World War II, and went on to beat the United States in the space race, but they were ultimately less successful in producing high-quality manufactured goods that would satisfy their people and generate hard currency revenue. What explains their failure? The answer is subject to dispute, but the leading accounts tend to emphasize the absence of price-setting markets, and the lack of a functional labor market in particular.

Under central planning, goods and services – including labor services – weren't allocated by prices in a context of voluntary exchange. They were instead allocated by targets and quotas dictated by central planners who had limited knowledge and foresight and therefore miscalculated both consumer demand and producer capacity on a regular basis. Imperfect information poses a problem in capitalist societies as well, to be sure, but price-setting markets force producers to address the problem; otherwise, they'll suffer grave losses and risk bankruptcy. Command economies had no comparable mechanism. Where producers met their targets, according to economist János Kornai, they did so by sacrificing quality – which is particularly hard to measure in the absence of market-determined prices – for quantity, and thereby made their products undesirable to a captive audience of buyers at home and unmarketable to better-off buyers abroad; hence the chronic export and foreign currency shortages in command economies. Where producers didn't meet their targets, however, they were bailed out by the governments for political as well as ideological reasons. "A firm can incur losses for years and years," explained Kornai, "and still survive because of the intervention of the bureaucracy" (Kornai 1985: 28; see also Kornai 1986a). Compare, by way of contrast, a market economy, in which continued losses would typically issue in bankruptcy – a risk that tends to force the firm to focus on profit maximization.[5]

The problem lay not only in the market for goods, however, but in the market for labor. Whereas indolent or ineffective workers are at risk of discipline and dismissal in a capitalist economy, and therefore tend to be replaced or transformed into more industrious workers over time, their socialist counterparts are almost immune from discipline, let alone dismissal, and therefore continue to underperform their goals or targets (Vodopivec 1990; Burawoy and Krotov 1992: 7). The result is a vicious circle in which productivity stagnates, pay suffers, and workers try to compensate by pursuing informal activities – often on company time – that take a further toll on their health and productivity (Kornai 1986b: 1714). For managers, moreover, there is effectively no labor market at all: their professional fates are almost entirely in the hands of high-ranking bureaucrats, and personal loyalty is therefore their dominant strategy (Kornai 1986b: 1694; Vodopivec 1990: 4–5).[6]

The parallels between high-ranking bureaucrat and feudal lord, on the one hand, and mid-level manager and medieval vassal, on the other, are perhaps not as surprising as they may seem at first glance. Central planning has frequently been portrayed as a sort of "industrial feudalism" in which the loyalty of the "vassal firm" buys the indulgence of the bureaucratic barons, and the vassals indulge their subordinates in turn (Boisot and Child 1988: 514; Teckenberg 1989: 62; Djilas 1991: 84; Gellner 1993: 150–1). These indulgences not only undermined the system's ability to produce high-quality goods and services at low cost but ensured that, when living standards stagnated or declined as a result, the population would blame, and challenge, the state itself, much as feudal peasants rebelled against their lords in times of crisis – an outcome predicted by sociologist Iván Szelényi more than a decade before the collapse of the Berlin Wall (Szelényi 1978: 73).

Industrialization through infant industry protection

Other late developers have also been portrayed as feudal or semi-feudal, of course, albeit for different reasons. The best-known cases are former European colonies in Africa, Asia, and particularly Latin America, where semi-servile labor relations survived in the countryside and anti-imperial ideologies emerged in the cities, borne by educated professionals who favored industrialization and condemned socialism for entirely predictable reasons: they expected to reap the rewards of industrialization, and the promised redistribution from North to South; and they worried that they would pay a price for socialism and the proposed redistribution from rich to poor. While revolutionaries like Lenin and Mao therefore pursued industrialization by means of central planning, their "middle-class nationalist" (Thomas 1965; Huntington 1968; Watkins 1978; Mamdani 1990) counterparts embraced not the command economy but a policy package known as import-substituting industrialization (ISI) that involved: *tariff and non-tariff barriers* designed to protect "infant industry" from foreign competition; and *preferential exchange rates* designed to subsidize the importation of capital and intermediate goods (e.g., plastics, sewing machines, steel, textiles, etc.).

The trade barriers are easy to understand: If policymakers impose a tariff on foreign toasters, for example, they'll make the purchase of domestically made toasters more appealing and, in so doing, make the local manufacture of toasters more profitable. *Somebody* will take advantage of the opportunity, ideally a local entrepreneur, occasionally a foreign investor, almost invariably with the support of middle-class professionals like lawyers, accountants, and engineers who share an interest in industrialization and an ideology of nationalism. But the potential toaster manufacturer can't start from scratch. She'll almost certainly have to import the machinery, metals, and electronics she'll need to outfit her toaster factory, and they're likely to prove costly, especially since she'll need to buy them in foreign currency.

What is to be done? This is where the preferential exchange rates come in. By offering the toaster manufacturer access to low-cost foreign currency, for example, policymakers could not only allow her to import her inputs at artificially low prices – since she'd get the dollars, yen, deutschmarks, or pounds she'd need to pay her suppliers for less than their free-market value – but effectively force the country's exporters – who would now receive an artificially *low* price for their export earnings – to pay the cost. If the free market says a peso is worth a dollar, by way of illustration, and the government insists it's worth two dollars, the importer gets two dollars per peso when she wants to trade pesos for dollars to buy machinery in New York, and the exporter gets 50 centavos – or half a peso – per dollar when he brings the fruits of his export earnings back *from* New York in greenbacks (Hirschman 1968).

In effect, therefore, the overvalued exchange rates that prevailed in the mid-twentieth century developing world constituted export taxes. They transferred real income from traditional exporters, including producers of primary products, to infant industries, especially producers of consumer goods, and in so doing encouraged disinvestment from activities like agriculture and mining and investment in manufacturing – particularly insofar as manufacturing was protected by tariff and non-tariff barriers. Let's take one example: In 1980, the US Department of Commerce conducted a survey of 49 national auto industries and found that import restrictions were *universal* in the 33 poor countries and absent in half of the 16 rich countries, particularly the wealthiest ones (USDOC 1980; see also Schrank 2017).

In theory, moreover, the poor countries would grow into a more laissez-faire trade posture as well. As producers of consumer goods learned the ropes, according to advocates of ISI, they would outgrow their need for protection, conquer foreign markets, generate the foreign exchange they used to consume, and allow industrial policymakers to shift their support to producers of capital and intermediate goods who would gradually "mature" as well. Over time, therefore, the urban industrial economy would expand – with all that entailed for imports, income, employment, and growth – and the rural primary product economy would contract, at least in theory.

In practice, however, things were rarely so simple. On the contrary, protected manufacturers found it easier to appeal for more protection – via political pressure and/or illicit inducements – than to compete with foreign producers, and local policymakers found it easier and/or more lucrative to meet their costly demands than to risk disinvestment and job loss by exposing them to the cold baths of international competition. Consequently, industry stagnated, debts mounted, and policymaking gained a reputation for inefficiency, favor trading, and outright corruption.

Nor did preferential exchange rates help. On the contrary, they encouraged arbitrage, speculation, and black-market foreign currency transactions – epitomized by touts outside of airports offering foreigners premium prices for their hard currency – and discouraged exports of both manufactured and primary products, given the presence of the de facto export tax imposed by the monetary authorities. "High levels of effective protection and overvalued exchange rates contributed to a situation in which domestically produced goods were often priced well above world prices," explain Eliana Cardoso and Ann Helwege. "In 1969, the Chilean price of electric sewing machines, bicycles, home refrigerators, and air conditioners was, respectively, three, five, six, and seven times higher than international prices" (Cardoso and Helwege 1992: 95–6). The bearers of these costs included not only powerful producers, like garment manufacturers, who preferred imported sewing machines, but myriad consumers, who exercised influence both at the polls and in the streets, and policymakers therefore responded by adopting compensatory measures – e.g., targeted tax breaks, government-backed loans, and price controls – that nonetheless aggravated the underlying imbalances.

Minimum wage laws provide one well-known example. They were frequently embraced by protectionist policymakers on the grounds that they would offset the costs of high-priced consumer goods and augment the size of the domestic market simultaneously (Portes 1983: 165; Zapata 1990: 380), in effect uniting producers and consumers behind ISI. But they have been derided as populist missteps by skeptics who blame their "premature adoption" (Sicat 2014) for: inflation, when producers responded by passing the costs along to consumers; informality, when employers responded by hiring workers off the books; and job loss, when bankruptcy constituted the only viable alternative (see also Guillén 2000a; Thoene 2019).

Nor are minimum wage laws atypical. On the contrary, the political foundations of ISI were almost always "*populist* policies that promote short-term compromise and income redistribution among interest groups, frequently at the expense of productivity growth and long-term prosperity" (Guillén 2000b: 365; see also Wallerstein 1974a: 11; de la Torre 1992: 389; Zhao and Hall 1994: 214; Biggart and Guillén 1999: 738–9; Fourcade-Gourinchas and Babb 2002: 558–9; Riley and Desai 2007: 842). Import substitution was like a game of whack-a-mole in which efforts to solve one problem, like inflation, by adopting regulations, such as price controls, created other problems, like corruption and capital flight. And import-substituting economies therefore descended into an endless succession of policy missteps and performance shortfalls. While they grew rapidly in the short run, when domestic demand was high and foreign inputs were available, they were vulnerable to foreign-exchange bottlenecks, inflation, debt, and crisis over the long run, when their governments could no longer appease their citizens or meet their hard currency obligations (Diamand 1977; Sachs 1989; Krueger 1993). And by the late twentieth century, therefore, the Global South had fallen into despair and the ISI model had fallen into disrepute.

The East Asian debate in the late twentieth century

East Asia has frequently been portrayed as the exception that proves the rule. After all, the HPAEs largely escaped the debt crisis that plagued Latin America and Africa in the 1980s, and more than doubled their per capita growth rates over the course of the next three decades. What followed was a vigorous debate over the sources of Asian growth and the rule that was being proven.

Early answers underscored the region's alleged retreat from ISI and embrace of a laissez-faire alternative that involved trade, labor market, and exchange-rate liberalization. While Korea and Taiwan rolled back ISI in the early 1960s, according to the conventional wisdom, their neighbors followed suit in the decades to follow, when they embraced their comparative advantages in labor and raw materials and became "deeply integrated into the global economy" (Radelet and Sachs 1997: 45). Beginning in the early 1980s, for example, Indonesia and Thailand lowered their average tariffs, consolidated their tariff structures, and removed non-tariff barriers on manufactured inputs in an effort to jump-start export-led growth (Nehru 1993: 5). And by the late 1980s, therefore, Bela Balassa of the World Bank would praise both the alleged neutrality of the East Asian incentive system, which eliminated ISI's anti-export bias, and the efficiency of the region's capital and labor markets, which allowed producers to pursue their comparative advantages in primary products and labor-intensive manufactured goods. "At the same time," he argued, "these factors are interdependent. For example, while export expansion requires well-functioning labor and capital markets, the neutrality and the stability of the incentives system will improve the operation of factor markets" (Balassa 1988a: S288; see also Balassa 1971; Krueger 1990).

In other words, the conventional wisdom held that development policy reform is a package deal. The costs of imperfections in one market are necessarily felt in neighboring markets, meaning that reforms in the first market almost inevitably drive reforms in the second market as well. Product and labor markets offer an example – insofar as manufacturers who are exposed to international competition will find labor and employment laws unbearable. But political economists go a step further and anticipate a virtuous cycle in which the winners from the first round of reform become the key drivers of the second. "Seen in this light," argued another World Bank economist, "a successful export-oriented set of trade policies forces the adoption of other efficiency and growth-enhancing liberalization policies. Those policies permit further gains to be realized from the trade strategy, and simultaneously induce further growth and yet greater complexity of the economic structure" (Krueger 1990: 111).

In a sense, this is an optimistic vision. Balassa and his associates arguably downplayed key factors that had contributed to Asian growth – including military rule, foreign aid, and a first-mover advantage in the market for manufactured exports – in an effort to portray the free-market model as both humane and replicable (Balassa 1971: 75, 1988a: S288, 1988b: 36). Asia's liberal lessons could and should be learned, they argued, and the sooner the better (Ranis 1985: 544). Others – including mainstream economists as well as neo-Marxists (see, e.g., Cline 1982) – disagreed vehemently and worried that widespread efforts to follow Asia's example would provoke protectionism in the North and poverty in the South. "When it comes to analyzing trade," argued Stephan Haggard, "it is political analysis, not economics, that is the dismal science" (Haggard 1986: 361). But the most dubious of all were a group of "revisionists" (Rodrik 1995: 56; Headey 2009: 712) who called the orthodox portrait of Asia itself into question.

Before delving too deep into the revisionist account, however, we'd do well to explicitly draw a distinction between orthodox optimists and orthodox pessimists. Orthodox optimists traced East Asia's success to presumably replicable liberal economic policies. By letting the market allocate resources, they argued, the region's governments ensured that their producers pursued their comparative advantages and, in so doing, ensured exports, growth, and employment creation for their people. Other countries could follow Asia's lead, moreover, if only they would abandon ISI. Orthodox pessimists essentially accepted the market-based account of Asian success but doubted its replicability in countries that lacked military rulers who could readily quell dissent; foreign aid from the United States; and/or a first-mover advantage in the export of labor-intensive manufactured goods. Abandoning ISI for a liberal alternative necessarily involves bankruptcy and job loss, they argued, and developing countries that lacked Asia's hard regimes and soft loans wouldn't be up to the task – especially once Asia itself had grabbed the lead in export-led industrialization.

Just how many low-wage export platforms does the world need? But the revisionists took a radically different view by arguing that the HPAEs had never abandoned ISI in the first place; on the contrary, they had imposed "performance standards" (Amsden 2001) on their infant industries and, in so doing, *forced* them to grow up – or, to put it more pointedly, they had just done ISI better than their rivals by refusing to give in to political pressure and illicit inducements.

The best-known performance standards were *local-content requirements* and *export targets*. Local-content requirements compelled beneficiaries of government support – including tariffs and subsidies – to gradually replace their imported inputs with locally made alternatives. Export targets conditioned government support on foreign sales. And performance standards thereby addressed ISI's tendency to foster high-priced, low-quality products, on the one hand, and balance-of-payments deficits, on the other, by forcing the local beneficiaries of protection and subsidy to compete with their foreign counterparts at home and abroad (Amsden 2001; Schrank 2017).

Exports are a particularly interesting performance benchmark for several reasons. First, they're deployed in a self-conscious effort to *augment* the production of high-quality, price-competitive, fashion-sensitive products that are competitive on world markets – that is, to *encourage* the very reactivity we discussed in chapter 2. Second, they're "easy to monitor" (Wade 1993: 158) by central customs authorities, and therefore economize on administrative resources that are allegedly lacking in the developing world (Evans 1992: 177). And, third, they combat balance-of-payments shortfalls that are of interest to fiscal sociologists in particular. Where exports are concentrated or unsustainable, for example, developing countries have trouble meeting their obligations and the "fiscal contract between the state and society" (Barlow and Peña 2022: 403) is placed in jeopardy; where they are broader-based and sustainable, however, net debtors become net creditors and stability is more likely (Block 2009: 74).

Other performance standards involved ownership, technology transfer, workforce development, and employment creation, and a 1982 survey by the US Department of Commerce found at least some performance standards in all seven HPAEs (USDOC 1985: 139–42). Even laissez-faire Hong Kong asked multinational companies to transfer a bit of technology, for example, and the larger HPAEs imposed an array of performance standards on the auto industry in particular (USDOC 1985: 140; see also USDOC 1980; Schrank 2017). The late Alice Amsden therefore referred to the "principle of reciprocity" as the key to East Asian development. "In exchange for subsidies," she argued, "the state has imposed performance standards on private firms" (Amsden 1989: 8).

Amsden was not alone. The Japanese government adhered to the revisionist line, claiming that targeted industrial policies had played an indispensable part in Asian growth (Wade 1996), and the World Bank eventually bowed to Japanese pressure by abandoning its "orthodox optimism" for a sort of revisionist pessimism that acknowledged both the *contributions* of "contest-based interventions" (Preston 1993: vii) that tied subsidies to performance, on the one hand, and the institutional *limits* to their replication, on the other. "The use of contests in Japan and Korea required competent and insulated civil servants," explained the Bank's exhaustive *East Asian Miracle* report. "In parts of sub-Saharan Africa and Latin America, and elsewhere in Asia where such institutional conditions are lacking, activist government involvement in the economy has usually gone awry" (World Bank 1993: 26). In effect, therefore, the Bank admitted that targeted industrial policy had proven successful in East Asia and simultaneously warned potential imitators not to "try this at home" (Chang 2011: 95; see also Easterly 2001: 211).

Table 4.1 summarizes the various interpretations of the East Asian miracle in terms of their answers to two questions: Do they think the miracle itself resulted from orthodox, free-market policies or from revisionist policies, including reciprocity? Are they optimistic or pessimistic about the miracle's replication?

Over time, it seems, the orthodox, optimistic account in the northwestern cell gave way to revisionist and/or pessimistic alternatives, ranging from "you got the story right but probably shouldn't generalize beyond your sample," in the southwestern quadrant, to "you don't even have the story right" in the eastern

Table 4.1 Perspectives on the East Asian miracle

		Origins of the East Asian Miracle	
		Orthodox	*Revisionist*
Replicability of the East Asian Miracle	*Optimistic*	Mainstream economics: Growth is a product of laissez-faire; no social or political prerequisites	Japanese government and heterodox economists: Growth is a replicable product of reciprocity
	Pessimistic	Orthodox pessimists: Growth is a product of laissez-faire and unique add-ons like US aid, autocracy, etc.	World Bank *East Asian Miracle* report: Growth is an inimitable product of reciprocity

column, with a second-order debate about generalization; that is, whether or not developing countries beyond East Asia should try to impose reciprocity at home.

From the World Bank to Weber and beyond

The World Bank's account had a twofold appeal to sociologists. By simultaneously highlighting the *indispensability* and the *peculiarity* of "economic technocrats insulated from narrow political pressures" (World Bank 1993: 158), it first reconciled modernization theory's faith in the *possibility* of development with neo-Marxism's doubts about its *likelihood*; and, second, echoed the portrait of impersonal rule painted by Max Weber in his classic work on bureaucracy. And a number of observers therefore remarked upon both the convergence of the sociological and World Bank interpretations of East Asian success (Haggard 2004: 61; Schrank 2015: 244) and the related challenges of "dependency management" (Bornschier and Trezzini 2001: esp. 211) in the early twenty-first century.

According to Weber, the "mechanization of the bureaucratic apparatus" (Gerth and Mills 1946: 208) that underpins modern society presupposes the lifetime appointment of well-paid experts; otherwise, public officials will lack the autonomy and/or expertise they need to carry out their appointed tasks and will instead prove venal, incompetent, or both. "The more complicated and specialized modern culture becomes," he explained, "the more its external supporting apparatus demands the personally detached and strictly 'objective' *expert*, in lieu of the master of older social structures, who was moved by personal sympathy and favor, by grace and gratitude" (Gerth and Mills 1946: 216). Where modern bureaucracies had not taken hold, therefore, Weber anticipated arbitrary rule by patrimonial authorities. And his descendants have explicitly challenged "the notion that patrimonial politics apply only to faraway places or bygone eras" (Charrad and Adams 2011: 8).

In fact, the World Bank's late-twentieth-century line was in some ways anticipated by dissident modernization theorists and neo-Marxists three decades earlier, and we can therefore connect this chapter and the last chapter by considering the surprisingly similar ways in which sociologists Reinhard Bendix, a prominent modernization theorist, and Fernando Henrique Cardoso, who claimed Marxist roots (Cammack 1989: 268; see also Cardoso in Sorj and Fausto 2011: 192), dealt with anomalies in their preferred accounts in the late 1960s. While Bendix abandoned teleology in favor of the analysis of "specific processes of industrialization," and acknowledged his debt to economic historian Alexander Gerschenkron in doing so (Bendix 1967: 316, esp. fn. 55), Cardoso underscored the "necessity of a historico-structural viewpoint," and invoked Gerschenkron simultaneously (Cardoso 1967: 112–13, esp. fn. 12; see also Cardoso and Faletto 1979: 19, fn. 4; and Gootenberg 2001: 78, fn. 39).

The point is not simply that their bibliographies were similar, however, but that despite their distinct intellectual origins their ideas had converged as well. When modernization theorists and neo-Marxists were debating the relative merits of their distinct teleologies, Gerschenkron and his offspring were coming to recognize that "backwardness" had advantages as well as disadvantages, and that their employment or abandonment would ultimately come down to politics. Late developers could leapfrog first-movers by adopting the latest techniques and technologies, Gerschenkron argued, but to do so they'd have to undergo a decidedly ugly transition under the auspices of a "coercive" state that was anything but universally available or successful for by now familiar reasons, including peasant uncertainty, landlord hostility, widespread illiteracy, and dependence on foreign capital, among other things (Gerschenkron 1962: esp. 354; see also Davidoff 2002). By the early 1970s, therefore, the fates of peripheral countries were being attributed less to the demonstration effect emphasized by modernization theory or the exploitation bemoaned by neo-Marxists than to the discipline and power of their states. "Gerschenkron's paradigm of European development and the experience of Japan suggest that the more backward a country, the more essential is initiative and direction by its government," argued Peter Evans in 1971. "Yet, governments of poor countries are often forced into roles more passive than those of governments in developed countries" (Evans 1971: 688), hence the distinctiveness of Japan.

Over the course of the next three decades, however, South Korea and Taiwan would take off and development sociology would take on a self-consciously Weberian – and slightly more upbeat – tone. While the advantages of backwardness would indeed be squandered by "predatory" states dominated by regime insiders, argued Evans, they'd be exploited by "developmental states" marked by "embedded autonomy," or Weberian organizational features, on the one hand, and dense ties to the private sector, on the other. "Embeddedness is necessary for information and implementation," explained Evans "but without autonomy embeddedness will degenerate into a supercartel, aimed, like all cartels, at protecting its members from changes in the status quo" (Evans 1992: 154; see also Evans 1995).

The concept of embedded autonomy has proven both influential and controversial. Some agree that a "coherent, meritocratic bureaucracy" (Evans 1992: 152) is a necessary but insufficient basis for late development, and thus view the addition of embeddedness as a valuable extension of the original Weberian model (Wright 1996). Others view embeddedness as a "methodologically

underspecified" (Form 1997: 189) complication that borders on
tautology: if development occurred, Evans implies, embeddedness
must be present; otherwise, it must be lacking. "As in so many
areas of sociological theorizing," argued Alejandro Portes, "an
earnest attempt to account for a complex phenomenon comes
to acquire a suspicious circularity" (Portes 1996: 176; see also
Moore 1998: 428–9). Evans would go on to relegate embeddedness to a footnote in a subsequent article on the relationship
between Weberian bureaucracies and growth (Evans and Rauch
1999: 752), which may be telling in this regard. But he and his
co-author would simultaneously report a powerful relationship
between "Weberianness" and growth in the period between 1970
and 1990, and in so doing reinforce the reigning sociological
consensus.

The developmental state in Northeast Asia

The broader problem with the Weberian account, however, is not
that it is wrong but that it is incomplete. After all, the same governments that imposed performance standards on their industrialists
in the 1970s and 1980s had been portrayed as singularly patrimonial in previous decades, when they failed to do so, and in many
cases beyond (Johnson 1986: 559; Biggart 1991: 223; Biggart and
Guillén 1999: 730; Lie 2015: 114–15). And the same governments
that failed to impose performance standards on their industrialists
had at one point been portrayed as models of bureaucratic competence, to be imitated by their East Asian peers (Chang 2011: 96),
and have at times made real gains in other areas, including health-
care provision (Sen 1981; Caldwell 1986; McGuire 2001; Schrank
2019), higher education (Ryu 2017; Kapur 2020: esp. 48), and
infrastructure development (Guillén 2004).

Efforts to rank countries on some sort of aggregate measure
of "state capacity" are therefore misguided (Kurtz and Schrank
2012: 616). As Ha-Joon Chang has noted, "different governments have competences in different areas" (Chang 2011: 95),
and the relevant question is not why some states have capacity

that others lack but "capacity for what" (Weiss 1998: 17; see also Hanson and Sigman 2021: 1496). Why did the HPAEs impose performance standards forgone by their peers? Macro-cultural answers are at best incomplete (Evans 1987; Gong and Jang 1998). They explain neither why the HPAEs failed to impose performance standards until the mid-1960s or 1970s, nor why their co-ethnics in North Korea and mainland China took a different path entirely. Military rule is at best a necessary but insufficient part of the story, given the prevalence of military dictatorships in Latin America and Africa at the same time (McGuire 1994: 212). And US support for Cold War allies, though frequently invoked by world-system theorists (Aseniero 1994; Bilotti 2010), is similarly insufficient, for the United States offered comparable support, developed and propagated by the very same advisers, to a number of Latin American countries at the same point in time (Schrank 2003).

A number of historical sociologists have therefore pointed to the survival of large-scale, labor-repressive landlords in most developing countries, and their elimination by land reform in East Asia, as the key difference between mid-twentieth century Korea and Taiwan, on the one hand, and their less prosperous peers, on the other (Evans 1987; Chibber 2002; D. Davis 2004; Schrank 2007). After all, the middle-class nationalists who undertook ISI hoped to build a "national bourgeoisie" (Chibber 2005; Schrank 2005). If the goal was to end dependency, they argued, the key was to develop industry that was owned and operated in the South. And the most likely source of capital that could fuel national industry was in the countryside, where landed aristocrats not only had enormous wealth at their disposal but exploited millions of impoverished peasants who were at risk of recruitment to the cause of communism. When Korea and Taiwan redistributed land from the aristocracy to the peasantry in an effort to head off revolution, therefore, they simultaneously unlocked human and material resources in the countryside and thus facilitated industrialization in three ways: first, by compensating dispossessed landlords with stocks and bonds that were reinvested in urban industry; second, by transforming ill-educated peasants into productive farmers, workers, and potential industrialists; and, third, by imposing ceilings on rents and acreage that made rural investment less appealing than industry more generally.

Consider, for example, Taiwan, where all three dynamics were on display. Landlords who gave up their titles were compensated with shares in the powerful cement, mining, textile, and machinery industries (Gold 1986: 66; Numazaki 1986: 490), among others. Their former tenants were in many cases "turned into farmers who turned into factory owners" in short order on "land they had obtained for free from the government" (Hamilton and Cheng-shu 2017: 40; see also Numazaki 1986: 491). And insofar as the factory owners bought their inputs from local suppliers, like the Taiwan Industrial Development Corporation (*Taiwan Review* 1964), and sold their output to "big buyers" and "brand-name merchandisers" (Hamilton and Cheng-shu 2017: 41), like Nike and Panasonic, they fueled the growth of decentralized manufacturing networks that linked firms of different sizes to national and global markets through both formal and informal arrangements (Numazaki 1986; Hamilton and Cheng-shu 2017; Looney 2020).[7]

The point is not to attribute Taiwan's growth to pre-existing social networks, however, but to understand the role of land reform in rewiring and reconstituting social as well as human and physical capital over time (Portes 1998; Chen 2002). Only by "forcing and facilitating" (Pack and Westphal 1986: 99) industrial investment could policymakers jump-start growth and development. And land reform forced industrial investment by expropriating traditional landlords and facilitated industrial investment by compensating them and offering their former tenants property and opportunity as well.

Not all of the dispossessed landlords and former tenants became successful industrialists, of course, but many of the most successful manufacturers in Taiwan and Korea trace their origins to the countryside (Numazaki 1986: 490–1; Shin 2006: 55; Hamilton and Cheng-shu 2017: 37–40; Looney 2020: 94) and, no less importantly, turned to industry only when land reform eliminated their rural redoubts (Barrett and Whyte 1982: 1079; Greenhalgh

1989: 94–5; Lie 1998: 16). They couldn't move their capital back into agriculture, due to newly established ceilings on rents and land ownership, or abroad, due to foreign currency controls, and therefore had little choice but to meet – or try to meet – the government's performance standards. When the opportunity cost to industrial investment is low, in other words, the government's bargaining power is high. The HPAEs didn't need state capacity in a global and abstract sense, therefore, but needed to subordinate a particular form of capital to distinct government regulations at a precise moment in time.

Where landed aristocrats were highly profitable, however, they had much more bargaining power and their capital had a much higher opportunity cost. Unlike their Northeast Asian counterparts, who'd been dispossessed by land reforms and had little alternative to industry, landlords in most of Latin America and parts of Africa and South Asia were doing well in agriculture and didn't see any need to take risks in the city (McGuire 1994; Schrank 2007). If they were to be drawn out of agriculture and into industry, therefore, they'd have to be guaranteed a very high rate of return on their investment; otherwise, they'd just as soon keep their capital in the countryside – or perhaps offshore. But performance standards would have reduced their rate of return in industry, at least in the short run, and in so doing scared them away. If the policymakers and professionals who were pushing industrialization beyond East Asia wanted to build a national bourgeoisie, in short, they'd have had little choice but to give their investors virtually free rein by ruling out performance requirements – and in many cases they did so.[8]

Policymakers could have imposed higher taxes on the landlords in order to draw them into manufacturing, but the overvalued exchange rates that constituted the key mechanism of taxation posed an independent threat to export-led industrialization (Schrank 2007). Would Americans really buy Mexican toasters, after all, if they first had to buy overpriced pesos? Would Mexican appliance manufacturers try to meet US standards, for that matter, if they had to worry about exchange-rate volatility? So policymakers in most of the developing world found themselves on the horns of a dilemma: if they wanted to draw capital from agriculture into manufacturing, they had little choice but to offer infant industry highly favorable terms; and if they abandoned performance standards in an effort to guarantee those terms, they'd condemn their industry to a state of permanent immaturity. Northeast Asian land reforms put paid to this dilemma in one fell swoop by generating urban industrialists and eliminating their rural exit option (McGuire 1994: 229; Kim 2021: 280).

But the land reforms also contributed to human development both directly, by drastically reducing inequalities in income and wealth, and indirectly, by encouraging education and training. Some landlords anticipated the reforms by selling off their land and investing the profits in their children's education (Sorensen 1994: 26). Others used their bonds to educate their own children and/or to establish private secondary schools and universities that had the unintended side effect of allowing the government to focus on primary education (Park 2013: 100; see also Shin 1998: 1342; Seth 2013: 45; Sung-Chan 2013: 30). And peasants at long last had both an incentive and the latitude to send their children to school, ensuring not only the growth of productivity on farms that were suddenly subject to commercial pressure but the birth of "a skilled workforce for industry" (Boyce, Rosset, and Stanton 2005; see also Kwon and Yi 2009: 775). One recent counterfactual exercise suggests that land reform alone explains approximately half the growth in Korean primary schooling between 1949 and 1960 (Woo and Kahm 2017: 203). Another finds that the effect extends to secondary school enrollment, and that the beneficiaries were disproportionately girls who'd been deprived of education prior to the reform "due to male offspring preference" (Hong and Kim 2020: 32).

Others have identified broadly similar dynamics in Taiwan (Wei 1976: 263), where they've been accompanied by a remarkable demographic transition. "With the shift of mobility opportunities away from agriculture toward occupations requiring education," explained anthropologist Susan Greenhalgh, "the costs and benefits of children moved in a direction favoring lower fertility" (Greenhalgh 1989: 98). The island's overall fertility rate therefore peaked at more than seven children per woman in 1951 and fell to just over two in 1983, with rural rates about 10 percent higher than their urban counterparts throughout the period.

The educational and demographic consequences of land reform are no less important than the industrial. Literacy and education, and female education in particular, not only contribute to life expectancy in the short run – by augmenting both the availability, appreciation, and utilization of health services among the rural poor – but fuel a "virtuous cycle" of fertility and mortality decline more generally (McGuire 2010: 211; see also Cohn 2021) as parents opt to invest more resources in fewer children. Rapid GDP growth thus went hand in hand with human development in Northeast Asia.

Populist societies in the developing world

Land reform is arguably the *differentia specifica* of Northeast Asia in the second half of the twentieth century. By breaking the back of the landed elite, it opened the door to rural education and mobility, closed the door to rural speculation and exploitation, and forced former landlords to submit to efficiency-enhancing performance standards when they redirected their capital into urban industry. It's worth remembering, therefore, that land reform was motivated less by economic imperatives than by political ones – particularly the effort to build a bulwark against communism in the countryside.

In this respect, moreover, land reform was successful. Several observers have noted not only the political links between the architects of land reform and their rural beneficiaries in Northeast Asia but the price of rural inequality in the rest of the developing world, and the contrast has been drawn most forcefully in Latin America (McGuire 1994; D. Davis 2004; Schrank 2007; Looney 2020; Cohn 2021). With the bargaining power afforded by land reform, they argue, Asian policymakers could educate the peasantry, discipline industry, and jump-start "shared growth" (McGuire 2001: 1678) that would redound to the benefit of both constituencies.

Rural support gave them the latitude they'd need to force city dwellers to subordinate their short-run desires to the long-run needs of the nation. When confronted by rural inequality in Latin America, however, policymakers found themselves indulging "fear of education" (Tendler 2002) in the countryside, forgoing performance standards in the city, and overvaluing their exchange rates in an effort to transfer surplus from rural to urban sectors by any means necessary; otherwise they'd have driven capital back to the countryside (or overseas), alienated the peasantry, deprived themselves of a key means of taxation, and/or provoked opposition among their allies in the cities.

The result was a "populist policy cycle" (Sachs 1989) of public spending and austerity that was inimical to both growth and human development. Infant industrialists and workers who backed the regime insisted on tariffs, regulations, and similar means of support. Policymakers endeavored to meet their demands by directly and indirectly taxing their opponents – including landed agriculture and extractive industry – in the countryside. Rural interests resisted, evaded, or fled the taxes, provoking foreign exchange shortfalls, budget deficits, and inflation. Policymakers had little choice but to ask international financial institutions (IFIs) like the IMF and the World Bank for support. And the IFIs conditioned their support on "structural adjustment" involving trade liberalization, market deregulation, and the privatization of state-owned enterprises.

In the absence of performance requirements, it seems, import-substituting industrialization fostered the worst of both worlds: predictable urban problems without the requisite industrial solutions. For instance, ISI drew enormous numbers of ill-educated peasants into the largely informal urban labor force, where they traded their political loyalty (or at least quiescence) for material payoffs that produced more budgetary pressure than human capital. It lured ill-prepared (and/or foreign) investors into the heavily protected urban industrial sector, where they consumed but didn't generate foreign exchange. And it left them exit options both in the countryside and overseas, where they could escape any export or local-content requirements that were imposed on them by "developmental" (or just desperate) officials who wanted to resolve their budget and balance-of-payments difficulties by boosting industrial productivity. Where exit options were foreclosed in East Asia, therefore, leaving capital little choice but to get competitive, they were accommodated elsewhere, leaving policymakers subject to holdup by relatively mobile investors.

What were the long-term consequences? Some expected the industrialists and their sponsors to eventually "win the struggle for support" by luring the masses into populist coalitions with promises of "public goods and political participation" (Kroneberg and Wimmer 2012: 199). Others doubted their ability to organize a coherent program and instead envisioned a never-ending cycle of "stop–go" (Merkx 1969: esp. 105; Schrank 2007: 194) growth that would reproduce both inefficiency and inequality. Writing about late-twentieth-century Brazil, for example, and drawing an explicit contrast with Korea and Taiwan, Edward Telles worried that inequality and segregation would pose a barrier to growth and human development by depriving the urban poor of access to schools, public services, and industrial labor markets (Telles 1995: 1219–20). Others identified similar dynamics elsewhere in the region (Margheritis and Pereira 2007: 30; Madariaga 2015: 46). And Kelly Hoffman and Miguel Angel Centeno asked whether "the size of the gulfs separating sections of the population, the absence of any long-term trend to ameliorate the injustices, and the stability of an untouchable population of informal workers seems [sic] to call for categories more closely resembling that of caste than of class" (Hoffman and Centeno 2003: 373) not only in Brazil but throughout Latin America.

The subsequent literature on social mobility in Latin America is largely consistent with their caveat. We've already alluded to the distinction between "structural mobility," which occurs when the occupational structure itself changes, and "exchange mobility," which occurs when individuals shift positions within a given occupational structure (Beckfield 2020: 23). While structural mobility almost inevitably grows in the course of industrialization and urbanization, as certain occupational categories expand (e.g., nonskilled manual worker) or contract (e.g., agricultural laborer), exchange mobility in Latin America tends to be either: inconsequential (Torche 2005: 422) in the middle and lower strata, where it reshuffles people among positions that share similar resources and rewards; or unusual at the upper end of the occupational distribution, where well-educated professionals and managers maintain a stranglehold over elite positions. Latin America's novelty in this regard is particularly noteworthy. Whereas poor children in rich countries could occasionally take advantage of social capital, like interpersonal networks and role models, to gain access to upward mobility, social capital itself tends to be inherited in Latin America, making such strategies unlikely (Binder and Woodruff 2002: 252; Torche 2014: 636; see also Portes 1998). In fact, Florencia Torche refers to a "particularly Latin American pattern of intergenerational class reproduction characterized by strong intergenerational persistence of the upper class" (Torche 2014: 630), or "elite closure" (Torche 2005: 422), and one careful study finds "near caste-like conditions" in Mexico, where the offspring of "managers are 15.6 times more likely to be immobile than mobile, whereas the offspring of US managers are only 2.3 times more likely to be immobile" (Huerta Wong, Burak, and Grusky 2015: 11–13).[9]

The mechanisms reproducing these conditions aren't entirely obvious but, insofar as the professional and managerial classes reap the bulk of the rewards, Torche emphasizes the distinct role of education in reproducing the region's "inherited meritocracy" (Torche 2014: 636). Whereas public school spending yields few returns in terms of social mobility, she elaborates, well-developed financial markets are more important – perhaps because Latin American governments devote a disproportionate share of their education budgets to universities, which benefit the upper classes, and leave the poor to borrow on private credit markets that are at best ill suited to educational lending (Torche 2014: 634; see also Torche 2010a). Almost half a century after being christened by Ronald Dore, therefore, the "diploma disease" (Dore 1976) continues to reproduce inequality by encouraging and empowering the elite to capture an outsized share of the education budget.

Educational inequalities are by no means the only source of elite reproduction in developing regions like Latin America. Assortative mating in which "like marries like" also plays a role, and is itself reproduced when people meet their partners in school (Torche 2010b: 483), as do racial and ethnic segregation and discrimination, which are themselves linked to social class, education, and mating patterns (Gullickson and Torche 2014; Telles, Flores, and Urrea 2015). Aaron Gullickson and Florencia Torche's work on racially assortative mating and status exchange – i.e., in which heteronomous (or mixed) marriages unite people with distinct status advantages – revealed a "generalized penalty for darkness" (Gullickson and Torche 2014: 835) in Brazil, where "interracial marriages are more likely to be formed by a less-educated white spouse and a more-educated black spouse" (Gullickson and Torche 2014: 854). Andrés Villarreal discusses a similar skin-color preference in Mexico, where the main legally recognized boundary is not based "on phenotypical differences, but rather on cultural practices and language use" (Villarreal 2010: 652). And Telles finds that a number of Latin American countries are "pigmentocracies," in which "skin color is a central axis of social stratification" (Telles 2014: 3).

Of course, Latin America is just one world region. It's hardly representative. Both China and India have more people than the combined populations of the entire Spanish- and Portuguese-speaking worlds, for example, and have been growing dramatically in recent years. But the best available evidence suggests that the Latin American combination of growing absolute mobility and limited exchange mobility is fairly typical in the Global South (Hvistendahl 2014; see, e.g., Bagchi 1991). It's Northeast Asia that's the exception, not Latin America.

More than 60 years ago, economist Simon Kuznets predicted that industrialization and urbanization would initially aggravate inequality, as they drew capital away from the countryside and toward a new urban elite, and eventually mitigate inequality, as the rural masses moved to the cities and took advantage of new opportunities (Kuznets 1955). But the HPAEs never experienced an initial spike in inequality, and the growth of inequality in today's low-income countries could itself impede long-run development by undermining human capital formation, political stability, and investment (Hvistendahl 2014: 833).

The high human developers: exceptions that prove the rule?

The principal exceptions to populist politics beyond East Asia are also marked by rural transformation, and these include non-communist as well as communist cases. Countries like Costa Rica in Central America, and states like Kerala in India, have long had at least two things in common: high human development, including literacy and life expectancy levels that put their periph-eral peers to shame; and dense populations of family farmers engaged in cash-crop agriculture, particularly for coffee. While the causal links between human development and commercial family farming aren't entirely clear, they probably lie on both the demand and the supply sides (Caldwell 1986: 183–4). On the demand side, commercial family farmers are ensconced in a transactional world of banks, accounts, and agents that presupposes literacy and numeracy (Molina and Palmer 2004: 181). Unlike their semi-servile feudal predecessors, they have reason to favor, rather than fear, education. On the supply side, education itself is cheaper, on a per capita basis, in densely populated areas (Boserup 1965: 75; Goldin 2016: 59). Widely dispersed populations are simply harder to reach, meaning not only that rural education tends to lag urban, in general, but that more remote and/or isolated peasants are more likely to be undereducated, in particular.

The implications are profound. After all, John Caldwell has identified education as the key determinant of health achievement in "high human developers" that have overperformed their per capita GDPs in terms of mortality and life expectancy more gen-erally (Caldwell 1986: esp. 179). Educated adults – and mothers, in particular – are more likely to demand and deploy improved nutrition and health-care services, he explains, and to join the health-care labor force themselves. "Where many rural girls are educated," Caldwell explained, "it is possible to recruit in every village young women to work cheaply as health auxiliaries or to be trained as midwives" (Caldwell 1986: 184). The relationship between fertility decline and mortality is less clear, but there's reason to believe that "steep fertility declines give rise to greater parental worries about child survival and hence encourage greater infant and child care and consequently mortality transition" (Caldwell 1986: 204).

It's worth taking a moment, moreover, to reflect upon the broader relationship between gender and development by distinguishing the *descriptive* association between the two variables and the *causal* relationships involved. On the one hand, gender gaps in health, education, employment, and the like are typically higher in developing countries than in their better-off counterparts. Men's advantages in education tend to be higher, women's advantages in life expectancy tend be lower, and attitudes toward gender roles tend to be more patriarchal in the Global South than in the Global North (Jayachandran 2015).

On the other hand, the underpinnings of the inequalities aren't obvious. Does development erode gender inequality? Is gender inequality itself an obstacle to development? Or is the relationship spurious? The answers are anything but clear, given the methodological challenges involved in their pursuit, but the overwhelming weight of the evidence suggests a bidirectional relationship between women's empowerment and development, especially *human* development. While industrialization and urbanization pose a threat to patriarchal norms, they're more likely to occur when women are free to delay family formation, attend school, enter the labor market, practice fertility control, and pass their knowledge and values down to a presumptively smaller next generation – and in so doing to fuel the shift from population "quantity" to population "quality" over time (Lagerlöf 2003; Reher 2011). It's something of a cliché at this point to say that "fighting poverty means fighting patriarchy" (ActionAid 2005; Elliott 2016) but that doesn't mean it's wrong. Women's status and empowerment are particularly powerful solvents in the educational sphere, where they're associated with higher overall attainment and lower gender disparity in the next generation (Afridi 2010; Koissy Kpein 2010).

A typology of late developing societies

The point is not to paint a passive portrait of the poor and working classes in the bulk of the Global South. They take individual and collective measures to improve their situations on a daily basis, and they're met with everything from political repression to pork and patronage; hence the persistence of the relationship between poverty and despotism, on the one hand, and populism, on the other. But Table 4.2 tries to distill the key variables and examples invoked in this chapter into a necessarily incomplete typology of late development trajectories – patrimonialism, developmentalism, revolution, and populism – and their respective states.

Our starting point, following Gellner, is the northwest cell, where the rural elite has survived and capitalist (or price-setting) markets are at best poorly developed. Patrimonial societies like these are by no means common in the early twenty-first century, and they're decidedly vulnerable, but they're not necessarily extinct or devoid of champions (Hammond 2011).

In the southeast corner, meanwhile, one finds the very opposite: late developing societies like Korea and Taiwan that have undergone profound rural transformation, typically amidst warfare, and fostered the growth of capitalist markets simultaneously. With

Table 4.2 A typology of late developing trajectories

		Rural elite	
		Accommodated	*Transformed*
Capitalist markets	*Underdeveloped*	Patrimonialism: feudal, caste, millet	Revolution: command economies
	Developed	Populism: Latin America, South Asia, Africa	Developmentalism: HPAEs

no rural retreat available, and exposed to the very real threat of liquidation, the elite had little choice but to take advantage of government support, invest in urban industry and/or education, and subject themselves to demanding performance standards as they did so. While many losses and bankruptcies occurred along the way, human capital was developed in both rural and urban areas, infant industries grew up under the guiding hand of the developmental state, and shared growth occurred.

In the northeast corner, one finds the leading Cold War alternative: distributive societies in which revolutionary governments destroyed the rural elite and ushered in communist, rather than capitalist, governments. While the revolutions broke the backs of the landed oligarchies, and built states and schools, central planning undermined long-run growth by giving managers and workers perverse incentives – and in so doing opened the door to market transitions that in many cases put their earlier human development gains at risk (Kuhn 2010).

And, finally, the bulk of the Global South looks like the southwest cell, where capitalism was built "with the ruins," rather than "on the ruins," of pre-capitalist societies (Stark 1996: 995), and powerful elites therefore had a wide array of potentially profitable investment outlets. Unlike their East Asian counterparts, who had little choice but to invest their surplus in cities on whatever terms the developmental state offered, the dominant classes in the bulk of the Global South could stay in the countryside, invest in the city, or take their capital abroad in search of the highest possible returns. What this meant, in practice, was that populist politicians could not impose performance requirements or taxes on investors for fear of provoking capital flight and job loss, and therefore had little choice but to steer a rudderless ship of state toward the twenty-first century.

The typology is obviously incomplete. Its brackets both the role and location of "predatory" states (Evans 1995) and leaves the line between "populist" and "patrimonial" societies blurry (cf. Mouzelis 1985: 340; Biggart and Guillén 1999: 741). It says nothing at all about China's alleged journey from the northeast to the southeastern cell (Amsden 2007: 9). It leaves "high health achievers" that aren't command economies in a somewhat ambiguous – but consistent – position. And it's more descriptive than explanatory, at least in the strict sense of the term. But it distills four distinct modes of social organization down to two key variables that are by overwhelming consensus critical, if by no means sufficient, to understanding different development outcomes in the late twentieth century.

Conclusion

In this chapter, I've tried to do three things. First, I've drawn a distinction between the pre-industrial societies that dominated most of human history and their industrial successors. Second, I've drawn additional distinctions between the development or under-development of capitalist markets and the accommodation or transformation of the rural elite in the course of industrialization. And, finally, I've used the resultant bivariate classification scheme to develop a typology of late developing societies, their stratification orders, and development dynamics over time. While the combination of rural transformation and price-setting markets is conducive to growth and human development, I've argued, material living standards and their cultural concomitants will likely lag in the absence of either or both processes. If chapter 4 addressed the divergence of late developing societies in the middle of the twentieth century, chapter 5 will discuss their partial convergence toward the end of the century and beyond.

In the meantime, however, I'd like you to consider the ways in which the same institution can play different roles in different contexts. So, for example, institutions like land reform, ISI, and meritocracy were common in late developers; however, only the HPAEs – and, really, Korea and Taiwan – achieved rapid economic growth with broad-based equity. Why didn't land reform foster growth with equity in Russia, Cuba, or for that matter revolutionary Mexico? Why didn't ISI produce rapid growth, let alone equity, in most of Latin America and South Asia? What about meritocracy? It's portrayed as the key to growth in Northeast Asia and a source of inequality and discontent elsewhere. There are at least three possible answers, each of which merits consideration.

The first is that these institutions only work in particular institutional contexts that are themselves package deals. When the Soviets expropriated their landlords and peasants in the aftermath of the Russian Revolution, for example, they didn't impose market discipline on their successors, and Soviet farmers, industrialists, and wage laborers therefore went on to produce high-cost, low-quality products. Similarly, when tariffs and subsidies were adopted outside of East Asia, they were rarely accompanied by performance standards, and import-substituting economies therefore failed to build competitive industry.

The second is that the concepts themselves have different meanings in different places and times. Consider, for example, the hereditary meritocracy found in contemporary Latin America (Torche 2014). Is it the same beast as the "meritocratic bureaucracy" (Evans 1992: 152) found in miracle-era East Asia, or a different animal entirely, doing different work institutionally as well as ideologically? For that matter, is Mexico's land reform, which "never came close to eliminating the large landlord class" (D. Davis 2004: 266), comparable to land reform in Korea and Taiwan? And might the answers affect our assessments of their correlates and consequences?

And the third is that development is relational, more like a football game than a footrace, and only so many miracles can occur in any given time period. On this account, it really didn't matter what the rest of the Global South did, or, perhaps does, because there's only so much room at the top.

My point isn't to take a position in this debate, of course. My suspicion is that all three accounts play a role, albeit to different degrees in regard to different institutions and contexts. But in thinking about their respective implications, both theoretical and observable, we'll get a better purchase on both development in general and the material to come.

5

The Diffusion and Demise of
Free-Market Reform in the
Post-Cold War Era

By the late 1980s the illiberal development strategies discussed
in chapter 4 had been largely discredited. Central planning was
about to be consigned to the "dustbin of history." The populist
policy cycle had given ISI a bad name. And East Asia's success was
still being attributed to a laissez-faire regime that looked more
like a libertarian fantasy than a land-reforming, infant-industry
protecting, and performance standard-imposing developmental
state. The result was a so-called Washington Consensus in favor
of trade liberalization, deregulation, budget rationalization, and
privatization.

The emergence of the Washington Consensus fostered a radical
shift in the economic sociology of development. If the puzzle in
the era of national development concerned the emergence and
consequences of distinct illiberal policy regimes in different
countries and regions, the puzzle in the era of globalization concerned their sudden abandonment for liberal alternatives, often
by their former architects and defenders. Why, for example,
did the former communists in Eastern Europe move toward the
Washington Consensus rather than some form of social democracy? Why did the seemingly successful high-performing Asian
economies (HPAEs) embrace at least a measure of free-market
reform? And why did stop–go cycles that had been taken for
granted for decades throughout Latin America at long last stop
in large parts of the region? While mainstream economists had
always taken the superiority of free-market policies for granted,

and therefore treated their embrace as little more than a rational reawakening, sociologists noted the limits to their account and offered a number of alternatives including the: coercive power of the international financial institutions (IFIs) and the developed market economies; influence of professional economists and their theories; and mimicry of foreign governments.

This chapter is designed to bring order to the literature by digging deeper into the history of the Washington Consensus before: first, discussing mainstream accounts of policy convergence and alternatives rooted in the "new institutionalism" (DiMaggio and Powell 1991) in organizational sociology; second, distilling them into a typology based on a twofold distinction between "rational" and "ideational" accounts of human behavior, on the one hand, and "structural" and "agentic" sources of political pressure, on the other; third, exploring the limits of the typology in light of more recent empirical and theoretical developments, including the rise of China, the breakdown of neoliberal globalization, and the proliferation of populism in the early twenty-first century; and, fourth, discussing the origins of institutions more generally. While both mainstream economics and the new institutionalism offered compatible – if by no means identical – explanations of policy convergence, I argue, they have a harder time explaining institutional origins, nationally as well as internationally, and I therefore conclude by offering a "contrarian" (Zuckerman 2012) approach that tries to bridge the "macro" and the "micro" by taking the interests, ideas, and agency of peripheral actors more seriously.

The Washington Consensus revisited

The term "Washington Consensus" was coined by economist John Williamson in 1989 to describe ten specific policies he thought "more or less everyone in Washington would agree were needed" if Latin America was to escape the populist policy cycle (Williamson 2009: 7). Examples included things like gradual – and qualified – import and investment liberalization, market-determined interest rates, the deregulation of business start-up, and the reordering of public spending priorities away from subsidies for the middle class (e.g., universities, gasoline) and toward basic education and health care (Williamson 1990). Williamson self-consciously left "neoliberal" ideas like "monetarism, supply-side economics, and minimal government" off the list on the grounds that they had never commanded a consensus in Washington and by the late 1980s had "been discarded as impractical or undesirable fads" (Williamson 2009: 9).

Over the course of the next decade, however, Williamson came to express four related reservations about his conceptual creation. First, he worried that the adjective "Washington" was at best misleading, insofar as the policies he'd originally had in mind had much broader origins and support, and at worst counterproductive insofar as it implied that they'd been imposed on developing countries by the United States and the IFIs when in many cases the developing countries themselves had taken the lead. Second, he recognized that despite his original caution the term had come to serve as a synonym or shorthand for neoliberal policies that were far from consensual and that he himself, among others, didn't endorse. Third, he discovered that the term had simultaneously come to denote not an approach to crisis management in Latin America in the short run but the "attitudes of the IMF and World Bank toward all developing countries" (Williamson 2003: 1476) all the time, and that those attitudes overlooked critical geographic as well as temporal differences. And, fourth, he worried that by associating Washington with "an extreme and dogmatic commitment to the belief that markets can handle everything" (Williamson 2000: 252) the term had done the causes of diplomacy and development policymaking more harm than good. In short, Williamson came to regret the way a term he'd coined to capture the least common denominator that a broad array of stakeholders in the development community would desire had come to imply the maximal conceivable platform the most extreme hardliners in Washington would demand.

With rare exception, however, developing countries were not adopting the market fundamentalist policies Williamson deplored in lieu of his original program of liberalization, privatization, rationalization, and deregulation. On the contrary, they were embracing his preferred policies and at times going beyond them by moving more rapidly or further than the conventional wisdom would have advised and/or adopting measures that lay outside the consensus entirely (e.g., capital account liberalization, intellectual property protection), and this opens a host of questions. Were they undertaking these reforms in pursuit of economic efficiency? At the behest of the United States and the IFIs? Or for some other reason? And why now? Had the populist era discussed in chapter 4 finally come to an end? Or was something else afoot?

Economic rationality and beyond

The most obvious account of policy convergence is economic competition. If policymakers don't adopt free-market measures, argue most economists, capital will flee, jobs will be lost, and people will stay poor. If they do adopt reforms, however, they can embrace their comparative advantages, lure investment and employment, and prosper. On this account, in short, policymakers in the developing world had learned, after 50 or more years of failed, illiberal experiments, to get with the program by adopting "rational," or neoclassical, economic policies.

These neoclassical approaches are "realist" in orientation. They assume that people are by their very nature actors with boundaries and preferences that are, at least to a large degree, independent of their environments; that their preferences include income and wealth maximization; and that they will pursue their preferences by advocating and exploiting a minimal set of universally desirable institutions including property rights and perhaps sovereignty (Meyer 2010: 4; see also North and Thomas 1973; Krasner 1999). On this account, therefore, growth and development should take hold everywhere over time.

The problems with this account are just as obvious. First, it's inconsistent with a large body of literature that suggests that "coordinated market economies" like Japan, Germany, and Sweden – not to mention Korea and Taiwan (Schneider 2009:

573) – are at least as competitive as their liberal counterparts (Hall and Soskice 2001). And, second, it can't explain the timing of reform. Given that most developing (and transitional) economies had been depressed and/or volatile long before the 1980s, after all, there was no explanation for why they hadn't learned earlier – let alone why they all learned simultaneously. The puzzle wasn't just the occurrence of reform, in other words, but the direction, extent, timing, and uniformity of the convergence. If the Washington Consensus marked the sudden emergence of "collective rationality" (Rodrik 1996: 12) in the developing world, it leaves us to ask about the persistence of collective irrationality in the decades prior, and sociologists have plenty to say about collective behavior.

Organizational ecologists traced collective rationality to market competition, and in that sense bore a resemblance to economists, but treated the "isomorphism" (or homogenization) that epitomizes rationality as a product of selection pressures rather than self-conscious adaptation (Hannan and Freeman 1977: 932–3). "Failing churches do not become retail stores," argued a seminal contribution, "nor do firms transform themselves into churches" (Hannan and Freeman 1977: 957). And most organizations therefore live and die in the form or structure in which they started. The ones that are well adapted to their environments survive, according to organizational ecology, and the ones that are ill adapted perish over time, leaving a broadly uniform population of organizations behind to fill any available niche.

Organizational ecology is a powerful tool that has brought light to many debates in economic sociology. But it probably doesn't explain the proliferation of free-market reform in the late twentieth century, when a number of parties and politicians who had traditionally defended ISI and deplored laissez-faire abandoned their birthrights and embraced the Washington Consensus – in effect turning churches into stores. In fact, policy reversals were sufficiently common in Latin America that scholars invoked the term "policy switcher" to describe newly minted neoliberals like Carlos Menem in Argentina and Alberto Fujimori in Peru (Murillo 2018: 3; see also Forteza and Tommasi 2006), who had started out as populists, and drew a firm distinction between "pragmatic converts" to free-market reform and "true believers" (Murillo 2009).

Was there a more plausible alternative to organizational ecology? In one of the most influential contributions to twentieth-century sociology, Paul DiMaggio and Walter Powell posited three mechanisms through which organizations could bring collective rationality, or organizational homogeneity, to their fields independently of market pressure or competition alone (DiMaggio and Powell 1983: 149), and all three – coercion, professionalization, and mimicry – have been invoked by political scientists and economists as well as sociologists in an effort to understand development policy convergence in the late twentieth century (Drezner 2001; Dobbin, Simmons, and Garrett 2007; Simmons, Dobbin, and Garrett, 2006). In fact, the concepts of coercive, normative, and mimetic isomorphism are among sociology's most successful recent exports.

Coercive isomorphism

The first mechanism posits coercion as an alternative to rational policymaking or profit maximization. The idea is that organizations, like firms, courts, and schools, converge in form not because the uniform outcome is more rational or profitable than what came before, or than some third alternative, but due to the coercive power of a superior authority. Imagine, for example, a government mandate that declared that all schools had to achieve a minimum average score on a common test to maintain their accreditation. Schools would not only force their students to take the test, which would entail one form of convergence, but would in all likelihood adjust their curricula, and in turn their faculty, to guarantee their performance and accreditation, which would entail further convergence. This could be interpreted as an example of coercive isomorphism.

Organizational sociologists pointed to similar dynamics at the international level in the late twentieth century. If the IMF conditioned bailouts or balance-of-payments support on exchange-rate devaluation and tariff reduction, which it did, indebted countries would begin to abandon ISI in favor of a free-market alternative (Babb 2007; Kentikelenis and Babb 2019). If rich countries treated patent and copyright protection as the price for their unilateral trade preferences, which they did, poor countries would begin to adopt and enforce demanding patent and copyright laws (Shadlen, Schrank, and Kurtz 2005). If Washington withheld aid from poor countries that refused to do its bidding, which it did, they'd come into line (Milner, Nielson, and Findley 2016). And insofar as the policies in question are controversial, rather than unambiguously rational, and bind developing country governments and firms, which is their intent, they constitute examples of coercive isomorphism.

Normative isomorphism

A neo-Marxist might look at these examples and say, "See, I told you all along!" After all, they imply – or at the very least do nothing to rule out – a powerful Global North dominated by the United States that dictates policies that are inimical to the Global South. Why not erase developing country debt, allow people in the Global South to use software, medicine, and fertilizer developed in the Global North at low cost, and free their policymakers from the imperial, patronizing oversight of the United States? And the neo-Marxist would have a point. Some of the reforms demanded by international organizations and northern governments are indefensible by almost any reasonable standard (see, e.g., Médecins Sans Frontières 2018). But the theoretical problem is that in many cases the developing countries themselves embraced these policies with little or no input from the Global North – or went beyond the recommendations of northern advisers to adopt even more extreme reforms (see, e.g., Connell and Dados 2014). In these cases, it's hard to pin the blame on coercion alone.

This is where professionalization comes in. Normative isomorphism occurs when the people who staff or lead an organization have been trained and socialized to take certain values for granted in the course of their professionalization – particularly in schools or professional associations, but during the course of certification, career advancement, accreditation, and the like as well. Consider, for example, the medical profession in the United States. If almost all doctors spend four years in a pre-medical program, four more years in medical school, and typically go on to a residency, perhaps a fellowship, and membership in the American Medical Association, and if hospitals have traditionally been run by doctors, is it surprising that most hospitals have similar features? Or that they'll adopt different practices and take on different features when they're taken over by non-clinicians with business degrees (Numerato, Salvatore, and Fattore 2012)?

A vast body of literature suggests that similar dynamics not only occur in public policymaking, in general, but go a long way toward explaining the spread of free-market reform, in particular. Where policymakers in the mid-twentieth century were frequently drawn from the "lower and middle professional, administrative, and intellectual strata" that had traditionally fueled the growth of "middle-class nationalism" (Hobsbawm 1962: 135), their late-twentieth-century successors frequently included professional managers and economists imbued with radically different ideas and norms, many of which they'd absorbed in northern business and graduate schools. Some have portrayed these technocrats as mere pawns – or perhaps members – of the upper classes, appointed to legitimate public policies that were ultimately in their own private interest (Silva 1993: 41–2). Others emphasize the power of professionalization itself. Just as military officers bristle at talk of surrender, they argue, no matter the cost of war, economists and MBAs take laissez-faire for granted, and find it hard to imagine – let alone endorse – alternatives (Markoff and Montecinos 1993; Fourcade 2001, 2006; Fourcade-Gourinchas and Babb 2002; Dobbin, Simmons and Garrett 2007).

Mimetic isomorphism

The obvious problem is that not all policy choices have a single professional norm attached, in part because the boundaries across the professions – and professional knowledge – are themselves socially constructed. Some policy terrains span professions (e.g., crime control, law, and social work), and most professions contain more than one perspective. The Washington Consensus offers some obvious examples; for instance, Williamson left capital account liberalization off his list because he didn't think it "did or should command a consensus in Washington" (Williamson 2009: 10) at the time, despite the fact that it had many champions, and came to see that the range of acceptable opinion vis-à-vis the exchange rate was quite broad as well. And the barriers to picking among competing norms are aggravated in the middle of a crisis, when the problem's not just risk but uncertainty; that is, when the unknowns are so numerous and vexing that you can't even place a probability on the bets you're making (Knight 1921).

What happens then? DiMaggio and Powell hold that mimicry becomes likely. Organizational leaders choose their respective peer group, if it hasn't already been chosen, and do what its members have done. Just as the presidents of Pac-12 schools or elite liberal arts colleges benchmark against their peers, for instance, the leaders of firms and governments benchmark against theirs, particularly in periods of uncertainty; hence the institutional similarities between countries that are found in the same region (Schwinn 2012; Guillén and Capron 2016), trace their roots to common cultural traditions (Huntington 1996; Beckfield 2008; Schrank 2021), and/or play similar roles in the international trading system (Henisz, Zelner, and Guillén 2005; Polillo and Guillén 2005).

Drivers of isomorphism

It's worth remembering that the institutional sources of isomorphism anticipated by DiMaggio and Powell predict the same outcome as market competition: collective rationality. In "highly structured organizational fields," they argue, "individual efforts to deal rationally with uncertainty and constraint often lead, in the aggregate, to homogeneity in structure, culture, and output" (DiMaggio and Powell 1983: 147). The question in these cases is less whether individual organizations adopt the rational form, which they will, than how the organizational field gets to the "tipping point" (DiMaggio and Powell 1983: 156) in the first place. What drives organizations to embrace the privileged form, whatever it may be? Where economists place their faith in the logic of competition, new institutionalists like DiMaggio and Powell pay more attention to learning, legal constraints, and legitimacy; that is, to the power of social approval and disapproval, formal and informal.[1]

But the differences among the distinct schools of thought shouldn't obscure their similarities, especially since the drivers of isomorphism "intermingle" with each other in practice (DiMaggio and Powell 1983: 150). Consider, for example, a car company that makes a fortune figuring out how to meet fuel-efficiency standards to the pleasure of its engineers, stockholders, and successful imitators in the industry. Economists will feel vindicated by its profitability, to be sure. But advocates of coercive isomorphism will note that it was motivated by the regulations; proponents of normative isomorphism will underscore the contributions of the engineers; and champions of mimicry will highlight the homogenization of the industry as a whole and discuss the role of peer effects. While old-school organization theory asked, "Why are there so many kinds of organizations?" and privileged methods that were "geared towards explaining variation" (DiMaggio and Powell 1983: 148), the new institutionalists asked why there were so few, and paid more attention to the underlying mechanisms.

One of the problems this poses is that the mechanisms in question are "not always empirically distinct" (DiMaggio and Powell 1983: 150; see also Mizruchi and Fein 1999: 657; Simmons et al. 2006: 803; Dobbin et al. 2007: 450), and it's hard to know what's doing the work in practice. Are developing countries adopting free-market reforms under the influence of the IMF? Neoclassical economists? Mobile investors? Peer countries? Other factors? Is there a way to distinguish them analytically? Are they, at a minimum, *conceptually* distinct? Table 5.1 distills the four categories of isomorphism – one competitive, three institutional – into a two-dimensional typology designed to bring clarity to the field.[2]

The first dimension is the degree to which isomorphic pressures are structural or agent-based. When they're products of

Table 5.1   Hypothesized drivers of policy convergence in the late twentieth century

		Drivers	
		Structural	*Agentic*
Motivation	*Rational*	Competitive	Coercive
	Ideational	Mimicry	Normative

diffuse pressures that are built into the system as a whole, they're structural. When they're products of identifiable individuals or organizations and are at least theoretically reversible, they're agent-based. The IMF and the economics profession could at least theoretically change their tunes and backtrack a bit; so coercive and normative isomorphism are agentic. But developing countries will always have peers and need capital, at least for the foreseeable future, and I therefore think of mimicry and competitive isomorphism as structural.

The second dimension is the extent to which motivations are rational or ideational. They're rational when they're in the interests of key stakeholders. They're ideational when they're ambiguous or contrary to the interests of key stakeholders but have gained so much normative or cultural traction that they're adopted anyway. When policymakers adopt risky reforms at the behest of peers or neoliberal advisers, for example, they're placing ideas ahead of reason. When they adopt risky reforms at the behest of bond rating agencies or the IMF, however, they're quite possibly being rational (Chwieroth 2007).

The result is a continuum that runs clockwise from the more realist approaches in the northwestern cell of Table 5.1 to the "constructivist" or "phenomenological" approaches in the southwest. While the actors who populate the normative and coercive accounts in the eastern column are heavily "socialized and constrained by a complex institutional environment," according to John Meyer, they nonetheless boast realist roots and a degree of agency. They're more than mere channels of their cultures, environments, and institutions. But the actors who populate the mimetic accounts that, according to Meyer, constitute the "creative core" of the new institutionalism tend to lack "the full awareness or purposiveness that actorhood ordinarily implies" and therefore lie entirely "outside the models of realist sociologies" (Meyer 2010: 4; see also Mizruchi and Fein 1999).

The limits to neoliberalism

These are blurry lines, to be sure, and all the more so given the definitional imprecision of terms like "identifiable," "agency," "interests," and "purposive." The methodological challenge is to understand how much harmonization is going on in the world, along which lines, and driven by which mechanisms. In an effort to find the answers, some sociologists have looked for statistical relationships between the timing of specific free-market reforms and indicators of competition, coercion, professionalization, and mimicry, respectively, in different countries. They've found support for each mechanism, albeit to different degrees and inconsistently (Dobbin et al. 2007; Gilardi 2012). Others have carried out careful studies of economic policymaking in specific countries and time periods. While their findings are absolutely fascinating, they're not necessarily consistent with each other, either within or between cases (cf. Babb 2001; Van Gunten 2015; Heredia 2018), and the literature on free-market reform therefore has an ad hoc character that's almost inescapable.

The problem's not simply that our understanding of reform is ad hoc, however, but that the most careful studies called the pervasiveness and power of neoliberalism itself into question. Some countries adopted free-market reforms in theory and ignored them in practice, for instance, in a process long known as "decoupling" (Meyer and Rowan 1977). When there's a "gap between ritual or ceremonial adoption and actual implementation," explain Mauro Guillén and Laurence Capron, decoupling is likely at work (Guillén and Capron 2016: 134; see also Helbardt, Hellmann-Rajanayagam, and Korff 2012). Others embraced free-market reforms and labor, environmental, and consumer protections simultaneously (Murillo and Schrank 2005; Schrank 2009, 2021) or replaced "at-the-border" initiatives that had been checked by the WTO with "behind-the-border" measures like "buy-national" campaigns and export incentives (Rickard and Kono 2014: 658; see also Schrank and Kurtz 2005). "Only by accounting for *both* weak enforcement of rules and policy substitution does it become apparent that developing countries do indeed have a wide range of options available to them," explained one careful observer (Intscher 2014: 20), and that the extent of neoliberalism – though vast – is therefore less powerful and uniform than believed.

By far the most common behind-the-border measures were research and development (R&D) subsidies (Chen et al. 2020: 1), and Ronald Dore therefore treated "the volume of public funding in the total research effort" as one of the "simplest measures" of the "role of industrial policy" in the early twenty-first century (Dore 2000: 237–8). Nor was he alone. Chalmers Johnson portrayed "government-sponsored research and development" as a key aspect of Japan's "market-conforming" industrial policy in the postwar era (Johnson 1982: 318). Peter Evans discussed the ratio of public to private R&D spending in late twentieth-century Korea (Evans 1995: 147). And Monica Merito and her colleagues hold that "public support to private R&D has been a traditional measure of industrial policy in Western countries" (Merito, Gianangelli, and Bonaccorsi 2010: 25) as well.

Is Gerschenkron's sense that the least developed countries require the most government intervention, which I discussed in chapter 4, consistent with their account? If so, we should see that the government share of R&D is inversely correlated with GDP per capita – with emerging economies more dependent on government, and rich countries more confident in their private sectors. Figure 5.1 speaks to the question by plotting the public share of R&D expenditure by GDP per capita in 39 upper- and middle-income countries in 2009, and reveals a strong inverse correlation. The wealthier the country, on average, the lower the government's share of R&D spending.[3]

The results not only bolster Gerschenkron's account of industrial policymaking in late developing countries but gainsay the

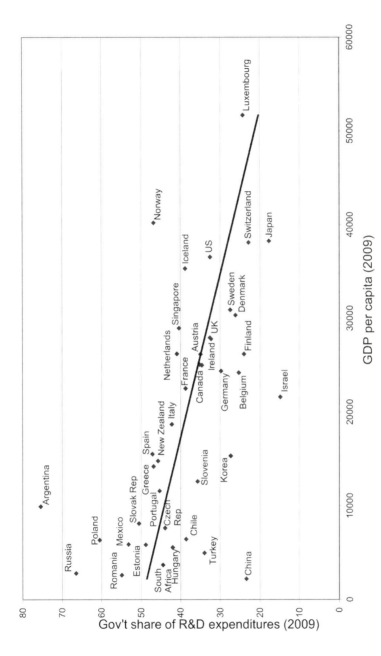

Figure 5.1 Government R&D spending by GDP per capita.

Source: Compiled with data from OECD (2013) and World Bank (2013).

omnipresence of neoliberalism in the early twenty-first century. The government share of R&D expenditures ranges from less than 20 percent in Israel to more than 70 percent in Argentina, and industrial policies defined more broadly are increasingly common. One recent survey holds that their rate of adoption "appears to be at an all-time high" (UNCTAD 2018: 128), and that more than 80 countries adopted some sort of industrial policy measure between 2013 and 2018 alone. And the era of neoliberalism would therefore appear to be over.

The problem with the convergence thesis isn't simply the proliferation of industrial policy, however, but that free-market reform itself has been delayed and, in some cases, reversed for at least three reasons: first, the rise of China; second, the demise of the World Trade Organization; and third, the growth of populism, especially in the United States.

The rise of China

Between 1990 and 2020, the Chinese economy grew at an average annual rate of almost 10 percent. China entered the period with an average per capita income of approximately US$1,000 and currently boasts a per capita income of more than US$10,000, in effect joining the HPAEs as a miracle economy (World Bank 2022). Unlike the HPAEs, however, China is enormous. With a population of almost 1.5 billion people, it is the largest country in the world, albeit losing ground to India, and by 2014 had overtaken the United States as the world's largest economy at purchasing power parity (Bird 2014).

China's rise posed a threat to free-market reform and globalization for several reasons. First, the Chinese have never accepted the merits of free trade and laissez-faire. On the contrary, they view their own success as a product of planning and industrial policy and the WTO as a threat to their growth. Second, their success discredited laissez-faire elsewhere in the Global South. When the fastest-growing economy in the world is an ardent advocate of industrial policy and a critic of free trade, potential imitators take notice. And, third, insofar as China aspires to great power status, it has an incentive to create parallel institutions that offer critics of the WTO – and US-dominated institutions more generally – an exit option (Wu 2016; Bradsher and Rappeport 2018).

The demise of the WTO

The street battles at the WTO's 1999 Ministerial Conference in Seattle further undermined the credibility of both the organization and its principles (Smith 2001). The failure to conclude the 2001 Doha Agreement signaled an organization on life support (Velthuis 2006). And the George W. Bush administration in the United States arguably heightened the threat by concluding a series of regional and bilateral trade agreements (RBTAs) in an effort to put pressure on the WTO. If the United States had an alternative to multilateralism, argued Ambassador Robert Zoellick, developing countries would bend over backward to open their markets and join the world trading system (Evenett and Meier 2008). And bending over backward typically entailed concessions to US demands on a host of issues that had little to do with trade per se, including financial liberalization, intellectual property protection, and military cooperation. For instance, the United States conditioned a number of trade deals on support for the Iraq War (Becker 2003; Miller 2021) and threatened to punish opponents of the broader "war on terror" with tariffs and trade sanctions (Armstrong 2003; see also Gowa and Mansfield 1993).

The result was a vicious circle. While developing countries preferred the multilateral WTO to plurilateral RBTAs, they preferred membership in RBTAs to wholesale marginalization by the United States and their competitors, and therefore joined plurilateral agreements that were neither in their obvious interests nor in the interests of the WTO itself (Shadlen 2008). Consequently, the US strategy of "competitive liberalization" turned out to be little more than "bilateral opportunism masquerading as high principle" (Evenett and Meier 2008: 63). In effect, it redistributed the gains from trade discussed in chapter 1 from poor countries to their wealthy trading partner and put the world trading system at risk.

The growth of populism

The third, and related, strike was the growth of populism around the world in the early twenty-first century. Chapter 4 described populism as an effort to build coalitions of potentially antagonistic interest groups (e.g., import-substituting industrialists and workers) by redistributing material resources to their members (Guillén 2000b: 365). While populism "need not involve nativism, xenophobic nationalism or indeed any kind of reference to cultural nationhood or ethnicity" (Brubaker 2020: 54), it frequently does, and populist discourse went hand in glove with protectionism in Russia (Quinn 2019), Brexit in the United Kingdom (Inglehart and Norris 2016), and "the return of economic nationalism to East Central Europe" (Varga 2021). When Donald Trump took office in 2016, moreover, and promised to "make America great again" by turning his back on a quarter of a century's worth of trade agreements, the era of globalization effectively came to an end (Alden 2018).

The broader point, of course, is that theories of isomorphism predict that organizations will converge in form but don't tell us which form, let alone when, where, or why. Structures that seemed eminently rational in the mid-1950s – like the closed national economy and active industrial policy – seemed completely anachronistic a half-century later and are nonetheless making a comeback today. The abandonment of outsourcing for vertical integration offers one example (Ewing 2022) and calls to mind the Ford Motor Company's mid-twentieth century ownership of mines, rubber plantations, ships, and steel mills, among other things. The revival of public ownership offers another (Musacchio, Lazzarini, and Aguilera 2015) and is expected to intensify in light of global challenges like climate change (Hsu, Liang, and Matos 2021; Wong 2022) and pandemic disease (Gaspar, Medas, and Ralyea 2020; Wright et al. 2021). And neither vertical integration nor state ownership is universal in any event. Many companies and countries continue to rely upon decentralization, privatization, and liberalization insofar as possible.

Lurking in the background of this chapter, therefore, is a socio-logically vexing omission alluded to in chapter 1: We tend to explain institutions by invoking other institutions. Free-market reform is a product of IMF pressure in the late twentieth century. The IMF is a product of the United Nations Monetary and Financial Conference (i.e., the Bretton Woods Agreement) sponsored by the United States in 1944. Industrial policy is a product of the developmental state in East Asia. The developmental state is a product of land reform, infant industry protection, and performance standards. And so on and so forth. We're left with "institutions all the way down" (Caporaso 2007: 404), not only in the chapter but in the book and, I worry, in development sociology writ large.

The origin of institutions

The challenge, therefore, is to explain the origins and shape of institutions in a non-tautological fashion. How do we explain the emergence of formal institutions, like vertical integration and public ownership, without simply invoking other formal institutions, like courts and parties? Given that there's no world government, the core institutions of global governance emerge in an institutional vacuum – and render the resort to tautology all but impossible. We can therefore gain unique insight into the origin of institutions *in general* by examining their international variants *in particular*.

In a series of classic works, Arrighi portrayed international institutions as the products and property of hegemonic nation-states. When they're at the peak of their powers, he argued, hegemons build institutions that legitimate and facilitate their rule and impose it on the rest of the world. So, for example, the United States built the IMF, the United Nations, and the WTO in the "long twentieth century" (Arrighi 1994: esp. 69) and placed less powerful countries on the horns of a dilemma: If they joined and participated in these institutions, they'd be reinforcing a decidedly inequitable system under the thumb of the United States; if they opted out, however, they'd forgo trade, investment, and diplomatic opportunities that would be in their own national interest. And most countries therefore opted into an asymmetrical arrangement – in much the same way that workers opt into arrangements that are exploitative, inequitable, and nonetheless better than unemployment.

International institutions are, on this account, sources as well as products of hegemonic influence. But they are by no means products of military and material power alone. Hegemonic rule requires a widespread perception that the national interests of the hegemon are consistent with the general interest of the system as a whole. The hegemonic power must therefore "mobilize consent and cooperation internationally" (Arrighi 2007: 214) no less than the employer must mobilize consent and cooperation in the workplace. And hegemons mobilize consent and cooperation in part by establishing credible – if not democratic or accountable – institutions; hence the survival of US-sponsored agencies like the IMF and the World Bank that garner legitimacy by imposing austerity arrangements in an effort to resolve debt crises of their own making (Arrighi 2007: 225). Peripheral countries can condemn the international financial institutions and the terms of their loans and bailouts, Arrighi implies, but they nonetheless find it difficult to walk away. Unless and until something better comes along, he concludes, IFIs like the World Bank are the best – if not quite the only – game in town.

But US hegemony isn't inevitable, argued Arrighi, and it won't last forever. China is already "out-competing Northern agencies by offering Southern countries more generous terms for access to their natural resources; larger loans with fewer political strings attached and without expensive consultant fees; and big and complicated infrastructure projects in distant areas at as little as half the cost of Northern competitors" (Arrighi 2007: 383). When they eventually put paid to US hegemony, moreover, the Chinese will build *international* institutions that meet their own needs for power, profit, and legitimacy, and the "epicenter of the global political economy" (Arrighi 2007: xi) will shift from North America to East Asia. Precocious examples of Chinese institution building include efforts to redefine the standards that govern the global cotton trade (Quark 2013), to develop an alternative monetary order based on the renminbi (Liao and McDowell 2016; cf. Hung 2022), and to challenge the legitimacy and efficacy of the WTO itself (Wu 2016; Bradsher and Rappeport 2018).

In short, Arrighi's account of global governance is highly sophisticated. It takes ideological as well as military and material factors seriously, and it seems prescient with regard to the rise of China. But for all of his sophistication Arrighi failed to *fully* address how the United States and, more recently China, became candidate hegemons in the first place. Why the United States and not Germany? Why China and not India? Why not Indonesia or Iran for that matter? Is it really "global institutions all the way down" (Block 2018: 27)?

Toward a contrarian alternative

Prevailing accounts of institutional origins – national as well as international – push the question of collective rationality back without answering it. Marxists make a convincing case that capitalism is both a necessary condition for hegemony and an unintended product of class conflict, but they can't account for the resolution of the conflict, if it's resolved at all. Weberians make a plausible case for the state's role in conflict resolution, but their account of state formation is lacking. Durkheimians offer a key caveat and contribution by invoking the social construction of institutions, but they don't tell us which constructions win or why. And we're therefore back where we started in chapter 1: unpersuaded by the classics and unaware of an alternative.

The problem is that none of the existing approaches to collective rationality – i.e., pure realism or pure constructivism – is fully plausible. Nobody really believes that their preferred structure or program is objectively the most rational or efficient, or that they could know or adopt it if it were. There are simply too many unknowns and uncontrollables. And nobody really believes that people's preferences are pure social constructs, unanchored in some social or human reality. For every bonkers belief that has found a substantial audience, there are a million more that not only haven't but almost certainly couldn't, and shouldn't, gain traction under any conceivable circumstance. Take, for example, drug safety. Reasonable minds can differ about how many trials a drug should undergo, or the minimal sample sizes, statistical procedures, and so on. But almost nobody would advocate complete deregulation, let alone the government procurement and distribution of placebos through the national healthcare system – perhaps in conjunction with a powerful propaganda campaign – in an effort to convince people they'd been rendered invulnerable, even if people believed it. And it's precisely in the gap between what people are *expected* to accept or appreciate and what they *do* accept or appreciate that politics comes in – when people take action to address the gap, whether by voting, demonstrating, running for office, taking up arms, or in any of the myriad ways in which people seek change. By ignoring that gap, moreover, both mainstream economics, with its Panglossian realism, and pure constructivism, where justice is in the eye of the beholder, abdicate politics entirely: the former by suggesting that everything is already for the best in the best of all possible worlds, making political action unnecessary or irrational; the latter by saying there's no clear basis for evaluating or assessing – let alone defending or advocating – what's "best" in the first place.[4]

In fact, Ezra Zuckerman argues that pure constructivism, no less than pure realism, is devoid of politics. While the pure realist accepts the validity of dominant interpretations, and thereby forgoes the opportunity to offer a critique or alternative, the pure constructivist has neither a fondness for dominant perspectives nor a "basis for challenging them or suggesting alternative arrangements since he believes all interpretations to be equally (in)valid" (Zuckerman 2010: 364). Ironically, therefore, the one principle on which the economic realists and the sociological constructivists agree is *de gustibus non est disputandum* (Zuckerman 2012: 232). And from an empirical perspective they suffer a similar problem: they have trouble explaining change, that is, the breakdown of collective rationality and, potentially, the emergence of new equilibria.

For Zuckerman, by way of contrast, change grows out of the gap between people's values and public valuations of assets or institutions. In essence, he argues, people take "contrarian" positions, and in so doing drive social change, when objective conditions provide at least "loose constraints on social valuations" (Zuckerman 2012: 231) that have become divorced from reality. His principal examples come from financial markets, where value investors buy up underpriced assets and take them private in an effort to gain access to their income streams, and short sellers borrow and sell "overvalued" stocks at their current prices, hoping to buy and pay back the shares at a lower price after a market correction has occurred (Zuckerman 2012). And financiers can certainly bring about social and economic change in this way (Burrough and Helyar 1990; Lewis 2010).

But the broader principle – that people stake out contrarian positions when public valuations are no longer plausible to them – has wider purchase. It suggests that macro-institutional change originates with contrarian beliefs and behavior at the micro level. When migrants take on debt in overvalued currencies to pay for journeys to countries with little inflation (Massey and Espinosa 1997; see also Robberson 1995; Asad and Garip 2019), aren't they effectively staking out contrarian positions against their home countries? If they bet right, they'll be able to pay off their loans in hard currency earned abroad once their debts are devalued at home. When garment "industry scouts" go to the ends of the earth to find low-cost export platforms, aren't they betting that their "new sources of supply" (Gereffi 1999: 53) are undervalued at current prices? On arrival, they hope to find more productive labor at lower cost than anticipated based on prior market signals. When microfinance organizations extend credit to borrowers who are denied by traditional banks (Doering 2018), aren't they effectively doing the same thing; that is, betting that conventional banks have been overly conservative in their credit assessments? And when people live or work underground or off the books (Portes and Sassen-Koob 1987), aren't they betting that the short-term costs of taxes and regulation outweigh the long-run benefits of legal protections or risks of evasion? While these might seem like discrete decisions that have little bearing on development outcomes, moreover, they have the potential to bring about large-scale social transformation.[5]

Whether they do so or not depends in part on the culturally mediated reactions, if any, of ancillary actors including peers, kin, consultants, credit-reporting agencies, policymakers, and parties. Does chain migration take hold? Are remittances invested productively? Do industry consultants and credit-rating agencies change their evaluations? Do policymakers and political parties notice and take action? When they do so, seemingly individual contrarian actions have the ability to scale up into broader, and perhaps systemic, change (Granovetter 1976).

Nor are these dynamics limited to what Albert Hirschman would label "exit," whether from countries, regulations, or markets. With some modification, they're applicable to his concept of "voice" (Hirschman 1970), or political protest, as well. When people believe that they're being overtaxed by the government, underpaid by their employers, or undercompensated for their land, for example, they're more likely to protest or go on strike (Flores Dewey and Davis 2013; Simmons 2014) – perhaps because their sense of justice has been violated, perhaps because they believe their claims and redress are more plausible. And in all of these cases – individual and collective, exit and voice – objective data of one sort or another provide "at least loose constraints on social valuations" (Zuckerman 2012: 231). Rarely do we see property owners asking for no tax at all, for example, or low-wage workers asking to become millionaires overnight.

Efforts to underestimate COVID mortality offer another illustration. COVID deaths have apparently been underestimated by orders of magnitude in countries like China, India, and Russia (Adam 2022; Mueller and Nolen 2022). There was bound to be some slippage between the official data and the underlying reality. Many countries lack the necessary data, and there are many unknowns and subjective decisions involved in their compilation and evaluation in any event. Is COVID mortality better estimated by means of hospital data, burial data, household surveys, estimates of excess mortality (i.e., the number of people who died during the pandemic versus the number expected to die during that period had there not been a pandemic), or a combination of some sort? And who decides? But the official figures and their defenders lose credibility when they begin to diverge radically from people's everyday experiences to the benefit of the politically powerful: when survivors begin to feel the pain; when medical professionals begin to speak out against the government; when the government responds with censorship; and when the consequences begin to redound back into the political and economic spheres by eroding trust in government and faith in institutions (see, e.g., Troianovski 2021).

In addition to bringing politics back in, therefore, Zuckerman's contrarian approach resolves a puzzle left unanswered in chapter 2. Why are struggles over performance indicators and benchmarks so intense? Why do politicians like Paul Kagame, firms like Hyundai, or organizations like the UNDP fight over which benchmarks to use and how they should be applied?

The answer is not obvious to either a pure realist or a pure constructivist. After all, the pure realist assumes that the indicators speak for themselves, and there's nothing more to be done to them. And the pure constructivist assumes that one metric is as good as any other and can't explain why Kagame, for example, tries to improve or perhaps manipulate Rwanda's performance on the HDI, where it still ranks well below the median, rather than simply come up with his own "development" indicator placing his country near the top; how Hyundai decides whether to meet fuel-economy standards or just assert that it does (Davenport and Vlasic 2014); and by what means consumers, citizens, and investors decide what to believe and disbelieve, or what to do with their doubts when they arise.

The contrarian approach addresses the puzzle in part by bridging the individual and the collective (cf. Krippner and Alvarez 2007) and in part by noting that valuations are socially constructed but they're not *pure* social constructs. Instead, they're anchored in more or less objective conditions, and when the gap between people's values and valuations gets too big legitimacy breaks down entirely, with perverse consequences for the actors, organizations, and societies in question. When exposed to chronic inflation, for example, Argentines can debate, doubt, or – in the case of policymakers – manipulate their consumer price index, but they can't ignore either the *inflación del changuito* (or "shopping cart inflation") that they see with their own eyes on a daily basis (Daniel and Lanata Briones 2019: 143; see also Barrionuevo 2011; Burke 2012) or its broader consequences – just as consumers and investors at least sometimes take notice when automobile makers sell flawed products (Stinchcombe 1997: esp. 17). Take, for example, the US Environmental Protection Agency's investigation into consumer complaints that Hyundai and Kia were exaggerating their fuel economy ratings in 2012; they ushered in both a record-setting financial penalty of US$300 million (Davenport and Vlasic 2014) and share price volatility as investors began to respond (Robles 2019).

This also explains why I spent so much time on literacy and numeracy in the first four chapters. It's not simply that they're an *indicator* or *reflection* of development; it's that they make the informational underpinnings of the contrarian positions that drive social change more widely available. If contrarian strategies presuppose that "there are right and wrong ways to evaluate objective conditions" (Zuckerman 2012: 225), after all, it's hard to believe they're not facilitated, on average, by formal education and deterred by illiteracy and innumeracy.

Information doesn't tell the whole story, of course. Interests are no less important, and there are winners and losers in all of these stories: incumbent politicians who want to keep sensitive information secret, and challengers who want it released; consumers who are overpaying for flawed products, and producers who are reaping the rewards; investors who are trying to arbitrage the differences, and rival investors who are taking opposing positions. The point is not to downplay the importance of material interests, therefore, but to note that contrarians and dissidents are better able to pursue their perceived interests and to effect social change when they have access to accurate information.

Is that social change likely to be for the better? That's a much harder question to answer, especially when some of the canonical contrarians include widely maligned financiers like John Paulson and Carl Icahn. Insofar as information asymmetries tend to redound to the benefit of political and economic oligarchs, however, I'm guardedly optimistic. I wouldn't go so far as John Kenneth Galbraith, who declared that nowhere "is there an illiterate peasantry that is progressive. Nowhere is there a literate peasantry that is not" (Galbraith 1962: 49). But I tend to think that formal education is valuable in its own right, and that on balance educated people are better able to defend their rights and pursue their ambitions.

This raises the related question of the internet and its role in development. Optimists hold that information and communications technology (ICT) will enhance efficiency and accelerate the diffusion of knowledge around the world – with enormous political as well as economic returns. In fact, the most optimistic accounts portray ICT as a veritable golden key that will unlock the door to entrepreneurship and "good government" in poor countries. But skeptics worry about censorship and surveillance, the fragmentation and isolation of user communities, and the digital divide between North and South. And Robert Wade goes farther still, worrying that "efforts to bridge the digital divide may have the effect of locking developing countries into a new form of dependency on the West" (Wade 2002: 443). After all, the dominant ICT firms, all of which are based in the Global North, have enormous market power due not only to their patents and copyrights but to their control over reigning standards and standard-setting bodies. The risk, therefore, is that developing countries will "introduce software and hardware systems that they have no capacity to maintain for themselves and that become crucial to the very functioning of their corporate and public sectors" (Wade 2002: 61).

It's almost certainly too soon to assess the relative costs and benefits of "ICT-for-development." On the one hand, Wade's concerns are legitimate. The risks to peripheral privacy and autonomy are real. But, on the other hand, so are the returns to technologies that dramatically increase the availability and lower the costs of information. And the results of the information revolution will almost certainly vary by country and context over time.

Conclusion

This chapter has tried to make five points. First, by the end of the twentieth century the era of national development – whether by central planning or import-substituting industrialization – had given way to a period of liberalization and globalization ushered in by free-market reform. Second, the apparent diffusion of free-market reform has been interpreted by economists as a product of competitive dynamics, and by sociologists as institutional isomorphism. Third, the advance of neoliberalism has nonetheless been stymied by decoupling and policy substitution, on the one hand, and the rise of China, demise of the WTO, and spread of populism, on the other. Fourth, theories of convergence that have been deployed to explain the initial diffusion of the Washington Consensus and free-market reform are unable to explain their origins and especially their demise. And, finally, the contrarian alternative to both realist economics and constructivist sociology offers a more propitious basis for the economic sociology of development in the years ahead. I hope to lay this out in more detail in the final chapter, with an eye toward distilling what we've learned and laying the foundation of what's to come. However, in the meantime, I'd like to foreshadow a more ambitious sociological agenda.

In an important article published more than a decade ago, Greta Krippner and Anthony Alvarez identified a tension between two superficially similar threads in the new economic sociology and their distinct approaches to the concept of *embeddedness*. The first thread operates at the individual, or micro, level and holds that people who are embedded in dense social networks and relationships are better positioned to carry out market transactions than their isolated counterparts. It privileges "the tools of network analysis to lay bare the relational bases of social action in economic contexts" (Krippner and Alvarez 2007: 234) and portrays embeddedness as an asset that improves individual performance in competitive markets. However, the second thread operates at the societal, or macro, level and portrays embeddedness less as a competitive asset in cutthroat markets than as a "defensive reaction against the extension of the self-regulating market" (Krippner and Alvarez 2007: 232). It draws from the late anthropologist Karl Polanyi's work on the emergence of social protection in Europe (Polanyi 1944) and is vulnerable to the charge of over-determination, especially insofar as the workers who allegedly call forth the defensive reaction are simply carrying out their historically assigned role. "It is in this sense," argue Krippner and Alvarez, "that many of Polanyi's formulations take on an air of inevitability" (Krippner and Alvarez 2007: 232). Since the micro perspective treats embeddedness as a "lubricant" that helps people pursue market exchange (Krippner and Alvarez 2007: 232), and the macro treats embeddedness as a shock absorber that insulates them from the market, conclude Krippner and Alvarez, the two views are almost entirely irreconcilable; they "cannot simply be stacked on top of one another, as is the case with micro- and macrolevel analyses in economics" (2007: 234).

To be clear, I don't think anything of value is "simple" in sociology. But I think the contrarian perspective has the potential to address Polanyi's functionalism and reconcile the micro and macro perspectives on embeddedness, and perhaps in economic sociology more generally. If I'm right, after all, moves toward laissez-faire will not only create opportunities for contrarian investors to reap rewards by betting against existing trends and institutions, and in so doing force corrections, but will simultaneously motivate social and political protest by contrarian citizens whose "expectations of the state" (Simmons 2014: 528) have been violated. Insofar as the individuals in question are embedded in dense social networks, moreover, their efforts will be imitated until they call forth a protective response. Beyond a certain point, I suspect, the protective response will call forth contrarian reactions in the other direction, which is why Polanyi speaks of a "double movement" between state and market. But my suspicion is that the hinge of that double movement lies in contrarians – investors, citizens, consumers, workers, and the like – who are embedded in dense social networks and that the key to linking the micro and macro may lie in their careful study.

6

What If Sociologists Were in Charge?

Sociologists have been extremely critical of development economists over the years. Their doubts have been expressed in informal
hallway chatter, outright condemnation, and the subtexts of their
writings on neoliberal technocrats (Lawson 2004: 124), among
other places. And insofar as economists have exerted influence
over development policymaking there's much to criticize. Poverty
remains entrenched in the Global South, as wealth accumulates
in New York, London, and Silicon Valley, and even peripheral
'success stories' have been marked by inequality, pollution, and
– with rare exceptions – political repression. But this raises the
obvious question: Would sociologists have done better? And, if
so, how and why? What would, and perhaps more importantly
should, we recommend if our turn comes?[1]

In this concluding chapter, I'll try to answer these questions in
three steps: first, by revisiting the grand and middle-range theories reviewed in this book and distilling their four key lessons;
second, by discussing more recent contributions and their limits;
and, third, by asking where we might go from here. In essence, I'll
argue that in moving from grand theories to more local accounts
sociologists have both made tremendous progress and left an enormous gap. The progress lies in a series of detailed studies – and
perhaps more importantly *concepts* and *methods* – that have shed
profound insight into the operations of developing country firms,
agencies, families, and communities. Insofar as contributions like
these aren't being – or likely to be – made by any other discipline,

they illuminate sociology's real comparative advantage in the study of development and developing societies and its roots in: the agnostic posture toward full employment and self-interest distilled into Table 1.4; the broadly relational approach to development discussed in chapter 2 and developed in chapters 3 and 4; and the contrarian approach to social change advanced in chapter 5. By treating both the balance between human needs and resources and the micro foundations of human behavior as socially constructed variables rather than theoretical assumptions, and recognizing that the social whole is invariably greater than the sum of its individual parts, sociology offers accounts and concepts that are unavailable to its cognate disciplines. But the gap lies in their aggregation: In the absence of grand or at least middle-range theories that have largely been abandoned or discredited, I'll argue, there's little to tie these accounts and concepts together, and there's a limit to how much they're likely to "scale" or accumulate over time. By way of conclusion, therefore, I try to offer some guiding principles for what a more cumulative economic sociology of development might look like in the years ahead based in part on what we already know and in part on what we think we know and could push harder to learn.

From grand theory to the middle range

We can think of the period between the end of World War II and the developing country debt crisis, more or less, as the era of grand sociological development theory. Modernization theorists and neo-Marxists weren't trying to understand the fates of particular countries and communities, let alone individuals; they were trying to paint broad, encompassing portraits of historical and global dynamics. If they got the details wrong here or there, that was simply the price of generality.

There's nothing inherently wrong with this approach. Science needs grand theories, and they're precisely what many of the most influential and valuable scientists have produced. So the real question concerns not the value of grand theory, in general, but the contributions of modernization theory and neo-Marxism, in particular, and here the record is mixed.

Despite coming in for enormous criticism – even contempt – from their successors, the most sophisticated modernization theorists had much to offer. They came up with influential concepts, like the "demonstration effect" and "involution," laid the foundation of many others, including "social capital" and "embeddedness" (Portes 1997; Woolcock 1998), and were ahead of the curve in studying phenomena like international diffusion and social networks that are central to sociology today. Furthermore, their empirical arguments were, in many cases, more right than wrong. For instance, the diffusion of ideas from North to South had an enormous impact on developing societies and their fates, if not always in the predicted direction, and there's a reason we still study foreign trade, investment, migration, and the diffusion of information more generally. They're of undeniable sociological import (see, e.g., Thornton 2001) and have arguably contributed to structural mobility in the international system.

Insofar as modernization theory's been abandoned rather than simply amended, moreover, it's less for theoretical or empirical reasons than for ideological ones. The modernization theorists were identified with US counterinsurgency efforts in Southeast Asia and discredited by the antiwar movement (Frank 1972). And their condemnation was in many cases warranted. To take the most obvious example, Rostow did serve as national security adviser in the Johnson administration and thereby played a key role in the atrocities carried out during the Vietnam War (Halberstam 1972). Long after his fellow "whiz kids" had developed doubts about the US counterinsurgency campaign, moreover, he held fast to his convictions (Stevenson 2017), which themselves were tightly coupled to his theory of development. It would be immoral, as well as naive, to ignore the connection.

But it would be no less immoral or naive to ignore the missteps of his critics. While the most sophisticated neo-Marxists made untold contributions to our understanding of the international system, and to the relational nature of development and underdevelopment in particular, they frequently backed parties, regimes, programs, and movements that themselves left much to be desired. The imperialism of the United States doesn't necessarily imply the "progressivism" of autocratic anti-imperialists, for example, let alone justify or explain their abuses. And despite neo-Marxist allusions to the "successes of the Democratic Peoples' Republic of Korea and of Vietnam" (Frank 1977), it was capitalist Northeast Asia that, for better or for worse, became a role model in the 1980s and, in so doing, pushed development sociology from the era of grand theory to an era of middle-range alternatives.

Robert Merton famously defined middle-range theories as those that lie "between the minor but necessary working hypotheses that evolve in abundance during day-to-day research and the all-inclusive systematic efforts to develop a uniform theory that will explain all the observed uniformities" (Merton 1949: 448) of interest to the investigator, and underscored their susceptibility to "empirical testing." If modernization theory and neo-Marxism constituted "all-inclusive" efforts to understand international development, moreover, efforts to bring the state back into development theory and understand institutional isomorphism were middle-range theories par excellence, and have been identified as such (Kang 2014: 225–6; Fine and Pollen 2018: 212; Nee 2018: 847). They're designed to address "specific sociological problems within an evolving and provisional framework" (Merton 1949: 453).

They also have much to recommend them empirically. It seems likely that reciprocity had something to do with the Asian miracle. It seems certain that policy convergence has multiple drivers. And it seems clear that both factors are mediated by a host of contextual conditions that deserve far more study than they've received to date. But they've hardly survived empirical testing unscathed, and they're far from a readymade alternative to mainstream development economics. After all, the high-performing Asian economies were hardly models of social justice and democracy, and it's not at all clear that they could be replicated on a large-scale in any event. Their "reciprocal control mechanisms" (Amsden 2001) almost certainly have too many preconditions, and the ecological consequences of worldwide Asian-like growth would be prohibitive.

Meanwhile, the literature on institutional isomorphism – for all of its merits – endeavored to explain the diffusion of neoliberal reform; it did little to explain its origin or demise and replacement.

What, then, have we learned from a century of development sociology? I'd point to four lessons that are distinctly sociological; that is, that are unlikely to be internalized, aggregated, and deployed in any other social science, and that as a result lay the foundation for a viable economic sociology of development in the years ahead.

First, development is a social fact that is manifest in indicators like GDP per capita and the HDI; it is not synonymous with them. "A miner, in a desolate mountain region, discovers a mine of gold or silver," explained nineteenth-century polymath John Ruskin. "He is just as poor as he was before because he is in the mountain desert alone" (Montgomery 1902: 41). Ruskin's point is obvious and more general: Wealth, money, income, urbanism, industrialization, and even literacy take on meaning exclusively in social context – and, it might be added, that context is constantly undergoing change.

Second, development is not a product of *conditions* like full employment and self-interest, which are themselves social constructs and context dependent; it's a product of cooperative and competitive *relationships* between and within workplaces, supply chains, communities, and countries. Some might say these relationships are fractal-like, insofar as the same patterns repeat themselves at higher and higher scale: workers are employed by firms in establishments; small firms supply larger firms in supply chains; and communities and countries assume buyer and supplier roles in a global division of labor, which happens to give the system as a whole a spatial aspect. But the highest returns tend to accrue to the most powerful actors, with power determined socially and politically and not just economically. Software companies don't just derive power from popular demand for their products, to take but one example. Insofar as they defend and depend upon an intellectual property regime that's enforced by their governments and naturalized by their schools and media outlets, they translate their power into popular demand for their products. And intellectual property is merely one example; one could just as easily point to antitrust institutions, labor law, fiscal and monetary policy, land tenure regimes, and a range of analogous policies, not to mention social and cultural institutions that have been "naturalized" by social scientists who treat variables as assumptions or conditions.

Third, these institutions and policies are underpinned by informal as well as formal relationships rooted in kin, community, class, caste, identity, and nationality, among other factors, that are themselves evolving in meaning and membership over time. Just as formal institutions like schools can be liberating and progressive in one context and affronts to human freedom elsewhere, informal institutions like ethnic identity and the extended family can either shelter or subjugate depending on context – or perhaps do both simultaneously. Alejandro Portes and Patricia Landolt have discussed the "downside of social capital" (1996) at some length. One could no less easily discuss the downsides of diffusion (Schrank 2020: 207), the developmental state (Kohli 2004: 10), meritocracy (Chua et al. 2021), or middle-class nationalism (Greenfeld 1996b) for that matter.

Fourth, and perhaps most controversially, institutional transformations demand collective action, albeit not necessarily self-conscious collective action. Sometimes individuals make seemingly discrete choices – about family planning, investment, voting, or the like – that in different contexts have broader consequences (Granovetter 1976: 1423–4). If their friends and neighbors imitate their own family planning practices, for example, the results could reverberate through the broader society in a completely unplanned fashion – with enormous social and economic consequences – and the likelihood of peer imitation is not randomly distributed (see, e.g., Cotts-Watkins 1990). On the contrary, it's shaped by the very formal and information institutions we've already discussed: kinship, community, language, and the like. We need to recognize, therefore, that causality need not flow "from big to small" but can sometimes flow "from small to large, from the arbitrary to the general, from the minor event to the major development" (Abbott 1988: 173).

Beyond the middle range

What, then, might we contribute to contemporary discussions of development theory and policymaking? In an effort to answer that question, I'll briefly allude to four bodies of literature that are distinctly sociological and have something to contribute – reflections on development concepts and indicators; quantitative analyses of social and political networks; social and political demography; and ethnographies of communities and organizations – before laying out a broader agenda. What all four bodies of literature hold in common, I'll argue, is that they employ concepts and methods that are high value, known to sociologists, unfamiliar to economists, and therefore well within our comparative advantage.

Development concepts and indicators

In chapter 2, I made reference to a growing body of sociological literature on concepts, benchmarks, and indicators, and chapter 5 brought that literature back into the discussion of realism and constructivism by taking the "middle ground" position that most of our concepts and indicators are social constructs *but not pure social constructs*; that is, that they can be benchmarked against more or less objective criteria drawn from people's lived experience. These claims, and the broader debates in which they're situated, have enormously important methodological as well as theoretical implications. After all, the realist approaches deployed by economists take the validity of key indicators for granted; in fact, quantitative methods classes in economics programs tend to dismiss issues of concept formation and measurement entirely (Kurtz and Schrank 2007: 563, fn. 1), and much of our empirical economic knowledge (or belief) thus presupposes the accuracy of indicators that have never been subject to systematic assessment and may well be plagued by inefficiency and/or bias.

Insofar as they've looked into these issues, moreover, sociologists have exposed these inefficiencies and biases by asking bigger-picture questions like: What's the goal being assessed?

Why? By whom? How do they know if they're measuring it accurately and, if not, why not and what might be done differently? These questions might be asked not only of "economic" variables like productivity and consumer prices (Block and Burns 1986; Neiburg 2006; de Santos 2009) but of performance indicators that purport to map political and ecological concepts like poverty, corruption, and environmental effluents that increasingly loom large in development debates as well (Korhonen-Kurki et al. 2013; Kurtz and Schrank 2020). The result would be a much richer approach to the study of development.

In chapter 2, for example, we discussed Paul Kagame and his efforts to exploit and perhaps "game" global development indicators in Rwanda. Kagame offers a convenient example, but he is far from alone. Goodhart's Law tells us that "when a measure becomes a target, it ceases to be a good measure" (Eldridge and Palmer 2009: 164; see also Chua, Morck, and Yeung 2021). But the timing, nature, and degree to which it becomes a bad measure are likely to vary enormously and systematically (Wade 2004: 407–8), as are the consequences, and the opportunities for sociological investigation are therefore boundless.

Political and economic networks

Lurking in the background of chapters 4 and 5 are interpersonal and cross-network ties between and among public and private sector officials and families. They're certainly the essence of the "embeddedness" introduced by Peter Evans in his discussion of the developmental state. They're no less important to patrimonial and populist societies, insofar as they underpin corruption, resource hoarding, and rent seeking (see, e.g., Padgett and Ansell 1993; McClean 2011). And they've been widely portrayed as the missing ingredient in the Washington Consensus which allegedly fell victim to a lack of social capital, according to some, or an excess of the "wrong" kind of social capital, according to others (Fukuyama 2002; Schuurman 2003; Li 2005: esp. 389).

While concepts like embeddedness and social capital have at times – and understandably – been condemned as underspecified, they're not intrinsically underspecified. On the contrary, a number of younger sociologists have teased out their observable implications and subjected them to falsifiable tests with the assistance of formal network analysis. For example, Steve Samford found that government efforts to disseminate new techniques to artisanal ceramics producers in Mexico are mediated by informal networks (Samford 2017). Chris Yenkey found that investors in the Nairobi stock exchange look to their co-ethnic peers for support when they distrust formal institutions (Yenkey 2015: 581). Laura Doering found that both "escalation of commitment," among loan officers, and compliance with credit terms, among borrowers, were heightened by interpersonal ties at a Latin American microfinance organization, at least up to a point (Doering 2018). And a number of analysts have studied the relationship between "elite closure" and the reproduction of inequality in Latin America and beyond (see, e.g., Torche 2005; Chua, Morck, and Yeung 2021).

More work in this vein would not only build upon sociology's comparative advantages but would help bridge the gap between the micro and the macro in the study of development more generally. Consider, for example, the long overdue outpouring of work on social networks and irrigation performance in the Global South. It's in a sense designed to address the deficit described in chapter 1, when donor agencies designed irrigation systems without regard for their users (Cernea 1993b), and it has produced a number of promising and policy-relevant results (Frija et al. 2017; Navarro-Navarro, Moreno-Vazquez, and Scott 2017; Miao et al. 2018; Basati et al. 2020). But it simultaneously speaks to much broader sociological questions of trust, governance, and development (Pokharel 2014).

Social and political demography

One obvious but underutilized source of comparative advantage is demography. Population dynamics are central to development, after all, and demography tends to loom large in sociology. But development sociologists and demographers have for the most part failed to exploit their proximity. The memberships of the development and population sections of the American Sociological Association are almost completely disjoint, for example, and the family section – which plays host to lots of demographers – fares even worse.

But why? Some might think that the arrival of the fertility transition, and the more or less global decline in birth rates, renders demography irrelevant to development, at least prospectively. But nothing could be further from the truth. Population and family dynamics are absolutely indispensable drivers of development outcomes (Ben Porath 1980). They play a role in everything from aging and the life course to health and mortality, education and human capital formation, and politics. The East Asian development model has been portrayed as a partial product of population density (Schrank 2017), for instance, and global populism has been attributed to the growth of pressure on social services, on the one hand, and conflict over immigration, on the other, that tend to accompany declining fertility and population aging in middle- and upper-income societies (Wachs 2021; see also Goldstone and Turchin 2020).

The time for reconciliation would therefore seem overdue. Demography has both substantive expertise and a vast toolkit that's relevant to development, and demographers are already making meaningful contributions to the field (Thornton 2001), whether consciously or unconsciously. By making these connections explicit and bidirectional, students of demography and development could generate more powerful payoffs for all parties concerned.

Organizational and community ethnography

A fourth body of literature deploys long-term ethnography to address puzzles that are difficult or impossible to resolve from the outside. Examples would include Stephen Bunker and Lawrence Cohen's assessment of the roles of cooperation and competition – themselves rooted in different residence patterns – in fueling or tempering official corruption among bureaucrats in the Brazilian Amazon (Bunker and Cohen 1983); Marco Garrido's effort to trace democratic backsliding in the Philippines not to "weak institutions" but to "contradictory" ones (Garrido 2021); and Javier Auyero and Debora Swistun's account of the "social production of toxic uncertainty" in an Argentine shantytown, which pays particularly careful attention to the "relational anchoring of risk perceptions" (Auyero and Swistun 2008).

Contributions like these are theoretically important, policy relevant, and empirically convincing, not least of all because they begin with clear puzzles and lay out their theoretical stakes and observable implications in a clear manner. They not only speak to issues in the core of sociology, moreover, but utilize concepts and methods that are likely to get at hard-to-study subject matter and are largely unfamiliar to other disciplines. Consequently, they're well within sociology's comparative advantage. They're also among the most difficult contributions to pull off, however, insofar as they require access, patience, and time.

I don't want to imply that these are the only paths forward for the economic sociology of development. There's plenty of good work being done – or to be done – with interviews, comparative history, or traditional statistical approaches, among others. Nor am I asking development sociologists to pursue the "science of leftovers" approach to their discipline (Granovetter 1990: 89). On the contrary, I think these topics and methods are valuable in their own right and therefore happen to constitute a propitious basis for a reconstituted development sociology. In fact, I think the "science of leftovers" claim has it backward: issues and methods involving boundaries, communities, and networks are not the province of sociology because they're left over by other disciplines, in my opinion. They're left over by other disciplines because they're the province of sociology, and particularly challenging, and by exploiting their comparative advantage in these fields and methods – among others – economic sociologists of development are likely to prove particularly influential.

It would be hard to argue, however, that the aforementioned literatures have *already* reconstituted the sociology of development. They've hardly replaced modernization theory and neo-Marxism, or even the middle-range alternatives that emerged in the late twentieth century, and development sociology therefore feels a bit ad hoc right now: awash in pathbreaking work but lacking a cumulative foundation.

Moving toward the future

What would a cumulative foundation look like? In an effort to answer the question I'd conclude by asking what features simultaneously unite the pathbreaking work alluded to in this chapter and distinguish it from work being carried out in other disciplines. By doing so, I believe, we'll deduce the principles underlying sociology's comparative advantage and guiding the discipline's contributions to the study of development in the years to come.

The first such principle, I'd argue, is a commitment to the Mertonian middle-range. Students of development processes return to middle-range approaches "again and again," according to Alejandro Portes and Douglas Kincaid, "long after the intellectual fashions of one or another grand synthesis have faded from view" (Portes and Kincaid 1989: 499). And they do so for good reason: it's in the middle range that theories are bold enough to yield cumulative insight and demanding enough to risk falsification and rejection.

The second principle is a commitment to a relational notion of inequality. Whether or not one shares the Marxist concerns about exploitation distilled into Table 2.2, it's no longer possible to view development as a purely gradational process. We live in a world of finite resources. The threats of climate change and other environmental catastrophes are upon us. And notwithstanding the possibility of ecological modernization, we have to operate from the conservative assumption that growth in one place and time exacts an ecological cost somewhere else. Given that very real likelihood and – in the short run – perhaps reality, we have to build a relational approach to development into our theories and worldviews.

The third principle is a commitment to social construction *within reason*. God did not come down from Heaven and announce that

GDP per capita was development and vice versa; nor did he, she, or they come down with two tablets inscribed with GDP per capita, the HDI, the government's share of R&D expenditures, the unemployment rate, and so on and so forth. These concepts and indicators are social constructs, as are the culturally mediated preferences – for employment, wealth, security, and the like – that drive them. But they're not *random* constructs; they're related to more or less objective human desires and indicators. Those relationships deserve and require testing, and when the relationship drifts too far, scholars need to take notice, just as their subjects do. Debates over these relationships are therefore of theoretical and substantive, as well as methodological, import. But to take one simple example, I'd argue that the human desire for a longer rather than shorter life expectancy is not a pure social construct. It would be very hard, perhaps even impossible, to construct a society in which people want to die young rather than old, or watch their children do so.

The fourth principle is sensitivity to mismatches between people's values and existing social valuations. It's when people adopt contrarian perspectives, in Zuckerman's terminology, that they bet against the system as individuals, rebel against the system as collectivities, and change the system in a variety of related ways. Existing accounts of social order, ranging from neoclassical accounts of equilibrium to sociological portraits of collective rationality, are remarkably insightful and profound. But they have little to say when the equilibrium breaks down, or rationality becomes irrational, and moments like these are the very essence of development.

After all, the process of development, above and beyond everything else, is constituted by change, not by equilibrium – which is precisely why postwar development theory was interdisciplinary. The development economists who reigned supreme in the mid-twentieth century didn't turn to sociologists, among others, for support because they wanted to; they did so because they recognized that a science founded on a notion of equilibrium could only take them so far if their goal was to understand dynamics, and this is no less true today. But this means that a development sociology worthy of the name need not be just an account of change but a *systematic* account of change – a consistent, cumulative story of when, how, and why people give up on existing institutions, stable and tolerable though they may have been, and make bets on new ones. I've tried to outline such a story in chapter 5, and while it may not be ideal it seems a useful starting point for an effort to transcend notions of equilibria and stasis and embrace a notion of development that's more process than place.

Notes

Preface

1 The term is defined by neither the bylaws of the American Sociological Association's official section on the sociology of development nor the website of the journal *Sociology of Development*, published by the University of California Press (University of California Press 2021). The ASA section claims to promote "the study of societal development within the discipline of sociology" (ASA 2021), without defining "societal development," and the journal addresses "issues of development, broadly considered," including "economic development and well-being, gender, health, inequality, poverty, environment and sustainability, political economy, conflict, social movements, and more." It's hard to know what's not eligible for inclusion.

Chapter I Introduction

1 While the Africans and their descendants who were enslaved in the New World at times had access to garden plots, and were able to "to accumulate, own, and trade property among themselves and with white people" (Penningroth 1997: 409), they did so informally and/or with the "tacit consent" of their owners, who often treated so-called slave gardens as a cost-saving substitute for their own provisions (Morris 1994: 219, 1998: 998). The law itself didn't recognize the ownership claims of enslaved peoples.
2 This is, of course, the "problem of order" that looms large in both Hobbes and contemporary sociology (Granovetter 1985).
3 See Schrank and Whitford (2011) for a broader elaboration of the distinction between mistakes and malfeasance in a different context.
4 Critics frequently bemoan both the Eurocentrism and the theoretical and methodological state of postwar sociology and, in so doing, imply that a more inclusive discipline would have been more theoretically and methodologically

catholic. It seems no less likely, however, that a more encompassing discipline would simply have imposed "metropolitan" theories and methods disdained by the critics (e.g., abstract empiricism, Parsonian functionalism) on the periphery.

5 Neo-Marxist analyses of international inequality thus bore a striking resemblance to the Marxist analyses of subnational inequality that were gaining ground in the United States and Western Europe at the time. While popular commentators had long invoked the "quantitative, spatial" imagery of lower, middle, and upper classes (Wright 1979: 5), thereby treating class as a synonym for income, Marxists defined classes in terms of their relationships to each other, and thus treated the income differences they produced not as synonyms but as symptoms of exploitative social structures. "Classes are not labeled along a continuum from lower to upper," explained Marxist sociologist Erik Olin Wright; "instead they have names such as capitalist class, working class; lord, serf; ruling class, subordinate class" (Wright 1979: 6) – the key point being that one class's toil is another's treasure. Giovanni Arrighi (1991) offers an explicitly *relational* approach to the international division of labor, and economist Pranab Bardhan sees no contradiction between the neoclassical idea that developing countries might gain from trade in the short run and the Marxist idea that they might nonetheless be "better off in the counterfactual world of a more egalitarian international distribution of assets" (Bardhan 1985: 550). I return to these themes in more detail in chapter 2.

6 Even the catastrophic COVID-19 pandemic "is likely go down in history as a short-term interruption to long improvements in life expectancy, and it is most unlikely that the improving trend in global life expectancy will not resume within a few years" (Shaw-Taylor 2020: E15). Of course, the fact that literacy and life expectancy have gone up monotonically for centuries need not imply that they'll continue to do so; a "cataclysmic collapse" (Cohn 2021: 200) is possible, especially in light of global challenges like climate change and nuclear proliferation.

7 This is consistent with DiMaggio and Powell's sense that sociologists "find institutions everywhere, from handshakes to marriages to strategic-planning departments" and "view behaviors as potentially institutionalizable over a wide territorial range, from understandings within a single family to myths of rationality and progress in the world system" (1991: 9).

8 Of course, the mere employment of "experts" with "cultural skills" need not entail – and could even substitute for – the inclusion of members of indigenous or marginalized communities in decision-making; that is, it too could provide window-dressing. Some would say the problem is social engineering itself, not the identities of the social engineers (Scott 1998).

9 This isn't particularly controversial: The United States Bureau of Labor Statistics publishes six different measures of "labor underutilization" and critics doubt that any of them fully captures the real employment situation (Callahan 2013).

Chapter 2 What Do We Mean by "Development?"

1 GDP also includes "depreciation, retained earnings of corporations, and the part of government revenue (taxes) that is not distributed back to households as cash transfers" (Anand and Segal 2008: 67), and thus exaggerates household income. Deaton draws upon hundreds of surveys from more than 100 countries over 21 years and finds that household income makes up less than 60 percent of GDP, on average, with a lot of temporal and spatial variation (Deaton 2005: 4).

2 Note that, in principle, this index isn't that different from the "the number of hours it takes an unskilled male to earn enough to buy 100 kilograms of the staple food grain" (Wade 1990: 39) alluded to in chapter 1.

3 Anand and Segal note that the differences between market and PPP exchange rates are interesting in their own right. While market and PPP rates should have converged in the era of globalization, as countries traded a growing share of their GDPs, they actually grew further apart in the late twentieth century. "The apparent divergence over time between inequality measured at market and at PPP exchange rates thus requires some explanation" (Anand and Segal 2008: 65).

4 Of course, different countries boost their GDPs in different ways as well (e.g., guns versus butter), and the differences in GDP are arguably even more opaque than the differences in HDI in light of the former figure's alleged unidimensionality.

5 This alleged trade-off between the "negative freedom" from coercion and the "positive freedom" to achieve desired goals (e.g., a long and healthy life, literacy, employment) was precisely what exercised Isaiah Berlin, the architect of the distinction between the "two concepts of liberty" (Berlin 1969) in the Cold War era.

6 See Conley and Laureau (2008) for a more thorough introduction to different perspectives on social class and Tomaskovic-Devey and Avent-Holt (2019) for a recent relational approach.

7 Roemer's thinking has evolved over the years; however, he still views exploitation as a "manifestation of differential ownership of capital whose genesis is immoral" (Roemer 2020: 138).

8 Clark (2016) arguably constitutes an exception.

Chapter 3 Is International Inequality Gradational or Relational?

1 See Peltonen (2008) on the distinction between the "Weber thesis," as simplified and popularized by contemporary social scientists, and the more complicated and controversial perspective of Weber himself, and Gorski (1993) on the relationship between ascetic Protestantism and state formation.

2 Geertz himself discussed the "narrow margin between overpopulation and

underpopulation," as well as the fluid definitions of an acceptable standard of living, in rural Java in the 1950s (Geertz 1956a: 141).

3 Keyfitz (1965: 507) treats Geertz's work on Indonesia as evidence that "in overpopulated countries the code of ethical behavior so shapes itself that it becomes good form for each person to offer as much employment as he can," as argued by Lewis (Lewis 1954: 142); however, he pays less attention to the marginal productivity of rural labor itself.

4 The semi-periphery is neither the sole deviation from Marxist and neo-Marxist orthodoxy nor anchored to particular products and places. On the contrary, Wallerstein holds that the products being produced and trade by different places at different points in time are driven by technology. "If in the sixteenth century," he explains, "peripheral Poland traded its wheat for core Holland's textiles, in the mid-twentieth-century world, peripheral countries are often textile producers whereas core countries export wheat as well as electronic equipment" (Wallerstein 1974a: 5). See Skocpol (1977) for a more thorough-going review of the world-system perspective and Babones (2015) for an updated assessment.

5 Geertz would later disdain neo-Marxism and world-systems theory, in particular, for their tendency "to get the relation between social theory and social research rather backward, so that the function of research is the aggrandisation of theory rather than the function of theory the enablement of research" (Geertz 1984: 517); and Arrighi would eventually embrace Philip Huang's faith in the possibility of "involutionary growth, something not noted in Clifford Geertz's original notion of 'agricultural involution'" (Huang 1990: 13; see Arrighi 2007: 39).

6 Perhaps ironically, given his invocation by the neo-Marxists, Tawney was well aware of the gap in living standards between the Western and non-Western worlds but was "strangely incurious" as to its origins and deeply Eurocentric in outlook, invoking Tennyson's dictum that he would rather have "fifty years of Europe than a cycle of Cathay" (Chambers 1971: 357).

Chapter 4 Explaining National Mobility in the Cold War Era

1 While per capita income, life expectancy, and secondary enrollment are themselves highly correlated, the rank correlations between industrialization – measured as a share of either GDP or employment at the country level – and GDP per capita, secondary school enrollment, life expectancy, and urbanization ranged from just over 0.5 to just below 0 in 2010. The relationship between liberal democracy and these variables is even less straightforward (Przeworski 2004).

2 While Scott has been accused of "making a point by exaggerating it" (Hammond 2011), particularly in regard to the alleged "post-literacy" of hill peoples in Southeast Asia, his reservations about rural education are largely

uncontroversial: traditional people are frequently unreceptive or hostile toward formal education, and their hostility poses a barrier to state-building.

3 Rigorous data on literacy rates are hard to come by and range from less than one-half to less than one-quarter of the population (Kline 1958: 17; Mironov 1991: 251; Darden and Grzylama-Busse 2006: 113).

4 In 1920, Lenin famously declared that communism meant "Soviet power + electrification of the whole country," but he added the less familiar caveat that "we cannot carry out electrification with the illiterates we have" (Lenin 1920).

5 Obvious exceptions include the US government's bank bailouts following the 2007 financial crisis (Lucas 2019). If the likelihood and extent of bailout are unknowable *ex ante*, however, market competition should still impose some degree of discipline.

6 By the same token, according to Iván Szelényi, people *had to work*, calling the broader existence of a labor market into question. "Everyone is obliged by law to sell his/her labour to bureaucratic labour-organisations; if someone is without a job he can, and frequently is, prosecuted" (Szelényi 1978: 75). Szelényi argued that the "non-market trade of labour" was the key distinguishing feature of "state socialist redistributive economies" (Szelényi 1978: 75).

7 The empirical details in this paragraph are relatively uncontroversial. However, I am to some degree glossing over an ongoing debate over their proper interpretation (cf. Hamilton and Biggart 1988; Numazaki 1991; Hsieh 2014) as well as minor differences with the Korean case, where compensated landlords loomed larger in the industrial elite and former tenants less so (see, e.g., Hsieh 2011: 370–1).

8 Of course, foreign investment provided another – and, from a nationalist perspective, inferior – source of capital, and in the larger countries, in particular, the prospect of captive markets drew multinational corporations. But they were no less hostile to performance standards than local landlords and had at least as much bargaining power.

9 While Latin American earnings or economic mobility is harder to assess, due to a lack of detailed, longitudinal data, the best available studies also "highlight an asymmetric pattern of intergenerational persistence that is characterized by strong reproduction at the top of the socioeconomic hierarchy combined with more fluidity across middle and lower segment" (Torche 2014: 632); however, earnings persistence is much higher in Latin America than in developed market economies like the United States (Torche 2014: 631–2).

Chapter 5 The Diffusion and Demise of Free-Market Reform in the Post-Cold War Era

1 I leave organizational ecology out of this discussion since the goal henceforth is to explain the adoption of reform and not the selection of better and worse reforms; organization ecology is primarily focused on selection.

2 This scheme has been heavily influenced by Drezner (2001), though he is in no way responsible for any errors or disagreements.

3 See Gerschenkron (1978: 76) on the conceptualization and measurement of relative backwardness.

4 Lest there be any doubt, moreover, the new institutionalism treads very close to the constructivist extreme. While the actors in DiMaggio and Powell's account bore at least the scars of a realist ontology (Meyer 2010: 3), the more constructivist aspects of their account have been by far the most influential (Mizruchi and Fein 1999). And John Meyer, who arguably constitutes the founding father of the new institutionalism, has explicitly crossed the "red line" (Meyer 2010: 4) between realism and constructivism.

5 One can find many examples of these dynamics in the realm of household decision making. In a classic work of economic sociology, for instance, Tamara Hareven reminds us that families in industrializing societies make "calculated trade-offs in order to achieve solvency: to buy a house, to facilitate children's education or their occupational advancement, to save for the future, and to provide for times of illness, old age, and death" (Hareven 1990: 216). Where conventional calculators are implicitly accepting existing valuations, and reproducing existing institutions, their contrarian counterparts are skeptical, and thus have the potential to provoke or inspire social change by, for example, spending rather than saving, renting rather than owning, or betting on education rather than employment.

Chapter 6 What If Sociologists Were in Charge?

1 This chapter is clearly inspired by Zuckerman (2010), though he bears no responsibility for its content.

References

Abbott, Andrew. 1988. "Transcending General Linear Reality." *Sociological Theory* 6(2): 169–86.

Abbott, Andrew. 2005. "The Idea of Outcome in US Sociology," in George Steinmetz (ed.), *The Politics of Method in the Human Sciences: Positivism and Its Epistemological Others*. Durham: Duke University Press, pp. 393–426.

Abel, James and Bond, Norman. 1929. *Illiteracy in the Several Countries of the World*. Department of the Interior: Bureau of Education. Washington: Government Printing Office.

Acemoglu, Daron Johnson, Simon, and Robinson, James. 2005. "The Rise of Europe: Atlantic Trade, Institutional Change, and Economic Growth." *American Economic Review* 95(3): 546–79.

ActionAid. 2005. *Rights First: Working Together to End Poverty and Patriarchy*. New Delhi: ActionAid India.

Adam, David. 2022. "The Effort to Count the Pandemic's Global Death Toll." *Nature* 601 (January 20): 312–16.

Afridi, Farzana. 2010. "Women's Empowerment and the Goal of Parity between the Sexes in Schooling in India." *Population Studies* 64(2): 131–45.

Alden, Edward. 2018. "Trump, China, and Steel Tariffs: The Day the WTO Died." New York: Council on Foreign Relations, March 9.

Alvarez, Michael, Cheibub, José Antonio, Limongi, Fernando, and Przeworski, Adam. 1996. "Classifying Political Regimes." *Studies in Comparative International Development* 31: 3–36.

Amin, Samir. 2017. "A Dependency Pioneer." Interview with Ingrid Harvold Kvangraven, in Ushehwedu Kufakurinani (ed.), *Dialogues on Development, Volume 1: Dependency*. New York: Institute for New Economic Thinking pp. 12–17.

Amsden, Alice. 1989. *Asia's Next Giant: South Korea and Late Industrialization*. Oxford: Oxford University Press.

References

Amsden, Alice. 2001. *The Rise of "The Rest": Challenges to the West from Late-Industrializing Economies*. Oxford: Oxford University Press.

Amsden, Alice. 2007. *Escape from Empire: The Developing World's Journey through Heaven and Hell*. Cambridge: MIT Press.

Anand, Sudhir. 2018. "Recasting Human Development Measures." International Inequalities Institute Working Paper 23. London: LSE.

Anand, Sudhir and Segal, Paul. 2008. "What Do We Know about Global Income Inequality?" *Journal of Economic Literature* 46(1): 57–94.

Andersen, David Delfs Erbo. 2018. "Does Meritocracy Lead to Bureaucratic Quality? Revisiting the Experience of Prussia and Imperial and Weimar Germany." *Social Science History* 42(2): 245–68.

Anderson, Benedict. 1983. *Imagined Communities: Reflections on the Origin and Spread of Nationalism*. London: Verso.

Ansoms, An. 2009. "Re-Engineering Rural Society: The Visions and Ambitions of the Rwandan Elite." *African Affairs* 108(431): 289–309.

Ansoms, An and Rostagno, Donatella. 2012. "Rwanda's Vision 2020 Halfway through: What the Eye Does Not See." *Review of African Political Economy* 39(133): 427–50.

Ansoms, An, Marijnen, Esther, Cioffo, Giuseppe, and Murison, Jude. 2017. "Statistics versus Livelihoods: Questioning Rwanda's Pathway out of Poverty." *Review of African Political Economy* 44(151): 47–65.

Arbouch, Mahmoud and Dadush, Uri 2019. "Measuring the Middle Class in the World and Morocco." Rabat: Policy Center for the New South.

Armstrong, David. 2003. "US Pays Back Nations that Supported War." *San Francisco Chronicle*, May 11.

Arnove, Robert and Graff, Harvey. 1987. "National Literacy Campaigns: Historical and Comparative Lessons." *Phi Delta Kappan* 69(3): 202–6.

Arrighi, Giovanni. 1966. "The Political Economy of Rhodesia." *New Left Review* I 39 (September/October): 35–65.

Arrighi, Giovanni. 1970. "Labour Supplies in Historical Perspective: A Study of the Proletarianization of the African Peasantry in Rhodesia." *Journal of Development Studies* 6(3): 197–234.

Arrighi, Giovanni. 1990. "The Developmentalist Illusion: A Reconceptualization of the Semiperiphery," in William Martin (ed.), *Semiperipheral States in the World Economy*. New York: Greenwood Press, pp. 11–42.

Arrighi, Giovanni. 1991. "World Income Inequalities and the Future of Socialism." *New Left Review* 189 (September/October): 39–65.

Arrighi, Giovanni. 1994. *The Long Twentieth Century: Money, Power and the Origin of Our Times*. London: Verso.

Arrighi, Giovanni. 2001. "Braudel, Capitalism, and the New Economic Sociology." *Review* 24(1): 107–23.

Arrighi, Giovanni. 2002. "The African Crisis: World-Systemic and Regional Aspects." *New Left Review* 15 (May/June): 5–36.

Arrighi, Giovanni. 2007. *Adam Smith in Beijing: Lineages of the Twenty-First Century*. London: Verso.

Arrighi, Giovanni. 2009. "The Winding Paths of Capital." Interview with David Harvey. *New Left Review* 56 (March/April): 61–94.

Arrighi, Giovanni and Drangel, Jessica. 1986. "The Stratification of the World Economy: An Exploration of the Semi-Peripheral Zone." *Review* 10(1): 9–74.

Arrighi, Giovanni and Saul, John. 1968. "Socialism and Economic Development in Tropical Africa." *Journal of Modern African Studies* 6(2): 141–69.

Arrighi, Giovanni and Saul, John. 1969. "Nationalism and Revolution in Sub-Saharan Africa," in Ralph Miliband and John Saville (eds), *The Socialist Register*. New York: Monthly Review Press, pp. 137–88.

Arrighi, Giovanni and Zhang, Lu. 2011. "Beyond the Washington Consensus: A New Bandung?" in Jon Shefner and Patricia Fernández Kelly (eds), *Globalization and Beyond: New Examinations of Global Power and Its Alternatives*. University Park: Pennsylvania State University Press, pp. 25–57.

Arrighi, Giovanni, Aschoff, Nicole, and Scully, Ben. 2010. "Accumulation by Dispossession and Its Limits: The Southern Africa Paradigm Revisited." *Studies in Comparative International Development* 45: 410–38.

Arrighi, Giovanni, Hopkins, Terence K., and Wallerstein, Immanuel. 1983. "Rethinking the Concepts of Class and Status-Group in a World-System Perspective." *Review* 6(3): 283–304.

ASA (American Sociological Association). 2003. *The Importance of Collecting Data and Doing Social Scientific Research on Race*. Washington: American Sociological Association.

ASA (American Sociological Association). 2021. "Section on the Sociology of Development: By-Laws." June. Washington: American Sociological Association.

Asad, Asad and Garip, Filiz. 2019. "Mexico–US Migration in Time: From Economic to Social Mechanisms." *Annals of the American Academy of Political and Social Science*. 684 (July): 60–84.

Aseniero, George. 1994. "South Korean and Taiwanese Development: The Transnational Context." *Review* 17(3): 275–336.

Auyero, Javier and Kilanski, Kristine. 2015. "From 'Making Toast' to 'Splitting Apples': Dissecting 'Care' in the Midst of Chronic Violence." *Theory & Society* 44(5): 393–414.

Auyero, Javier and Swistun, Debora. 2008. "The Social Production of Toxic Uncertainty." *American Sociological Review* 73(3): 357–79.

Avineri, Shlomo. 1969. "Marx and Modernization." *Review of Politics* 31(2): 172–88.

Babb, Sarah. 2001. *Managing Mexico: Economists from Nationalism to Neoliberalism*. Princeton: Princeton University Press.

Babb, Sarah. 2007. "Embeddedness, Inflation, and International Regimes: The

IMF in the Early Postwar Period." *American Journal of Sociology* 113(1): 128–64.

Babb, Sarah. 2013. "The Washington Consensus as Transnational Policy Paradigm: Its Origins, Trajectory and Likely Successor." *Review of International Political Economy* 20(2): 268–97.

Babones, Salvatore. 2015. "What *is* World-systems Analysis? Distinguishing Theory from Perspective." *Thesis Eleven* 127(1): 3–20.

Bagchi, Amiya Kumar. 1991. "From a Fractured Compromise to a Democratic Consensus: Planning and Political Economy in Post-Colonial India." *Economic and Political Weekly* 26(11/12): 611–28.

Baker, David, Goesling, Brian, and Letendre, Gerald K. 2002. "Socioeconomic Status, School Quality, and National Economic Development: A Cross-National Analysis of the 'Heyneman-Loxley Effect' on Mathematics and Science Achievement." *Comparative Education Review* 46(3): 291–312.

Balassa, Bela. 1971. "Industrial Policies in Taiwan and Korea." *Weltwirtschaftliches Archiv* 106: 55–77.

Balassa, Bela. 1988a. "The Lessons of East Asian Development: An Overview," *Economic Development and Cultural Change* 36(3): S273–90.

Balassa, Bela. 1988b. "The Adding Up Problem." Background Paper for the 1988 World Development Report. Washington: World Bank.

Balbo, Marcello. 2014. "Beyond the City of Developing Countries: The New Urban Order of the 'Emerging City.'" *Planning Theory* 13(3): 269–87.

Baracco, Luciano. 2004. "The Nicaraguan Literacy Crusade Revisited: The Teaching of Literacy as a Nation-Building Project." *Bulletin of Latin American Research* 23(3): 339–54.

Bardhan, Pranab. 1985. "Marxist Ideas in Development Economics: A Brief Evaluation." *Economic and Political Weekly* 20(13): 550–5.

Barlow, Matt and Peña, Alejandro Milcíades. 2022. "The Politics of Fiscal Legitimacy in Developmental States: Emergency Taxes in Argentina under Kirchnerism." *New Political Economy* 27(3): 403–25.

Barrett, Richard and Whyte, Martin. 1982. "Dependency Theory and Taiwan: Analysis of a Deviant Case." *American Journal of Sociology* 87(5): 1064–89.

Barrionuevo, Alexei. 2011. "Kirchner Achieves an Easy Victory in Argentina Presidential Election." *New York Times*, October 23.

Basati, Hamid, Poursaeed, Alireza, Allahyari, Mohammad S., Eshraghi Samani, Roya, and Amin, Hamed. 2020. "Social Network Analysis of Local Water User Associations' Actors: Evidence from Iran." *Meteorology Hydrology and Water Management* 8(1): 90–7.

Bearak, Max. 2019. "25 Years after Genocide, Rwanda Commemorates Those Killed – but Omits One Group that Was Almost Wiped Out." *Washington Post*, April 5.

Bearman, Peter. 2010. "Just-so Stories: Vaccines, Autism, and the Single-bullet Disorder." *Social Psychology Quarterly* 73(2): 112–15.

References

Becker, Elizabeth. 2003. "US and Singapore Sign Free Trade Pact." *New York Times*, May 6.

Beckfield, Jason. 2008. "The Dual World Polity: Fragmentation and Integration in the Network of Intergovernmental Organizations." *Social Problems* 55(3): 419–42.

Beckfield, Jason. 2020. "Rising Inequality Is Not Balanced by Intergenerational Mobility." *Proceedings of the National Academy of Sciences* 117(1): 23–5.

Beetz, Simone. 2017. *External Democracy Promotion and Diversity among International Agencies: Evaluating Variances in the Impact of the UNDP and the EC in Rwanda*. Toronto: Budrich UniPress.

Benanav, Aaron. 2019. "Demography and Dispossession: Explaining the Growth of the Global Informal Workforce, 1950–2000." *Social Science History* 43: 679–703.

Bendix, Reinhard. 1967. "Tradition and Modernity Reconsidered." *Comparative Studies in Society and History* 9(3): 292–346.

Ben Porath, Yoram. 1980. "The F-Connection: Families, Friends, and Firms and the Organization of Exchange." *Population & Development Review* 6(1): 1–30.

Benson, Devyn Spence. 2016. *Antiracism in Cuba: The Unfinished Revolution*. Chapel Hill: University of North Carolina Press.

Berger, Peter, Berger, Brigitte, and Kellner, Hansfried. 1973. *The Homeless Mind: Modernization and Consciousness*. New York: Random House.

Berlin, Isaiah. 1969. "Two Concepts of Liberty," in Isaiah Berlin (ed.), *Four Essays on Liberty*. London: Oxford University Press, pp. 166–217.

Berry, Heather, Kaul, Aseem, and Lee, Narae. 2021. "Follow the Smoke: The Pollution Haven Effect on Global Sourcing." *Strategic Management Journal* 42(13): 2420–50.

Best, Joel. 2018. *American Nightmares: Social Problems in an Anxious World*. Berkeley: University of California Press.

Beswick, Danielle. 2010. "Managing Dissent in a Post-genocide Environment: The Challenge of Political Space in Rwanda." *Development & Change* 41(2): 225–51.

Bevins, Vincent. 2016. "To Understand 2016's Politics, Look at the Winners and Losers of Globalization: An Interview with Economist Branko Milanovic." *New Republic*, December 20.

Bhola, H. S. 1984. "A Policy Analysis of Adult Literacy Promotion in the Third World: An Accounting of Promises Made and Promises Fulfilled." *International Review of Education* 30(3): 249–64.

Biggart, Nicole Woolsey. 1991. "Explaining Asian Economic Organization: Toward a Weberian Institutional Perspective." *Theory & Society* 20(2): 199–232.

Biggart, Nicole Woolsey and Guillén, Mauro. 1999. "Developing Difference: Social Organization and the Rise of the Auto Industries of South Korea, Taiwan, Spain, and Argentina." *American Sociological Review* 64(5): 722–47.

References

Bilotti, Edvige. 2010. "Models of Economic Development from a World-Systems Perspective: Moving Beyond Universalism." *Review* 33(4): 271–94.

Binder, Melissa and Woodruff, Christopher. 2002. "Inequality and Intergenerational Mobility in Schooling: The Case of Mexico." *Economic Development and Cultural Change* 50(2): 249–67.

Bird, Mike. 2014. "China Just Overtook US as the World's Largest Economy, IMF Says." *Christian Science Monitor*, October 8.

Block, Fred. 2009. "Read Their Lips: Taxation and the Right-Wing Agenda," in Isaac William Martin, Ajay K. Mehrota, and Monica Prasad et al. (eds), *The New Fiscal Sociology: Taxation in Comparative and Historical Perspective*. Cambridge: Cambridge University Press, pp. 68–85.

Block, Fred. 2018. "Contesting Markets All the Way Down." *Australian Journal of Political Economy* 68: 27–40.

Block, Fred and Burns, Gene. 1986. "Productivity as a Social Problem: The Uses and Misuses of Social Indicators." *American Sociological Review* 51(6): 767–80.

Boianovsky, Mauro. 2010. "A View from the Tropics: Celso Furtado and the Theory of Economic Development in the 1950s." *History of Political Economy* 42(2): 221–66.

Boianovsky, Mauro. 2018. "Beyond Capital Fundamentalism: Harrod, Domar and the History of Development Economics." *Cambridge Journal of Economics* 42: 477–504.

Boisot, Max and Child, John. 1988. "The Iron Law of Fiefs: Bureaucratic Failure and the Problem of Governance in the Chinese Economic Reforms." *Administrative Science Quarterly* 33(4): 507–27.

Bornschier, Volker and Trezzini, Bruno. 2001. "World Market for Social Order, Embedded State Autonomy and Third World Development." *Competition & Change* 5: 201–44.

Boserup, Ester. 1965. *The Conditions of Agricultural Growth: The Economics of Agrarian Change under Population Pressure*. London: Allen & Unwin.

Bottomore, T. B. 1962. "Recent Theories of Development." *European Journal of Sociology* 3(2): 312–25.

Bottomore, T. B. 1971. *Sociology: A Guide to Problems and Literature*. New York: Pantheon.

Bourdieu, Pierre. 1986. "The Forms of Capital," in John Richardson (ed.), *Handbook of Theory and Research for the Sociology of Education*. Westport: Greenwood, pp. 241–58.

Boyce, James, Rosset, Peter, and Stanton, Elizabeth A. 2005. "Land Reform and Sustainable Development." UMass PERI Working Paper 98. University of Massachusetts Amherst.

Bradsher, Keith and Rappeport, Alan. 2018. "The Trade Issue That Most Divides US and China Isn't Tariffs." *New York Times*, March 26.

Breen, Richard and Rottman, David B. 1998. "Is the National State the Appropriate Unit for Class Analysis?" *Sociology* 32(1): 1–21.

Brenner, Robert. 1976. "Agrarian Class Structure and Economic Development in Pre-industrial Europe." *Past & Present* 70(1): 30–75.

Brenner, Robert. 1977. "The Origins of Capitalist Development: A Critique of Neo-Smithian Marxism." *New Left Review* 104: 28–92.

Brenner, Robert. 1986. "The Social Bases of Economic Development," in John Roemer (ed.), *Analytical Marxism*. Cambridge: Cambridge University Press, pp. 23–53.

Broad, Robin. 2007. "'Knowledge Management': A Case Study of the World Bank's Research Department." *Development in Practice* 17(4/5): 700–8.

Brubaker, Rogers. 2020. "Populism and Nationalism." *Nations & Nationalism* 26(1): 44–66.

Buckingham, Marcus. 2015. *Stand Out 2.0*. Boston: Harvard Business Review Press.

Bunker, Stephen. 1985. *Underdeveloping the Amazon: Extraction, Unequal Exchange, and the Failure of the Modern State.* Urbana: University of Illinois Press.

Bunker, Stephen and Cohen, Lawrence. 1983. "Collaboration and Competition in Two Colonization Projects: Toward a General Theory of Official Corruption." *Human Organization* 42(2): 106–14.

Burawoy, Michael. 1974. "Race, Class, and Colonialism." *Social and Economic Studies* 23(4): 521–50.

Burawoy, Michael and Krotov, Pavel. 1992. "The Soviet Transition from Socialism to Capitalism: Worker Control and Economic Bargaining in the Wood Industry." *American Sociological Review* 57(1): 16–38.

Burke, Hilary. 2012. "Analysis: Newfound Accuracy in Argentine Data Raises Eyebrows." Reuters, July 11.

Burrough, Brian and Helyar, John. 1990. *Barbarians at the Gate: The Fall of RJR Nabisco*. New York: Harper Business.

Buttel, Fred. 2003. "Environmental Sociology and the Explanation of Environmental Reform." *Organization & Environment* 16(3): 306–44.

Butty, James. 2015. "Rwanda Denies Existence of Unofficial Detention Centers." Voice of America News, September 25.

Cahill, Miles. 2005. "Is the Human Development Index Redundant?" *Eastern Economic Journal* 31(1): 1–5.

Caldwell, John. 1986. "Routes to Low Mortality in Poor Countries." *Population and Development Review* 12(2): 171–220.

Callahan, David. 2013. "The Most Bogus Unemployment Number: Discouraged Workers." Demos, September 6. Available at https://www.demos.org/blog/most-bogus-unemployment-number-discouraged-workers

Cammack, Paul. 1989. "Bringing the State Back In?" *British Journal of Political Science* 19(2): 261–90.

Campos, José Edgardo and Root, Hilton. 1996. *The Key to the Asian Miracle: Making Shared Growth Credible*. Washington: Brookings Institution.

References

Caporaso, James. 2007. "The Promises and Pitfalls of an Endogenous Theory of Institutional Change: A Comment." *West European Politics* 30(2): 392–404.

Cardoso, Eliana and Helwege, Ann. 1992. *Latin America's Economy: Diversity, Trends, and Conflicts.* Cambridge: MIT Press.

Cardoso, Fernando H. 1967. "The Industrial Elite," in Seymour Martin Lipset and Aldo Solari (eds), *Elites in Latin America.* New York: Oxford University Press, pp. 94–114.

Cardoso, Fernando Henrique and Faletto, Enzo. 1979. *Dependency and Development in Latin America.* Berkeley: University of California Press.

Carling, Alan. 1991. *Social Division.* London: Verso.

Carruthers, Ian. 1990. "Economic and Social Perspectives in New Irrigation Technology." *Agricultural Water Management* 17: 283–94.

Centeno, Miguel Angel. 1997. "Blood and Debt: War and Taxation in Nineteenth-Century Latin America." *American Journal of Sociology* 102(6): 1565–1605.

Centeno, Miguel Angel and Cohen, Joseph. 2012. "The Arc of Neoliberalism." *Annual Review of Sociology* 38: 317–40.

Cernea, Michael. 1991. "Knowledge from Social Science for Development Policies and Projects," in Michael Cernea (ed.), *Putting People First: Sociological Variables in Rural Development*, 2nd edn. Oxford: Oxford University Press/ World Bank, pp. 1–42.

Cernea, Michael. 1993a. "The Sociologist's Approach to Sustainable Development." *Finance & Development* (December): 11–13.

Cernea, Michael. 1993b. "Culture and Organization: The Social Sustainability of Induced Development." *Sustainable Development* 1(2): 18–29.

Cernea, Michael. 1993c. "Sociological Work within a Development Agency: Experiences in the World Bank." Washington: World Bank.

Chambers, J. D. 1971. "The Tawney Tradition." *Economic History Review* 24(3): 355–69.

Chang, Ha-Joon. 2002. *Kicking Away the Ladder: Development Strategy in Historical Perspective.* New York: Anthem Press.

Chang, Ha-Joon. 2011. "Industrial Policy: Can We Go beyond an Unproductive Confrontation?" in Justin Yifu Lin and Boris Pleskovic (eds), *Lessons from East Asia and the Global Financial Crisis.* Washington: World Bank, pp. 83–109.

Charrad, Mounira and Adams, Julia. 2011. "Introduction: Patrimonialism, Past and Present." *Annals of the American Academy of Political and Social Science* 636 (July): 6–15.

Chen, Ming-chi. 2002. "Industrial District and Social Capital in Taiwan's Economic Development: An Economic Sociological Study on Taiwan's Bicycle Industry." PhD dissertation, Yale University.

Chen, Yu, Wang, Yuandi, Hu, Die, and Zhou, Zhao. 2020. "Government R&D Subsidies, Information Asymmetry, and the Role of Foreign Investors: Evidence from a Quasi-natural Experiment on the Shanghai-Hong Kong Stock Connect." *Technological Forecasting & Social Change* 158: 1–11.

Cheng, Yinghong and Manning, Patrick. 2003. "Revolution in Education: China and Cuba in Global Context, 1957–76." *Journal of World History* 14(3): 359–91.

Chibber, Vivek. 2002. "Bureaucratic Rationality and the Developmental State." *American Journal of Sociology* 107(4): 951–89.

Chibber, Vivek. 2005. "Reviving the Developmental State: The Myth of the 'National Bourgeoisie,'" in Leo Panitch and Colin Leys (eds), *Socialist Register 2005: Empire Reloaded*. New York: Monthly Review Press, pp. 114–65.

Chirot, Daniel. 1980. "Review of *The Capitalist World-Economy* by Immanuel Wallerstein and *National Development and the World System: Educational, Economic, and Political Change, 1950–1970*, edited by John W. Meyer and Michael T. Hannan." *Social Forces* 59(2): 538–43.

Chirot, Daniel and Ragin, Charles. 1982. "World-System Theory." *Annual Review of Sociology* 8: 81–106.

Chua, Vincent, Morck, Randall, and Yeung, Yin Bernard. 2021. "The Singaporean Meritocracy: Theory, Practice, and Policy Implications." Unpublished manuscript. National University of Singapore.

Chwieroth, Jeffrey. 2007. "Neoliberal Economists and Capital Account Liberalization in Emerging Markets." *International Organization* 61(2): 443–63.

Clark, Charles. 1993. *Doloi negramotnost'! The Literacy Campaign in the RSFSR, 1923–1927*. PhD dissertation, University of Illinois.

Clark, Rob. 2016. "Examining Mobility in International Development." *Social Problems* 63(3): 329–50.

Cline, William. 1982. "Can the East Asian Model of Development Be Generalized?" *World Development* 10(2): 81–90.

Cohn, Samuel. 2021. *All Societies Die: How to Keep Hope Alive*. Ithaca: Cornell University Press.

Collin, Finn. 2011. *Science Studies as Naturalized Philosophy*. New York: Springer.

Collins, Jane. 1987. "Labor Scarcity and Ecological Change," in Peter D. Little, Michael Horowitz, and A. Endre Nyerges (eds), *Lands at Risk in the Third World: Local-Level Perspectives*. Boulder: Westview, pp. 19–37.

Congressional Research Service. 2018. "Rwanda: In Brief." February 7. Washington: CRS.

Conley, Dalton and Lareau, Annette. 2008. *Social Class: How Does It Work?* New York: Russell Sage Foundation.

Connell, R. W. 1997. "Why Is Classical Theory Classical?" *American Journal of Sociology* 102(6): 1511–57.

Connell, Raewyn. 2010. "Periphery and Metropole in the History of Sociology." *Sociologisk Forskning* 47(1): 72–86.

Connell, Raewyn and Dados, Nour. 2014. "Where in the World Does Neoliberalism Come From? The Market Agenda in Southern Perspective." *Theory & Society* 43(2): 117–38.

References

Convert, Bernard and Heilbron, Johan. 2007. "Where Did the New Economic Sociology Come From?" *Theory & Society* 36(1): 31–54.

Cotts-Watkins, Susan. 1990. "From Local to National Communities: The Transformation of Demographic Regimes in Western Europe, 1870–1960." *Population and Development Review* 16(1): 241–72.

Coulter, Charles. 1935. "Problems Arising from Industrialization of Native Life in Central Africa." *American Journal of Sociology* 40(5): 582–92.

Crosby, Alfred. 1986. *Ecological Imperialism: The Biological Expansion of Europe, 900–1900*. New York: Cambridge University Press.

Dadush, Uri. 2014. "Converging Economic Destinies." *Current History* (January 26–29).

Dadush, Uri and Ali, Shimelse. 2012. "In Search of the Global Middle Class: A New Index." Washington: Carnegie Endowment for International Peace.

Dale, Britt. 2002. "An Institutionalist Approach to Local Restructuring: The Case of Four Norwegian Mining Towns." *European Urban and Regional Studies* 9(1): 5–20.

Daniel, Claudia and Lanata Briones, Cecilia. 2019. "Battles over Numbers: The Case of the Argentine Consumer Price Index (2007–2015)." *Economy & Society* 48(1): 127–51.

Darden, Keith and Grzymala-Busse, Anna. 2006. "The Great Divide: Literacy, Nationalism, and the Communist Collapse." *World Politics* 59(1): 83–115.

Dasgupta, Susmita, Laplante, Benoit, Wang, Hua, and Wheeler, David. 2002. "Confronting the Environmental Kuznets Curve." *Journal of Economic Perspectives* 161(1): 147–68.

Davenport, Coral and Vlasic, Bill. 2014. "US Fines Automakers Hyundai and Kia for Misstating Mileage." *New York Times*, November 3.

Davidoff, Nicholas. 2002. *The Fly Swatter: How My Grandfather Made His Way in the World*. New York: Pantheon.

Davies, Richard. 2020. "The Huge Hidden Economy Is Missing from and Distorting Our Data." *Financial Times*, March 11.

Davis, Diane. 2004. *Discipline and Development: Middle Classes and Prosperity in East Asia and Latin America*. Cambridge: Cambridge University Press.

Davis, Mike. 2004. "Planet of Slums: Urban Involution and the Informal Proletariat." *New Left Review* 26 (March/April): 5–34.

Dawson, Neil. 2018. "Leaving No-one Behind? Social Inequalities and Contrasting Development Impacts in Rural Rwanda." *Development Studies Research* 5(1): 1–14.

Deaton, Angus. 2005. "Measuring Poverty in a Growing World (or Measuring Growth in a Poor World)." *Review of Economics and Statistics* 87(1): 1–19.

de Brun, Susanne and Elling, Ray H. 1987. "Cuba and the Philippines: Contrasting Cases in World-System Analysis." *International Journal of Health Services* 17(4): 681–701.

de la Torre, Carlos. 1992. "The Ambiguous Meanings of Latin American Populisms." *Social Research* 59(2): 385–414.

DeLong, J. Bradford. 1989. "The 'Protestant Ethic' Revisited: A Twentieth-Century Look." *Fletcher Forum* 13(2): 229–42.

de Miranda, Luis. 2020. *Ensemblance: The Transnational Genealogy of Esprit de Corps*. Edinburgh: Edinburgh University Press.

de Santos, Martín. 2009. "Fact-Totems and the Statistical Imagination: The Public Life of a Statistic in Argentina 2001." *Sociological Theory* 27(4): 466–89.

de Sardan, Jean-Pierre Olivier. 2005. *Anthropology & Development: Understanding Contemporary Social Change*. London: Zed Books.

Diamand, Marcelo. 1977. "Towards a Change in the Economic Paradigm through the Experience of Developing Countries." Boston University Center for Latin American Development Studies. Discussion Paper 24.

DiMaggio, Paul and Powell, Walter. 1983. "The Iron Cage Revisited: Institutional Isomorphism and Collective Rationality in Organizational Fields." *American Sociological Review* 48(2): 147–60.

DiMaggio, Paul and Powell, Walter. 1991. "Introduction," in Paul DiMaggio and Walter Powell (eds), *The New Institutionalism in Organizational Analysis*. Chicago: University of Chicago Press, pp. 1–40.

Djilas, Milovan. 1991. "The Legacy of Communism in Eastern Europe." *Fletcher Forum* 15(1): 83–92.

Dobbin, Frank, Simmons, Beth, and Garrett, Geoffrey. 2007. "The Global Diffusion of Public Policies: Social Construction, Coercion, Competition, or Learning?" *Annual Review of Sociology* 33: 449–72.

Doering, Laura. 2018. "Risks, Returns, and Relational Lending: Personal Ties in Microfinance." *American Journal of Sociology* 123(5): 1341–81.

Domar, Evsey. 1970. "On the Causes of Slavery or Serfdom: A Hypothesis." *Journal of Economic History* 30(1): 18–32.

Dore, Ronald. 1975. "The Prestige Factor in International Affairs." *International Affairs* 51(2): 190–207.

Dore, Ronald. 1976. *The Diploma Disease: Education, Qualification, and Development*. Berkeley: University of California Press.

Dore, Ronald. 2000. *Stock Market Capitalism: Welfare Capitalism: Japan and Germany versus the Anglo-Saxons*. New York: Oxford University Press.

Drabble, Sam, Ratzmann, Nora, Hooorens, Stijn, Khodyakov, Dmitry, and Yaqub, Ohid. 2015. "The Rise of a Global Middle Class." Rand Europe.

Drake, St Clair. 1951. "The International Implications of Race and Race Relations." *Journal of Negro Education* 20(3): 261–78.

Drechsler, Wolfgang. 2020. "Good Bureaucracy: Max Weber and Public Administration Today." *Max Weber Studies* 20(2): 219–24.

Dreze, Jean and Loh, Jackie. 1995. "Literacy in India and China." *Economic and Political Weekly* 30(45): 2868–78.

References

Drezner, Daniel. 2001. "Globalization and Policy Convergence." *International Studies Review* 3(1): 53–78.

Durkheim, Emile. 1982. *The Rules of Sociological Method*, ed. and intro. Steven Lukes, trans. W. D. Halls. New York: The Free Press.

Easterly, William. 2001. *The Elusive Quest for Growth: Economists' Adventures and Misadventures in the Tropics*. Cambridge: MIT Press.

Eckstein, Susan. 1982. "The Impact of Revolution on Social Welfare in Latin America." *Theory & Society* 11(1): 43–94.

Economist. 2018. "The Mac Strikes Back." January 20.

Economist. 2020. "Economics Brief: Culture." September 5.

Ehrhardt-Martinez, Karen, Crenshaw, Edward M., and Jenkins, J. Craig. 2002. "Deforestation and the Environmental Kuznets Curve: A Cross-National Investigation of Intervening Mechanisms." *Social Science Quarterly* 83(1): 226–43.

Eisenstadt, S. N. 1992. "The Breakdown of Communist Regimes and the Vicissitudes of Modernity." *Daedalus* 121(2): 21–41.

Eisenstein, Elizabeth. 1979. *The Printing Press as an Agent of Change: Communications and Cultural Transformations in Early Modern Europe*. Cambridge: Cambridge University Press.

El Amine, Loubna. 2016. "Beyond East and West: Reorienting Political Theory through the Prism of Modernity." *Perspectives on Politics* 14(1): 103–20.

Eldridge, Cynthia and Palmer, Natasha. 2009. "Performance-based Payment: Some Reflections on the Discourse, Evidence and Unanswered Questions." *Health Policy and Planning* 24(3): 160–6.

Elliott, Michael. 2016. "Fighting Poverty Means Fighting Sexism." *OECD Yearbook 2016*. Paris: OECD.

Elster, Jon. 1986. "The Theory of Combined and Uneven Development: A Critique," in John Roemer (ed.), *Analytical Marxism*. Cambridge: Cambridge University Press, pp. 54–75.

Erlanger, Steven. 2020. "Spread of Virus Could Hasten the Great Coming Apart of Globalization." *New York Times*, February 25.

Escobar, Arturo. 1995. *Encountering Development: The Making and Unmaking of the Third World*. Princeton: Princeton University Press.

Espeland, Wendy. 1997. "Authority by the Numbers: Porter on Quantification, Discretion, and the Legitimacy of Expertise." *Law & Social Inquiry* 22(4): 1107–33.

Espeland, Wendy and Sauder, Michael. 2007. "Rankings and Reactivity: How Public Measures Recreate Social Worlds." *American Journal of Sociology* 113(1): 1–40.

Espeland, Wendy and Stevens, Mitchell. 1998. "Commensuration as a Social Process." *Annual Review of Sociology* 24: 313–43.

Espeland, Wendy and Stevens, Mitchell. 2008. "A Sociology of Quantification." *European Journal of Sociology* 49(3): 401–36.

Evans, Peter. 1971. "National Autonomy and Economic Development: Critical Perspectives on Multinational Corporations in Poor Countries." *International Organization* 25(3): 675–92.

Evans, Peter. 1987. "Class, State and Dependence in East Asia: Some Lessons for Latin Americanists," in Frederic Deyo (ed.), *The Political Economy of the New Asian Industrialism*. Ithaca: Cornell University Press, pp. 203–26.

Evans, Peter. 1992. "The State as Problem and Solution: Predation, Embedded Autonomy, and Structural Change," in Stephan Haggard and Robert Kaufman (eds), *The Politics of Economic Adjustment: International Constraints, Distributive Conflicts and the State*. Princeton: Princeton University Press, pp. 139–81.

Evans, Peter. 1995. *Embedded Autonomy: States and Industrial Transformation*. Princeton: Princeton University Press.

Evans, Peter and Rauch, James. 1999. "Bureaucracy and Growth: A Cross-National Analysis of the Effects of 'Weberian' State Structures on Economic Growth." *American Sociological Review* 64(5): 748–65.

Evenett, Simon and Meier, Michael. 2008. "An Interim Assessment of the US Trade Policy of 'Competitive Liberalization.'" *World Economy* 31(1): 31–66.

Ewing, Jack. 2022. "Why Tesla Soared as Other Companies Struggled to Make Cars." *New York Times*, January 8.

Fairbrother, Malcolm. 2013. "Rich People, Poor People, and Environmental Concern: Evidence across Nations and Time." *European Sociological Review* 29(5): 910–22.

Fairbrother, Malcolm. 2016. "Externalities: Why Environmental Sociology Should Bring Them in." *Environmental Sociology* 2(4): 375–84.

Feder, Ernest. 1976. "McNamara's Little Green Revolution: World Bank Scheme for Self-Liquidation of Third World Peasantry." *Economic and Political Weekly* 11(14): 532–41.

Feldman, Arnold and Hurn, Christopher. 1966. "The Experience of Modernization." *Sociometry* 29(4): 378–95.

Feldmann, Andreas and Durand, Jorge. 2008. "Die-offs at the Border." *Migración y Desarrollo* 10(1): 11–34.

Fine, Ben and Pollen, Gabriel. 2018. "The Developmental State Paradigm in the Age of Financialization," in G. Honor Fagan and Ronaldo Munck (eds), *Handbook on Development and Social Change*. Cheltenham: Edward Elgar, pp. 211–27.

Fiss, Owen. 1983. "The Bureaucratization of the Judiciary." *Yale Law Journal* 92(8): 1442–68.

Flores Dewey, Onesimo and Davis, Diane. 2013. "Planning, Politics, and Urban Mega-Projects in Developmental Context: Lessons from Mexico City's Airport Controversy." *Journal of Urban Affairs* 35(5): 531–51.

Fordham, Paul. 1983. *One Billion Illiterates. One Billion Reasons for Action.* Report and Extracts from Papers of an International Seminar on Co-operating for Literacy. Berlin: International Council for Adult Education, October.

Form, William. 1997. "Review of *Embedded Autonomy: States and Industrial Transformation,* by Peter Evans." *Administrative Science Quarterly* 42(1): 187–9.

Forteza, Alvaro and Tommasi, Mariano. 2006. "On the Political Economy of Pro-Market Reform in Latin America," in Jose M. Fanelli and Gary McMahon (eds), *Understanding Market Reforms.* Palgrave Macmillan, London, pp. 193–228.

Foster-Carter, Aidan. 1978. "The Modes of Production Controversy." *New Left Review* 1(107).

Fourcade, Marion. 2001. "Politics, Institutional Structures and the Rise of Economics: A Comparative Study." *Theory and Society* 30(3): 397–447.

Fourcade, Marion. 2006. "The Construction of a Global Profession: The Transnationalization of Economics." *American Journal of Sociology* 112(1): 145–95.

Fourcade, Marion. 2011. "Cents and Sensibility: Economic Valuation and the Nature of 'Nature.'" *American Journal of Sociology* 116(6): 1721–77.

Fourcade, Marion and Healy, Kieran. 2007. "Moral Views of Market Society." *Annual Review of Sociology* 33: 285–311.

Fourcade Gourinchas, Marion and Babb, Sarah. 2002. "The Rebirth of the Liberal Creed: Paths to Neoliberalism in Four Countries." *American Journal of Sociology* 108(3): 533–79.

Frank, Andre Gunder. 1972. "Politics and Bias." *Economic & Political Weekly* 7(38): 1917–20.

Frank, Andre Gunder. 1976. "That the Extent of Internal Market Is Limited by International Division of Labour and Relations of Production." *Economic and Political Weekly* 11(5/7): 171–90.

Frank, Andre Gunder. 1977. "Long Live Transideological Enterprise! Socialist Economies in Capitalist International Division of Labour." *Economic & Political Weekly* 12(6/8): 297–348.

Frank, Andre Gunder. 1984. "World Economic Crisis and Third World in Mid-1980s." *Economic and Political Weekly* 12(19): 799–804.

Frija, Aymen, Zaatra, Abderraouf, Frija, Iheb, and AbdelHafidh, Hassen. 2017. "Mapping Social Networks for Performance Evaluation of Irrigation Water Management in Dry Areas." *Environmental Modeling and Assessment* 22: 147–58.

Fröbel, Folker, Heinrichs, Jürgen, and Kreye, Otto. 1978. "The World Market for Labor and the World Market for Industrial Sites." *Journal of Economic Issues* 12(4): 843–58.

References

Fukuyama, Francis. 2002. "Social Capital and Development." *SAIS Review* 22(1): 23–37.

Furtado, Celso. 1953. "La formación de capital y el desarrollo económico." *El Trimestre Económico* 77(1): 88–121.

Furtado, Celso. 1969. "Esferas de influência e desenvolvimento: o caso da América Latina." *Análise Social* 7(25–6): 50–66.

Furtado, Celso. 1976. "El conocimiento económico de América Latina." *Estudios Internacionales* 9(36): 11–23.

Furtado, Celso. 1979. "El desarrolo desde el punto de vista interdisciplinario." *El Trimestre Económico* 46(181): 5–33.

Galbraith, John Kenneth. 1962. *Economic Development in Perspective.* Cambridge: Harvard University Press.

Ganev, Venelin. 2009. "Postcommunist Political Capitalism: A Weberian Interpretation." *Comparative Studies in Society and History* 51(3): 648–74.

Garrido, Marco. 2021. "Democracy as Disorder: Institutionalized Sources of Democratic Ambivalence among the Upper and Middle Class in Manila." *Social Forces* 99(3): 1036–59.

Gaspar, Vitor, Medas, Paulo, and Ralyea, John. 2020. "State-Owned Enterprises in the Time of COVID-19," IMF Blog, May 7, International Monetary Fund. Available at https://blogs.imf.org/2020/05/07/state-owned-enterprises-in-the-time-of-covid-19/

Geertz, Clifford. 1956a. "Religious Belief and Economic Behavior in a Central Javanese Town: Some Preliminary Considerations." *Economic Development and Cultural Change* 4(2): 134–58.

Geertz, Clifford. 1956b. "The Development of the Javanese Economy: A Socio-Cultural Approach." Center for International Studies. Cambridge: MIT Press.

Geertz, Clifford. 1956c. "Capital-Intensive Agriculture in a Peasant Society: A Case Study." *Social Research* 23(4): 433–49.

Geertz, Clifford. 1963. *Agricultural Involution: The Processes of Ecological Change in Indonesia.* Berkeley: University of California Press.

Geertz, Clifford. 1977. "The Judging of Nations: Some Comments on the Assessment of Regimes in the New States." *European Journal of Sociology* 18(2): 245–61.

Geertz, Clifford. 1984. "Culture and Social Change: The Indonesian Case." *Man* 19(4): 11–32.

Geertz, Clifford. 1991. "Change Without Progress in a Wet Rice Culture." *Current Contents* 12 (March 25): 8.

Geertz, Clifford. 1995. *After the Fact: Two Countries, Four Decades, One Anthropologist.* Cambridge: Harvard University Press.

Gellner, Ernest. 1975. "Cohesion and Identity: The Maghreb from Ibn Khaldun to Emile Durkheim." *Government & Opposition* 10(2): 203–18.

Gellner, Ernest. 1982. "The Industrial Division of Labour and National Cultures." *Government & Opposition* 17(3): 268–78.

Gellner, Ernest. 1983. *Nations and Nationalism*. Ithaca: Cornell University Press.

Gellner, Ernest. 1987. "Nationalism and the Two Forms of Cohesion in Complex Societies," in Ernest Gellner (ed.), *Culture, Identity, and Politics*. Cambridge: Cambridge University Press, pp. 6–28.

Gellner, Ernest. 1993. "Homeland of the Unrevolution." *Daedalus* 122(3): 141–53.

Gereffi, Gary. 1999. "International Trade and Industrial Upgrading in the Apparel Commodity Chain." *Journal of International Economics* 48: 37–70.

Gerschenkron, Alexander. 1962. *Economic Backwardness in Historical Perspective*. Cambridge: Harvard University Press.

Gerschenkron, Alexander. 1966. "The Modernization of Entrepreneurship," in Myron Weiner (ed.), *Modernization: The Dynamics of Growth*. New York: Basic Books, pp. 246–57.

Gerschenkron, Alexander. 1978. "Time Horizon in Balzac and Others." *Proceedings of the American Philosophical Society* 122(2): 75–91.

Gerth, H. H. and Mills, C. Wright. 1946. *From Max Weber: Essays in Sociology*. New York: Oxford University Press.

Giebler, Heiko, Ruth, Saskia P., and Tanneberg, Dag. 2018. "Why Choice Matters: Revisiting and Comparing Measures of Democracy." *Politics and Governance* 6(1): 1–10.

Gilardi, Fabrizio. 2012. "Transnational Diffusion: Norms, Ideas, and Policies," in Walter Carlsnaes, Thomas Risse, and Beth A. Simmons (eds), *Handbook of International Relations*. London: Sage, ch. 17.

Giljum, Stefan and Eisenmenger, Nina. 2004. "North–South Trade and the Distribution of Environmental Goods and Burdens: A Biophysical Perspective." *Journal of Environment & Development* 13(1): 73–100.

Gilman, Nils. 2002. "Involution and Modernization: The Case of Clifford Geertz," in Jeffrey Cohen and Norbert Dannhaeuser (eds), *Economic Development: An Anthropological Approach*. Lanham: Rowman & Littlefield, pp. 3–22.

Gold, Thomas. 1986. *State and Society in the Taiwan Miracle*. Armonk: M. E. Sharpe.

Goldin, Claudia. 2016. "Human Capital," in C. Diebolt and M. Haupert (eds), *Handbook of Cliometrics*. Berlin: Springer-Verlag, pp. 55–86.

Goldstone, Jack. 2000. "Whose Measure of Reality?" *American Historical Review* 105(2): 501–8.

Goldstone, Jack and Turchin, Peter. 2020. "Welcome to the 'Turbulent Twenties.'" *Noema Magazine*, September 10. Available at https://www.noema mag.com/welcome-to-the-turbulent-twenties/

Gong, Yooshik and Jang, Wonho. 1998. "Culture and Development: Reassessing Cultural Explanations of East Asian Economic Development." *Development and Society* 27(1): 77–97.

Gootenberg, Paul. 2001. "*Hijos* of Dr Gerschenkron: 'Latecomer' Conceptions in Latin American Economic History," in Miguel Angel Centeno and Fernando

López-Alves (eds), *The Other Mirror: Grand Theory through the Lens of Latin America*. Princeton: Princeton University Press, pp. 55–80.

Gordon, Neve. 1996. "The Comparative Advantage of Exploiting Children." *Chicago Tribune*, October 1.

Gorski, Philip. 1993. "The Protestant Ethic Revisited: Disciplinary Revolution and State Formation in Holland and Prussia." *American Sociological Review* 99(2): 265–316.

Gough, Kathleen. 1982. "Commentary on Immanuel Wallerstein's 'The USA in Today's World.'" *Contemporary Marxism* 5 (Summer): 158.

Gowa, Joanne and Mansfield, Edward. 1993."Power Politics and International Trade." *American Political Science Review* 87(2): 408–20.

Granovetter, Mark. 1976. "Threshold Models of Collective Behavior." *American Journal of Sociology* 83(6): 1420–46.

Granovetter, Mark. 1979. "The Idea of 'Advancement' in Theories of Social Evolution and Development." *American Journal of Sociology* 85(3): 489–515.

Granovetter, Mark. 1985. "Economic Action and Social Structure: The Problem of Embeddedness." *American Journal of Sociology* 91(3): 481–510.

Granovetter, Mark. 1990. "The Old and New Economic Sociology: A History and an Agenda," in Roger Friedland and A. F. Robertson (eds), *Beyond the Marketplace: Rethinking Economy and Society*. New York: Aldine de Gruyter, pp. 89–112.

Granovetter, Mark. 1992. "Economic Institutions as Social Constructions: A Framework for Analysis." *Acta Sociologica* 35(1): 3–11.

Granovetter, Mark. 1995. "The Economic Sociology of Firms and Entrepreneurs," in Alejandro Portes (ed.), *The Economic Sociology of Immigration: Essays on Networks, Ethnicity, and Entrepreneurship*. New York: Russell Sage Foundation, pp. 128–65.

Granovetter, Mark and Swedberg, Richard. 2011. *The Sociology of Economic Life*, 3rd edn. Boulder: Westview.

Greenberg, Stanley. 1980. *Race and State in Capitalist Development*. New Haven: Yale University Press.

Greenfeld, Liah. 1996a. "Nationalism and Modernity." *Social Research* 63(1): 3–40.

Greenfeld, Liah. 1996b. *Nationalism: Five Roads to Modernity*. Cambridge, MA: Harvard University Press.

Greenhalgh, Susan. 1989. "Land Reform and Family Entrepreneurship in East Asia." *Population & Development Review* 15 (suppl.): 77–118.

Grose, Timothy. 2010. "The Xinjiang Class: Education, Integration, and the Uyghurs." *Journal of Muslim Minority Affairs* 30(1): 97–109.

Guillén, Mauro. 2000a. "Organized Labor's Images of Multinational Enterprise: Divergent Foreign Investment Ideologies in Argentina, South Korea, and Spain." *ILR Review* 53(3): 419–42.

Guillén, Mauro. 2000b. "Business Groups in Emerging Economies: A Resource-Based View." *Academy of Management Journal* 43(3): 362–80.

Guillén, Mauro. 2004. "Modernism without Modernity: The Rise of Modernist Architecture in Mexico, Brazil, and Argentina, 1890–1940." *Latin American Research Review* 39(2): 6–34.

Guillén, Mauro and Capron, Laurence. 2016. "State Capacity, Minority Shareholder Protections, and Stock Market Development." *Administrative Science Quarterly* 61(1): 125–60.

Gullickson, Aaron and Torche, Florencia. 2014. "Patterns of Racial and Educational Assortative Mating in Brazil." *Demography* 51(3): 835–56.

Gussman, Boris. 1953. "Industrial Efficiency and the Urban African: A Study of Conditions in Southern Rhodesia." *Africa: Journal of the International African Institute* 23(2): 135–44.

Habakkuk, H. J. 1961. "Review of *The Stages of Economic Growth: A Non-Communist Manifesto* by W. W. Rostow." *Economic Journal* 71(283): 601–4.

Hagen, Everett. 1960. "Turning Parameters into Variables in the Theory of Economic Growth." *American Economic Review* 50(2): 623–8.

Hagen, Everett. 1966. "Western Economics in a Non-Western Setting." *Challenge* 14(5): 28–31.

Haggard, Stephan. 1986. "The Newly Industrializing Countries in the International System." *World Politics* 38(2): 343–70.

Haggard, Stephan. 2004. "Institutions and Growth in East Asia." *Studies in Comparative International Development* 38(4): 53–81.

Halberstam, David. 1972. *The Best and the Brightest.* New York: Random House.

Hall, Derek. 2009. "Pollution Export as State and Corporate Strategy: Japan in the 1970s." *Review of International Political Economy* 16(2): 260–83.

Hall, Peter and Soskice, David. 2001. *Varieties of Capitalism.* New York: Oxford University Press.

Hall, Stuart. 1992. "The West and The Rest: Discourse and Power," in David Morley (ed.), *Essential Essays, Volume 2: Identity and Diaspora.* Durham: Duke University Press, pp. 185–227.

Hamilton, Gary and Biggart, Nicole Woolsey. 1988. "Market, Culture, and Authority: A Comparative Analysis of Management and Organization in the Far East." *American Journal of Sociology* 94 (suppl.): S52–S94.

Hamilton, Gary and Cheng-shu, Kao. 2017. *Making Money: How Taiwanese Industrialists Embraced the Global Economy.* Stanford: Stanford University Press.

Hammond, Phillip. 1989. "Constitutional Faith, Legitimating Myth, Civil Religion." *Law & Social Inquiry* 14(2): 377–91.

Hammond, Ruth. 2011. "The Battle Over Zomia." *Chronicle of Higher Education,* September 4.

Hannan, Michael and Freeman, John. 1977. "The Population Ecology of Organizations." *American Journal of Sociology* 82(5): 929–64.

Hanson, Jonathan and Sigman, Rachel. 2021. "Leviathan's Latent Dimensions: Measuring State Capacity for Comparative Political Research." *Journal of Politics* 83(4): 1495–1510.

Hareven, Tamara. 1990. "A Complex Relationship: Family Strategies and the Processes of Economic and Social Change," in Roger Friedland and A. F. Robertson (eds), *Beyond the Marketplace: Rethinking Economy and Society.* New York: Aldine de Gruyter, pp. 215–44.

Harms, John. 1981. "Reason and Social Change in Durkheim's Thought: The Changing Relationship between Individuals and Society." *Pacific Sociological Review* 24(4): 393–410.

Harris, Kevan. 2013. "The Rise of the Subcontractor State: Politics of Pseudo-Privatization in the Islamic Republic of Iran." *International Journal of Middle East Studies* 45(1): 45–70.

Harris, Paul. 2016. *Global Ethics and Climate Change.* Edinburgh: Edinburgh University Press.

Harrison, Graham. 2017. "Rwanda and the Difficult Business of Capitalist Development." *Development & Change* 48(5): 873–98.

Hasselskog, Malin. 2018. "A Capability Analysis of Rwandan Development Policy: Calling into Question Human Development Indicators." *Third World Quarterly* 39(1): 140–57.

Hauser-Schäublin, Brigata. 2015. "From *Homo Politicus* to Immobilized Icon: Clifford Geertz and Shifts in Anthropological Paradigms." *Bijdragen tot de Taal-, Land- en Volkenkunde* 171(2/3): 220–48.

Headey, Derek. 2009. "Appraising a Post-Washington Paradigm: What Professor Rodrik Means by Policy Reform." *Review of International Political Economy* 16(4): 698–28.

Helbardt, Sascha, Hellmann-Rajanayagam, Dagmar, and Korff, Rüdiger. 2012. "Isomorphism and Decoupling: Processes of External and Internal Legitimation in Southeast Asia." *Sociologus* 62(1): 25–46.

Henisz, Witold, Zelner, Bennet A., and Guillén, Mauro F. 2005. "The Worldwide Diffusion of Market-Oriented Infrastructure Reform, 1977–1999." *American Sociological Review* 70(6): 891–907.

Heredia, Mariana. 2018. "The International Division of Labor in Economists' Field: Academic Subordination in Exchange for Political Prerogatives in Argentina." *Historical Social Research* 43(3): 303–28.

Hettne, Björn. 1983. "The Development of Development Theory." *Acta Sociologica* 26(3/4): 247–66.

Heyneman, Stephen and Loxley, William. 1983. "The Effect of Primary-School Quality on Academic Achievement across Twenty-nine High- and Low-Income Countries." *American Journal of Sociology* 88(6): 1162–94.

Hickel, Jason, Sullivan, Dylan, and Zoomkawala, Huzaifa. 2021. "Rich

References

Countries Drained $152tn from the Global South since 1960." *Al Jazeera,* May 6.

Himbara, David. 2015. Testimony by David Himbara on Developments in Rwanda, House Committee on Foreign Affairs, Subcommittee on Africa, Global Health, Global Human Rights, and International Organizations, May 20. Available at https://docs.house.gov/meetings/FA/FA16/20150520/103498 /HHRG-114-FA16-Wstate-HimbaraD-20150520.pdf

Hirschman, Albert. 1968. "The Political Economy of Import-Substituting Industrialization in Latin America." *Quarterly Journal of Economics* 82(1): 1–32.

Hirschman, Albert. 1970. *Exit, Voice, and Loyalty: Responses to Decline in Firms, Organizations, and States.* Cambridge: Harvard University Press.

Hirschman, Albert. 1980. "La matriz social y política de la inflación: elaboración sobre la experiencia latinoamericana." *El Trimestre Económica* 47(187): 679–709.

Hirschman, Albert. 1981. *Essays in Trespassing: Economics to Politics and Beyond.* Cambridge: Cambridge University Press.

Ho, P. Sai-wing. 2012. "Revisiting Prebisch and Singer: Beyond the Declining Terms of Trade Thesis and on to Technological Capability Development." *Cambridge Journal of Economics* 36(4): 869–93.

Hobsbawm, Eric. 1962. *The Age of Revolution: Europe 1789–1848.* London: Weidenfeld & Nicholson.

Hoffman, Kelly and Centeno, Miguel Angel. 2003. "The Lopsided Continent: Inequality in Latin America." *Annual Review of Sociology* 29: 363–90.

Hong, Jea-Hwan and Kim, Duol. 2020. "Tenancy, Land Redistribution, and Economic Growth: A Case of Korea, 1920–1960." KDI School of Public Policy and Management, Development Discussion Series 11. Seoul: Korea Development Institute.

Hooker, J. R. 1965. "The Role of the Labour Department in the Birth of African Trade Unionism in Northern Rhodesia." *International Review of Social History* 10(1): 1–22.

Hopkins, Terence and Wallerstein, Immanuel. 1977. "Patterns of Development of the Modern World-System." *Review* 1(2): 111–45.

Horowitz, Irving Louis. 1964. "Sociological and Ideological Conceptions of Industrial Development." *American Journal of Economics and Sociology* 23(4): 351–74.

Hoselitz, Bert. 1952. "Non-Economic Barriers to Economic Development." *Economic Development and Cultural Change* 1(1): 8–21.

Hsieh, Michelle. 2011. "Similar Opportunities, Different Responses: Explaining the Divergent Patterns of Development between Taiwan and South Korea." *International Sociology* 26(3): 364–91.

Hsieh, Michelle Fei-yu. 2014. "Hollowing Out or Sustaining? Taiwan's SME Network-based Production System Reconsidered, 1996–2011." *Taiwanese Sociology,* 28 December: 149–91.

Hsu, Po-Hsuan, Liang, Hao, and Matos, Pedro. 2021. "Leviathan Inc. and Corporate Environmental Engagement." ECGI Working Papers in Finance 256/2017. Brussels: European Corporate Governance Institute.

Huang, Philip C. C. 1990. *The Peasant Family and Rural Development in the Yangzi Delta, 1350–1988*. Stanford: Stanford University Press.

Huerta Wong, Juan, Burak, Esra, and Grusky, David B. 2015. "Is Mexico the Limiting Case: Social Mobility in the New Gilded Age." Centro de Estudios Espinosa Yglesias. Documento de trabajo numero 17/2015.

Hung, Ho-Fung. 2022. "It's Too Soon to Announce the Dawn of a Chinese Century." Interview with Daniel Finn. *Jacobin* (January).

Huntington, Samuel. 1968. *Political Order in Changing Societies*. New Haven: Yale University Press.

Huntington, Samuel. 1996. *The Clash of Civilization and the Remaking of World Order*. New York: Simon & Schuster.

Hvistendahl, Mara. 2014. "While Emerging Economies Boom, Equality Goes Bust: Inequality Spikes in Developing Nations around the World." *Science* 344(6186): 832–35.

IMF (International Monetary Fund). 2016. "Behind the Scenes with Data at the IMF: An IEO Evaluation." Independent Evaluation Office of the IMF. Washington: IMF.

Ingelaere, Bert. 2010. "Do We Understand Life after Genocide? Center and Periphery in the Construction of Knowledge in Postgenocide Rwanda." *African Studies Review* 53(1): 41–59.

Inglehart, Ronald and Norris, Pippa. 2016. "Trump, Brexit, and the Rise of Populism: Economic Have-Nots and Cultural Backlash." Harvard Kennedy School Working Paper RWP 16-026, August. Cambridge: Harvard University.

Intscher, Nicholas. 2014. "The Rise of 'Murky Protectionism': Changing Patterns of Trade-Related Industrial Policies in Developing Countries: A Case Study of Indonesia." DESTIN International Development Working Paper Series 14–157. London: LSE.

Islam, Nazrul. 2014. "Beware, the Middle Class is Being Hijacked by the World Bank!" *Bangladesh e-Journal of Sociology* 11(2): 7–28.

Ito, Takatoshi. 1994. "Comment," in John Page (ed.), "The East Asian Miracle: Four Lessons for Development Policy." *NBER Macroeconomics Annual* (1994) 9: 274–80.

James, Harold. 2020. "Could Coronavirus Bring about the 'Waning of Globalization'?" World Economic Forum, March 4.

James, Ian. 2019. "This Mexican City Was Transformed by Factories: Its People Pay a Heavy Price." *Desert Sun*, December 15.

Jayachandran, Seema. 2015. "The Roots of Gender Inequality in Developing Countries." *Annual Review of Economics* 7: 63–89.

Jepperson, Ronald and Meyer, John. 2011. "Multiple Levels of Analysis and the

Limitations of Methodological Individualisms." *Sociological Theory* 29(1): 54–73.

Johnson, Chalmers. 1982. *MITI and the Japanese Miracle: The Growth of Industrial Policy.* Stanford: Stanford University Press.

Johnson, Chalmers. 1986. "The Nonsocialist NICs: East Asia." *International Organization* 40(3): 557–65.

Johnson, Paul and Papageorgiou, Chris. 2020. "What Remains of Cross-Country Convergence?" *Journal of Economic Literature* 58(1): 129–75.

Jonas, Susanne and Dixon, Marlene. 1979. "Proletarianization and Class Alliances in the Americas." *Synthesis* 3(1): 1–13.

Jones, Will and Murray, Sally. 2018. "Consolidating Peace and Legitimacy in Rwanda." London: LSE-Oxford Commission on State Fragility, Growth and Development.

Jorgenson, Andrew. 2016. "The Sociology of Ecologically Unequal Exchange, Foreign Investment Dependence and Environmental Load Displacement: Summary of the Literature and Implications for Sustainability." *Journal of Political Ecology* 32: 334–49.

Jorgenson, Andrew and Clark, Brett. 2012. "Are the Economy and the Environment Decoupling? A Comparative International Study, 1960–2005." *American Journal of Sociology* 118(1): 1–44.

Jütting, Johannes and de Laiglesia, Juan. 2009. "Is Informal Normal? Toward More and Better Jobs." OECD Policy Brief, March.

Kang, Nahee. 2014. "Towards Middle-Range Theory Building in Development Research: Comparative (Historical) Institutional Analysis of Institutional Transplantation." *Progress in Development Studies* 14(3): 221–35.

Kapur, Devesh. 2020. "Why Does the Indian State Both Fail and Succeed?" *Journal of Economic Perspectives* 34(1): 31–54.

Katz, Richard. 1998. *Japan, The System That Soured: The Rise and Fall of the Japanese Economic Miracle.* Armonk: M. E. Sharpe.

Kautsky, John. 1997. "Centralization in the Marxist and in the Leninist Tradition." *Communist and Post-Communist Studies* 30(4): 379–400.

Kelley, Allen. 1991. "The Human Development Index: 'Handle with Care.'" *Population and Development Review* 17(2): 315–24.

Kenez, Peter. 1982. "Liquidating Illiteracy in Revolutionary Russia." *Russian History* 9(2/3): 173–86.

Kentikelenis, Alexander and Babb, Sarah. 2019. "The Making of Neoliberal Globalization: Norm Substitution and the Politics of Clandestine Institutional Change." *American Journal of Sociology* 124(6): 1720–62.

Keyfitz, Nathan. 1965. "Indonesian Population and the European Industrial Revolution." *Asian Survey* 5 (1): 503–14.

Keyfitz, Nathan. 1982. "Development and the Elimination of Poverty." *Economic Development and Cultural Change* 30(3): 649–70.

Keyfitz, Nathan. 1985. "An East Javanese Village in 1953 and 1985: Observations on Development." *Population and Development Review* 11(4): 695–719.

Keyfitz, Nathan. 1995. "Inter-Disciplinary Contradictions and the Influence of Science on Policy." *Policy Sciences* 28(1): 28–31.

Killick, Tony. 1993. *The Adaptive Economy: Adjustment Policies in Small, Low-Income Countries.* Washington: The World Bank.

Kim, Sungjo. 2021. "Land Reform and Postcolonial Poverty in South Korea, 1950–1970." *Agricultural History* 95(2): 276–310.

Kim, Yun Tae. 2007. "The Transformation of the East Asian States: From the Developmental State to the Market-Oriented State." *Korean Social Science Journal* 34(2): 31–60.

Kirkwood, Michael. 1991. "'Glasnost', 'the National Question' and Soviet Language Policy." *Soviet Studies* 43(1): 61–81.

Klein, Philip. 1989. "Institutionalism Confronts the 1990s." *Journal of Economic Issues* 23(2): 545–53.

Kline, George. 1958. "Education toward Literacy." *Current History* 35(203): 17–21.

Knight, Franklin. 1921. *Risk, Uncertainty, and Profit.* Boston: Houghton Mifflin.

Kogut, Bruce and Macpherson, J. Muir. 2011. "The Mobility of Economists and the Diffusion of Policy Ideas: The Influence of Economics on National Policies." *Research Policy* 40: 1307–20.

Kohli, Atul. 2004. *State-Directed Development: Political Power and Industrialization in the Global Periphery.* Cambridge: Cambridge University Press.

Koissy Kpein, Sandrine Aïda. 2010. "The Greater Mothers' Empowerment, the Higher Girls' Schooling: Evidence from DHS Monogamous Households." CEPS Instead Working Paper 2010–19.

Korhonen-Kurki, Kaisa, Brockhaus, Maria, Duchelle, Amy E., Atmadja, Stibniati, Thuy, Pham Thu, and Schofield, Lydia. 2013. "Multiple Levels and Multiple Challenges for Measurement, Reporting and Verification of REDD+." *International Journal of the Commons* 7(2): 344–66.

Kornai, János. 1985. "Hungary's Reform: Halfway to the Market." *Challenge* 28(2): 22–31.

Kornai, János. 1986a. "The Soft Budget Constraint." *Kyklos* 39: 3–30.

Kornai, János. 1986b. "The Hungarian Reform Process: Visions, Hopes, and Reality." *Journal of Economic Literature* 24(4): 1687–1737.

Kowalewski, Stephen A. and Saindon, Jacqueline J. 1992. "The Spread of Literacy in a Latin American Peasant Society: Oaxaca, Mexico, 1890 to 1980." *Comparative Studies in Society and History* 34(1): 110–40.

Krasner, Stephen. 1999. *Sovereignty: Organized Hypocrisy.* Princeton: Princeton University Press.

Krippner, Greta and Alvarez, Anthony. 2007. "Embeddedness and the Intellectual Projects of Economic Sociology." *Annual Review of Sociology* 33: 219–40.

Kroneberg, Clemens and Wimmer, Andreas. 2012. "Struggling over the Boundaries of Belonging: A Formal Model of Nation Building, Ethnic Closure, and Populism." *American Journal of Sociology* 118(1): 176–230.

Krouglov, Alex. 2021. "Language Planning and Policies in Russia through a Historical Perspective." *Current Issues in Language Planning.* Available at: doi: 10.1080/14664208.2021.2005384

Krueger, Anne. 1990. "Asian Trade and Growth Lessons." *American Economic Review* 80(2): 108–12.

Krueger, Anne. 1993. "Virtuous and Vicious Circles in Economic Development." *American Economic Review* 83(2): 351–5.

Krugman, Paul. 1991. *Geography and Trade.* Cambridge: MIT Press.

Kuhn, Randall. 2010. "Routes to Low Mortality in Poor Countries Revisited." *Population & Development Review* 36(4): 655–92.

Kunkel, Benjamin. 2011. "How Much Is Too Much?" *London Review of Books* 33(3): 1–13.

Kurtz, Marcus and Schrank, Andrew. 2007. "Growth and Governance: Models, Measures, and Mechanisms." *Journal of Politics* 69(2): 538–54.

Kurtz, Marcus and Schrank, Andrew. 2012. "Capturing State Strength: Experimental and Econometric Approaches." *Revista de Ciencia Política* 32(3): 613–21.

Kurtz, Marcus and Schrank, Andrew. 2020. "The Social Construction of the Regulatory Burden: Methodological and Substantive Considerations." *Social Forces* 99(3): 1013–35.

Kuznets, Simon. 1955. "Economic Growth and Income Inequality." *American Economic Review* 45(1): 1–28.

Kwon, Huck-ju and Yi, Ilcheong. 2009. "Economic Development and Poverty Reduction in Korea: Governing Multifunctional Institutions." *Development & Change* 40(4): 769–92.

Lagerlöf, Nils-Petter. 2003. "Gender Equality and Long-Run Growth." *Journal of Economic Growth* 8(4): 403–26.

Lakner, Christoph and Milanovic, Branko. 2016. "Global Income Distribution: From the Fall of the Berlin Wall to the Great Recession." *World Bank Economic Review* 30(2): 1–30.

Landes, David. 1998. *The Wealth and Poverty of Nations: Why Some Are So Rich and Some So Poor.* New York: W. W. Norton.

Lange, Matthew. 2005. "The Rule of Law and Development: A Weberian Framework of States and State–Society Relations," in Matthew Lange and Dietrich Rueschemeyer (eds), *States and Development: Historical Antecedents of Stagnation and Advance.* New York: Palgrave Macmillan, pp. 48–65.

Larudee, Mehrene. 1998. "Integration and Income Distribution under the North American Free Trade Agreement: The Experience of Mexico," in Dean Baker (ed.), *Globalization and Progressive Economic Policy.* Cambridge: Cambridge University Press, pp. 272–92.

References

Lauglo, Jon. 1988. "Soviet Education Policy 1917–1935: From Ideology to Bureaucratic Control." *Oxford Review of Education* 14(3): 285–99.

Lawson, Chappell. 2004. "Review of *Mexico's Neoliberal Democracy and Its Critics* by Sarah Babb." *Latin American Politics & Society* 46(3): 115–29.

Leander, Anna. 2005. "Shifting Political Identities and Global Governance of the Justified Use of Force," in Markus Lederer and Philipp S. Müller (eds), *Criticizing Global Governance*. London: Palgrave Macmillan, pp. 125–43.

Lee, Jong-Wha and Barro, Robert. 2001. "Schooling Quality in a Cross-Section of Countries." *Economica* 68(272): 465–88.

Leed, Eric. 1982. "Elizabeth Eisenstein's *The Printing Press as an Agent of Change and the Structure of Communications Revolutions*." *American Journal of Sociology* 88(2): 413–29.

Leibenstein, Harvey. 1957. "The Theory of Underemployment in Backward Economies." *Journal of Political Economy* 65(2): 91–103.

Leibold, James. 2019. "Interior Ethnic Minority Boarding Schools: China's Bold and Unpredictable Educational Experiment." *Asian Studies Review* 43(1): 3–15.

Lenin, Vladimir. 1920. "Communism Is Soviet Power + Electrification of the Whole Country." Report on the Work of the Council of People's Commissars, December 22. Available at https://soviethistory.msu.edu/1921-2/electrification-campaign/communism-is-soviet-power-electrification-of-the-whole-country/

Lewis, Michael. 2010. *The Big Short: Inside the Doomsday Machine*. New York: W. W. Norton.

Lewis, W. Arthur. 1954. "Economic Development with Unlimited Supplies of Labour." *Manchester School* 22(2): 139–91.

Lewis, W. Arthur. 1955. *The Theory of Economic Growth*. London: George Allen & Unwin.

Lewis, W. Arthur. 1968. "Reflections on Unlimited Labour." Development Research Project, Discussion Paper No. 5, Woodrow Wilson School, Princeton University.

Lewis, W. Arthur. 1984. "The State of Development Theory." *American Economic Review* 74(1): 1–10.

Lewis, William. 2004. *The Power of Productivity: Wealth, Power, and the Threat to Global Stability*. Chicago: University of Chicago Press.

Li, Tania Murray. 2005. "Beyond 'The State' and Failed Schemes." *American Anthropologist* 107(3): 383–94.

Liao, Steven and McDowell, Daniel. 2016. "No Reservations: International Order and Demand for the Renminbi as a Reserve Currency." *International Standards Quarterly* 60: 272–93.

Lie, John. 1998. *Han Unbound: The Political Economy of South Korea*. Stanford: Stanford University Press.

Lie, John. 2015. "The Wreck of the Sewol: The Sinking South Korean Body Politic." *Georgetown Journal of International Affairs* 16(2): 111–21.

References

Linz, Juan. 1990. "Transitions to Democracy." *Washington Quarterly* 13(3): 143–64.

Llavador, Humberto, Roemer, John, and Silvestre, Joaquim. 2015. *Sustainability for a Warming Planet*. Cambridge: Harvard University Press.

London, Jonathan. 2018. *Welfare and Development in Marketizing East Asia*. London: Palgrave Macmillan.

Looney, Kristen. 2020. *Mobilizing for Development: The Modernization of Rural East Asia*. Ithaca: Cornell University Press.

Love, Joseph. 1980. "Raúl Prebisch and the Origins of the Doctrine of Unequal Exchange." *Latin American Research Review* 15(3): 45–72.

Lucas, Deborah. 2019. "Measuring the Cost of Bailouts." *Annual Review of Financial Economics* 11: 85–108.

Lukes, Steven. 1982. "Introduction," in Emile Durkheim (author) and Steven Lukes (ed.), *The Rules of Sociological Methods*. New York: The Free Press, pp. 1–30.

Lutz, Catherine. 2014. "The US Car Colossus and the Production of Inequality." *American Ethnologist* 41(2): 232–45.

Madariaga Espinoza, M. A. Aldo. 2015. "The Political Economy of Neoliberal Resilience: Developmental Regimes in Latin America and Eastern Europe." PhD dissertation, University of Cologne.

Maddison, Angus. 2001. *The World Economy: A Millennial Perspective*. Paris: OECD.

Malinowski, Bronislaw. 1943. "The Pan-African Problem of Culture Contact." *American Journal of Sociology* 48(6): 649–65.

Mamdani, Mahmood. 1990. "State and Civil Society in Contemporary Africa: Reconceptualizing the Birth of State Nationalism and the Defeat of Popular Movements." *Africa Development* 15(3/4): 47–70.

Mandle, Jay. 1980. "Marxist Analyses and Capitalist Development in the Third World." *Theory & Society* 9(6): 865–76.

Mann, Michael. 2013. "The Recent Intensification of American Economic and Military Imperialism: Are They Connected?" in George Steinmetz (ed.), *Sociology and Empire: The Imperial Entanglement of a Discipline*. Durham: Duke University Press, pp. 213–44.

Margavio, A. V. and Mann, S. A. 1989. "Modernization and the Family: A Theoretical Analysis." *Sociological Perspectives* 32(1): 109–27.

Margheritis, Ana and Pereira, Anthony W. 2007. "The Neoliberal Turn in Latin America: The Cycle of Ideas and the Search for an Alternative." *Latin American Perspectives* 34(3): 25–48.

Markoff, John and Montecinos, Verónica. 1993. "The Ubiquitous Rise of Economists." *Journal of Public Policy* 13(1): 37–68.

Marquart-Pyatt, Sandra. 2004. "A Cross-National Investigation of Deforestation, Debt, State Fiscal Capacity, and the Environmental Kuznets Curve." *International Journal of Sociology* 34(1): 33–51.

References

Marsh, Robert. 2008. "Convergence in Relation to Level of Societal Development." *Sociological Quarterly* 49(4): 797–824.

Martin, Philip. 2013. "The Global Challenge of Managing Migration." *Population Bulletin* 68(2): 1–16.

Martinez-Alier, Joan. 1995. "Distributional Issues in Ecological Economics." *Review of Social Economy* 53(4): 511–28.

Massey, Douglas and Espinosa, Kristin. 1997. "What's Driving Mexico–US Migration? A Theoretical, Empirical, and Policy Analysis." *American Journal of Sociology* 102(4): 939–99.

Massing, Michael. 2003. "Does Democracy Avert Famine?" *New York Times*, March 1.

McDonnell, Erin Metz. 2020. *Patchwork Leviathan: Pockets of Bureaucratic Effectiveness in Developing States.* Princeton: Princeton University Press.

McGuire, James. 1994. "Development Policy and Its Determinants in East Asia and Latin America." *Journal of Public Policy* 14(2): 205–42.

McGuire, James. 2001. "Social Policy and Mortality Decline in East Asia and Latin America." *World Development* 29(10): 1693–7.

McGuire, James. 2010. *Wealth, Health, and Democracy in East Asia and Latin America.* Cambridge: Cambridge University Press.

McLean, Hugh. 2021. "The Ground beneath Our Feet," in Susannah Hares and Justin Sandefur (eds), *The Pathway to Progress on SDG 4: A Symposium.* Washington: Center for Global Development, pp. 56–70.

McLean, Paul. 2011. "Patrimonialism, Elite Networks, and Reform in Late-Eighteenth-Century Poland." *Annals of the American Academy of Political and Social Science* 636 (July): 88–110.

McNeill, Kristen and Pierotti, Rachael. 2021. "Reason-Giving for Resistance: Obfuscation, Justification and Earmarking in Resisting Informal Financial Assistance." *Socio-Economic Review.* Available at https://doi.org/10.1093/ser/mwab034

McNeill, William. 1963. *The Rise of the West: A History of the Human Community.* Chicago: University of Chicago Press.

McNeill, William. 1990. "'The Rise of the West' after Twenty-Five Years." *Journal of World History* 1(1): 1–21.

Médecins Sans Frontières. 2018. "USTR Priority Watch List Calls out Countries for Protecting Public Health." Press release, 27 April.

Merito, Monica, Gianangelli, Silvia, and Bonaccorsi, Andrea. 2010. "Do Incentives to Industrial R&D Enhance Research Productivity and Firm Growth? Evidence from the Italian Case." *International Journal of Technology Management* 49(1/2/3).

Merkx, Gilbert. 1969. "Sectoral Clashes and Political Change: The Argentine Experience." *Latin American Research Review* 4(3): 89–114.

Merton, Robert. 1949. "On Sociological Theories of the Middle Range," in

Robert Merton (ed.), *Social Theory and Social Structure*. New York: Simon & Schuster, pp. 39–53.

Meyer, John. 2010. "World Society, Institutional Theories, and the Actor." *Annual Review of Sociology* 36: 1–20.

Meyer, John and Rowan, Brian. 1977. "Institutionalized Organizations: Formal Structure as Myth and Ceremony." *American Journal of Sociology* 83(2): 340–63.

Meyer, John, Boli, John, Thomas, George M., and Ramirez, Francisco O. 1997. "World-Society and the Nation-State." *American Journal of Sociology* 103(1): 144–81.

Miao, Shanshan, Heijman, Wim J. M., Zhu, Xueqin, Qiao, Dan, and Lu, Qian. 2018. "Income Groups, Social Capital, and Collective Action on Small-Scale Irrigation Facilities: A Multigroup Analysis Based on a Structural Equation Model." *Rural Sociology* 83(4): 882–911.

Mihályi, Péter and Szelényi, Iván. 2017. "The Role of Rents in the Transition from Socialist Redistributive Economies to Market Capitalism." *Comparative Sociology* 16: 1–26.

Milanovic, Branko. 2014. "Winners of Globalization: The Rich and the Chinese Middle Class. Losers: The American Middle Class." *World Post*, November 26.

Milanovic, Branko. 2015. "Global Inequality of Opportunity: How Much of Our Income Is Determined by Where We Live?" *Review of Economics and Statistics* 97(2): 452–60.

Milanovic, Branko. 2016. *Global Inequality: A New Approach for the Age of Globalization*. Cambridge: Harvard University Press.

Milanovic, Branko. 2020. "The Real Pandemic Danger Is Social Collapse." *Foreign Affairs*, March 19.

Miller, Geoffrey. 2021. "How 9/11 Changed New Zealand's Foreign Policy." *The Diplomat*, September 10.

Milner, Helen, Nielson, Daniel L., and Findley, Michael G. 2016. "Citizen Preferences and Public Goods: Comparing Preferences for Foreign Aid and Government Programs in Uganda." *Review of International Organizations* 11: 219–45.

Mironov, Boris. 1991. "The Development of Literacy in Russia and the USSR from the Tenth to the Twentieth Centuries." *History of Education Quarterly* 31(2): 229–52.

Mizruchi, Mark and Fein, Lisa. 1999. "The Social Construction of Organizational Knowledge: A Study of the Uses of Coercive, Mimetic, and Normative Isomorphism." *Administrative Science Quarterly* 44(4): 653–83.

Mohr, John and Friedland, Roger. 2008. "Theorizing the Institution: Foundations, Duality, and Data." *Theory & Society* 37(5): 421–6.

Mol, Arthur, Spaargaren, Gert, and Sonnenfeld, David A. 2014. "Ecological Modernization Theory: Taking Stock, Moving Forward," in S. Lockie,

References

D. A. Sonnenfeld, and D. Fisher (eds), *Handbook of Environmental Sociology*. London: Routledge, pp. 15–30.

Molina, Iván and Palmer, Steven. 2004. "Popular Literacy in a Tropical Democracy: Costa Rica, 1850–1950." *Past & Present* 184 (August): 169–208.

Montgomery, J. S. 1902. *John Ruskin: The Voice of the New Age*. Cincinnati: Jennings & Pye.

Moore, Jina. 2020. "What African Nations Are Teaching the West About Fighting the Coronavirus." *New Yorker*, May 26.

Moore, Mick. 1998. "Review of *Embedded Autonomy: States and Industrial Transformation* by Peter Evans." *Economic Development and Cultural Change* 46(2): 427–32.

Moore, Wilbert. 1948. "Primitives and Peasants in Industry." *Social Research* 15(1): 44–81.

Morey, Steven. 1998. "Pool Duration Influences Age and Body Mass at Metamorphosis in the Western Spadefoot Toad: Implications for Vernal Pool Conservation." Department of Biology, University of California at Riverside.

Morris, Christopher. 1994. "Review Essays – Challenging the Masters: Recent Studies on Slavery and Freedom." *Florida Historical Quarterly* 73(2): 218–24.

Morris, Christopher. 1998. "The Articulation of Two Worlds: The Master–Slave Relationship Reconsidered." *Journal of American History* 85(3): 982–1007.

Morrow, Daniel. 2006. "Possible World Bank Assistance to North Korea: Issues and Challenges." *Asian Perspective* 30(3): 37–67.

Mouzelis, Nicos. 1985. "On the Concept of Populism: Populist and Clientelist Modes of Incorporation in Semiperipheral Politics." *Politics & Society* 14(3): 329–48.

Mueller, Benjamin and Nolen, Stephanie. 2022. "Death Toll During Pandemic Far Exceeds Totals Reported by Countries, WHO Says." *New York Times*, May 6.

Murillo, María Victoria. 2009. *Political Competition, Partisanship, and Policy Making in Latin American Public Utilities*. Cambridge: Cambridge University Press.

Murillo, María Victoria. 2018. "Latin American Democracies: Breaking the Left-Wing Tide or Electoral Alternation with a Plebiscitarian Flavor?" *Columbia University Journal of Politics & Society* 26(2): 2–6.

Murillo, María Victoria and Schrank, Andrew. 2005. "With a Little Help from my Friends: Partisan Politics, Transnational Alliances, and Labor Rights in Latin America." *Comparative Political Studies* 38(8): 971–99.

Musacchio, Aldo, Lazzarini, Sergio G., and Aguilera, Ruth V. 2015. "New Varieties of State Capitalism: Strategic and Governance Implications." *Academy of Management Perspectives* 29(1): 115–31.

Myint, Hla. 1954–5. "The Gains from International Trade and the Backward Countries." *Review of Economic Studies* 22(2): 129–42.

References

Myint, Hla. 1965. "Economic Theory and the Underdeveloped Countries." *Journal of Political Economy* 73(5): 477–91.

Naím, Moisés. 2000. "Washington Consensus or Washington Confusion?" *Foreign Policy* 118 (Spring): 86–103.

NASA. 2010. "Road Transportation Emerges as Key Driver of Warming." NASA News & Feature Releases, February 18.

Navarro-Navarro, Luis Alan, Moreno-Vazquez, Jose Luis, and Scott, Christopher A. 2017. "Social Networks for Management of Water Scarcity: Evidence from the San Miguel Watershed, Sonora, Mexico." *Water Alternatives* 10(1): 41–64.

Nee, Victor. 2018. "Middle-Range Theories of Institutional Change." *Sociological Forum* 33(4): 845–54.

Nehru, Vikram. 1993. "How International Economic Links Affect East Asia." Washington: World Bank.

Neiburg, Federico. 2006. "Inflation: Economists and Economic Cultures in Brazil and Argentina." *Comparative Studies in Society and History* 48(3): 604–33.

Nelson, Janet. 2007. "The Dark Ages." *History Workshop Journal* 63(1): 191–201.

Newman, R. A. 1987. "Effects of Density and Predation on *Scaphiopus couchi* Tadpoles in Desert Ponds." *Oecologia* 71(2): 301–7.

North, Douglass and Thomas, Robert Paul. 1973. *The Rise of the Western World*. Cambridge: Cambridge University Press.

Numazaki, Ichiro. 1986. "Networks of Taiwanese Big Business: A Preliminary Analysis." *Modern China* 12(4): 487–34.

Numazaki, Ichiro. 1991. "State and Business in Postwar Taiwan: Comment on Hamilton and Biggart." *American Journal of Sociology* 96(4): 993–9.

Numerato, Dino, Salvatore, Domenico, and Fattore, Giovanni. 2012. "The Impact of Management on Medical Professionalism: A Review." *Sociology of Health & Illness* 34(4): 626–44.

Nunes, Evelyn Monteiro Pereira. 2016. *Essays on Development and Human Capital Investment*. PhD dissertation, Pennsylvania State University.

Nussbaum, Martha. 2011. *Creating Capabilities*. Cambridge: Harvard University Press.

OECD (Organisation for Economic Co-operation and Development). 2013. *Main Science and Technology Indicators* 2021(2).

Offe, Claus and Wiesenthal, Helmut. 1980. "Two Logics of Collective Action: Theoretical Notes on Social Class and Organizational Form," *Political Power and Social Theory* 1: 6–115.

O'Hearn, Denis. 2001. *The Atlantic Economy: Britain, the US, and Ireland*. Manchester: Manchester University Press.

Olsen, Johan. 2005. "Maybe It Is Time to Rediscover Bureaucracy." *Journal of Public Administration Research and Theory* 16: 1–24.

Olson, Mancur. 1965. *The Logic of Collective Action: Public Goods and the Theory of Groups*. Cambridge: Harvard University Press.

References

Öniş, Ziya and Kutlay, Mustafa. 2010. "The Global Political Economy of Right-wing Populism: Deconstructing the Paradox." *The International Spectator* 55(2): 108–26.

Oster, Emily. 2012. "You're Dividing the Chores Wrong." *Slate*, November 21.

Pack, Howard and Westphal, Larry. 1986. "Industrial Strategy and Technological Change: Theory versus Reality." *Journal of Development Economics* 22(1): 87–128.

Padgett, John and Ansell, Christopher. 1993. "Robust Action and the Rise of the Medici, 1400–1434." *American Journal of Sociology* 98(6): 1259–1319.

Palma, Gabriel. 1978. "Dependency: A Formal Theory of Underdevelopment or a Methodology for the Analysis of Concrete Situations of Underdevelopment." *World Development* 6: 881–924.

Pamuk, Şevket and Shatzmiller, Maya. 2014. "Plagues, Wages, and Economic Change in the Islamic Middle East, 700–1500." *Journal of Economic History* 74(1): 196–229.

Park, Myung-Ho. 2013. "Land Reform in Korea." Knowledge Sharing Program. Seoul: Ministry of Strategy and Finance.

Parsons, Talcott. 1970. "Theory in the Humanities and Sociology." *Daedalus* 99(2): 495–523.

Patrinos, Harry and Psacharopoulos, George. 2011. "Education: Past, Present and Future Global Challenges." Policy Research Working Paper 5616. Washington: World Bank.

Pellow, David and Nyseth-Brehm, Hollie. 2013. "An Environmental Sociology for the Twenty-First Century." *Annual Review of Sociology* 39: 229–50.

Peltonen, Matti. 2008. "The Weber Thesis and Economic Historians." *Max Weber Studies* 8(1): 79–98.

Penningroth, Dylan. 1997. "Slavery, Freedom, and Social Claims to Property among African Americans in Liberty County, Georgia, 1850–1880." *Journal of American History* 84(2): 405–35.

Pinheiro, Diogo, Chwieroth, Jeffrey, and Hicks, Alexander. 2015. "Do International Nongovernmental Organizations Inhibit Globalization? The Case of Capital Account Liberalization in Developing Countries." *European Journal of International Relations* 21(1): 146–70.

Piore, Michael. 1973. "Fragments of a 'Sociological' Theory of Wages." *American Economic Review* 63(2): 377–84.

Pokharel, Atul. 2014. "A Theory of Sustained Cooperation with Evidence from Irrigation Institutions in Nepal." PhD dissertation Cambridge: MIT.

Polanyi, Karl. 1944. *The Great Transformation*. New York: Farrar and Rinehart.

Polillo, Simone and Guillén, Mauro. 2005. "Globalization Pressures and the State: The Worldwide Spread of Central Bank Independence." *American Journal of Sociology* 110(6): 1764–802.

Popp Berman, Elizabeth. 2022. *Thinking Like an Economist: How Efficiency Replaced Equality in US Public Policy*. Princeton: Princeton University Press.

References

Portes, Alejandro. 1983. "The Informal Sector: Definition, Controversy, and Relation to National Development." *Review* 7(1): 151–74.

Portes, Alejandro. 1996. "Review of *Embedded Autonomy: States and Industrial Transformation*, by Peter Evans." *Contemporary Sociology* 25(2): 175–6.

Portes, Alejandro. 1997. "Neoliberalism and the Sociology of Development: Emerging Trends and Unanticipated Facts." *Population & Development Review* 23(2): 229–59.

Portes, Alejandro. 1998. "Social Capital: Its Origins and Applications in Modern Sociology." *Annual Review of Sociology* 24: 1–24.

Portes, Alejandro. 2006. "Institutions and Development: A Conceptual Reanalysis." *Population & Development Review* 32(2): 233–62.

Portes, Alejandro and Kincaid, A. Douglas. 1989. "Sociology and Development in the 1990s: Critical Challenges and Empirical Trends." *Sociological Forum* 4(4): 479–503.

Portes, Alejandro and Koob, Saskia Sassen. 1987. "Making It Underground: Comparative Material on the Informal Sector in Western Market Economies." *American Journal of Sociology* 93(1): 30–61.

Portes, Alejandro and Landolt, Patricia. 1996. "The Downside of Social Capital." *The American Prospect* 26: 18–22.

Postiglione, Gerard and Jiao, Ben. 2009. "Tibet's Relocated Schooling: Popularization Reconsidered." *Asian Survey* 49(5): 895–914.

Prebisch, Raúl. 1959. "Commercial Policy in the Underdeveloped Countries." *American Economic Review* 49(2): 251–73.

Preston, Lewis. 1993. "Foreword," in World Bank, *The East Asian Miracle: Economic Growth and Public Policy*. Oxford: Oxford University Press, pp. v–vii.

Pritchett, Lant. 2009. "Is India a Flailing State? Detours on the Four Lane Highway to Modernization." HKS Faculty Research Working Paper Series RWP09-013, John F. Kennedy School of Government, Harvard University.

Pritchett, Lant and Summers, Lawrence. 1996. "Wealthier Is Healthier." *Journal of Human Resources* 31(4): 841–68.

Przeworski, Adam. 2004. "The Last Instance: Are Institutions the Primary Cause of Economic Development?" *European Journal of Sociology* 45(2): 165–88.

Qin, Amy. 2020. "In China's Crackdown on Muslims, Children Have Not Been Spared." *New York Times*, October 15.

Qizilbash, Mozafar. 1996. "Capabilities, Well-Being and Development: A Survey." *Journal of Development Studies* 33(2): 143–62.

Quark, Amy. 2013. *Global Rivalries: Standards Wars and the Transnational Cotton Trade*. Chicago: University of Chicago Press.

Quinn, Aine. 2019. "Putin's Costly Protectionism Experiment Is a Lesson for Trump." *Bloomberg*, October 2.

Radelet, Steven and Sachs, Jeffrey. 1997. "Asia's Reemergence." *Foreign Affairs* 76(6): 44–59.

References

Ram, Rati. 2015. "International Income Inequality, 2005–2011: What a Difference 6 Years Can Make." *Applied Economics* 47(56): 6148–54.

Ranis, Gustav. 1985. "Can the East Asian Model of Development Be Generalized? A Comment." *World Development* 13(4): 543–5.

Rediker, Marcus. 1987. *Between the Devil and the Deep Blue Sea: Merchant Seamen, Pirates and the Anglo-American Maritime World, 1700–1750.* Cambridge: Cambridge University Press.

Reher, David. 2011. "Economic and Social Implications of the Demographic Transition." *Population & Development Review* 37: 11–33.

Reyntjens, Filip. 2011. "Constructing the Truth, Dealing with Dissent, Domesticating the World: Governance in Post-Genocide Rwanda." *African Affairs* 110(438): 1–34.

Rice, James. 2007. "Ecological Unequal Exchange: Consumption, Equity, and Unsustainable Structural Relationships within the Global Economy." *International Journal of Comparative Sociology* 488(1): 43–72.

Rickard, Stephanie and Kono, Daniel. 2014. "Think Globally, Buy Locally: International Agreements and Government Procurement." *Review of International Organizations* 9(3): 333–52.

Riley, James. 2005. "Estimates of Regional and Global Life Expectancy, 1800–2001." *Population and Development Review* 31(3): 537–43.

Riley, Dylan and Desai, Manali. 2007. "The Passive Revolutionary Route to the Modern World: Italy and India in Comparative Perspective." *Comparative Studies in Society and History* 49(4): 815–47.

Ríos-Figueroa, Julio and Staton, Jeffrey. 2014. "An Evaluation of Cross-National Measures of Judicial Independence." *Journal of Law, Economics, & Organization* 30(1): 104–37.

Ritzer, George. 2011. *Sociological Theory*, 8th edn. New York: McGraw-Hill.

Roberts, Anthea. 2020. "How Globalization Came to the Brink of Collapse." *Barron's*, April 2.

Robberson, Tod. 1995. "Peso Crisis Spurs Migrants' Quest for Dollars." *Washington Post*, January 28. Available at https://www.washingtonpost.com/archive/politics/1995/01/28/peso-crisis-spurs-migrants-quest-for-dollars/40ee21ee-98d0-443c-bc4b-1472fbcff91b/

Robles, Jorge. 2019. "Hyundai Motor: Restructuring Efforts Led By Activist Hedge Fund Manager Elliott Could Unlock Huge Returns." *Seeking Alpha*, January 28.

Rodrik, Dani. 1995. "Getting Interventions Right: How South Korea and Taiwan Grew Rich." *Economic Policy* 10(20): 53–107.

Rodrik, Dani. 1996. "Understanding Economic Policy Reform." *Journal of Economic Literature* 34(1): 9–41.

Roemer, John. 1982. "Property Relations vs. Surplus Value in Marxian Exploitation." *Philosophy & Public Affairs* 11(4): 281–314.

Roemer, John. 1988. *Free to Lose: An Introduction to Marxian Economic Philosophy.* Cambridge: Harvard University Press.

Roemer, John. 2020. "What Egalitarianism Requires: An Interview with John E. Roemer." Interview with Akshath Jitendranath and Marina Uzunova. *Erasmus Journal of Politics and Economics* 13(2): 127–76.

Romer, Paul. 1986. "Increasing Returns and Long-Run Growth." *Journal of Political Economy* 94(5): 1002–37.

Romer, Paul. 1993. "Two Strategies for Economic Development: Using Ideas and Producing Ideas," in *Proceedings of the World Bank Annual Conference on Development Economics* 6(1): 63–92. Washington: World Bank.

Rostow, W. W. 1956. "The Take-Off into Self-Sustained Growth." *Economic Journal* 66(261): 25–48.

Rostow, W. W. 1957. "The Interrelation of Theory and Economic History." *Journal of Economic History* 17(4): 509–23.

Rostow, W. W. 1959. "The Stages of Economic Growth." *Economic History Review* 12(1): 1–16.

Rostow, W. W. 1960. *The Stages of Economic Growth: A Non-Communist Manifesto*. Cambridge: Harvard University Press.

Rostow, W. W. 1963. "Introduction and Epilogue," in W. W. Rostow (ed.), *The Economics of Take-Off into Sustained Growth*. New York: Palgrave Macmillan, pp. xxiii–xxvi.

Rostow, W. W. 1970. "A Reply to Professor Felix." *Journal of Economic History* 30(1): 196–200.

Rostow, W. W. 1982. "Review of *Population and Technological Change: A Study of Long-Term Trends*, by Ester Boserup." *Journal of Economic History* 42(1): 265–6.

Rowden, Rick. 1998/9. "Developing Savages, Spreading Democracy: Popular Conceptions of North–South Relations." *Berkeley Journal of Sociology* 43: 149–87.

Rueschemeyer, Dietrich. 1994. "Variations on Two Themes in Durkheim's 'Division du travail': Power, Solidarity, and Meaning in Division of Labor." *Sociological Forum* 9(1): 59–71.

Rueschemeyer, Dietrich. 2005. "Building States – Inherently a Long-Term Process? An Argument from Theory," in Matthew Lange and Dietrich Rueschemeyer (eds), *States and Development: Historical Antecedents of Stagnation and Advance*. New York: Palgrave Macmillan, pp. 143–64.

Ruggie, John Gerard. 1998. "What Makes the World Hang Together? Neo-Utilitarianism and the Social Constructivist Challenge." *International Organization* 52(4): 855–85.

Rwakakamba, Morrison. 2016. "Harvard Platform is Justice for Kagame and Rwanda." *Harvard Crimson*, March 2.

Ryu, Jung-Hyun. 2017. "Building World-Class Universities in Developing Systems: The Success Case of the Indian Institutes of Technology." *Issues and Ideas in Education* 5(1): 39–57. Cambridge: National Bureau of Economic Research.

References

Sachs, Jeffrey. 1989. "Social Conflict and Populist Policies in Latin America." NBER Working Paper Series 2897. Cambridge: National Bureau of Economic Research.

Sachs, Jeffrey. 2000. "Notes on a New Sociology of Economic Development," in Lawrence Harrison and Samuel Huntington (eds), *Culture Matters: How Values Shape Human Progress*. New York: Basic Books, pp. 29–43.

Samford, Steven. 2017. "Networks, Brokerage, and State-Led Technology Diffusion in Small Industry." *American Journal of Sociology* 122(5): 1339–70.

Samuelson. Paul. 1971. "Understanding the Marxian Notion of Exploitation: A Summary of the So-Called Transformation Problem between Marxian Values and Competitive Prices." *Journal of Economic Literature* 9(2): 399–431.

Sánchez, Omar. 2003. "The Rise and Fall of the Dependency Movement: Does It Inform Underdevelopment Today?" *Estudios Interdisciplinarios de América Latina y el Caribe* 14(2): 31–50.

Sandilands, Roger. 2015. "Globalization and the Ladder of Comparative Advantage," in Toshiaki Hirai (ed.), *Capitalism and the World Economy*. New York: Routledge, ch. 4.

Sangiovanni, Andrea. 2011. "Global Justice and the Moral Arbitrariness of Birth." *The Monist* 94(4): 571–83.

Sayer, Derek. 1992. "A Notable Administration: English State Formation and the Rise of Capitalism." *American Journal of Sociology* 97(4): 1382–415.

Schleicher, Andreas. 2019. *PISA 2018: Insights and Interpretations*. Paris: OECD.

Schneider, Ben Ross. 2009. "Hierarchical Market Economies and Varieties of Capitalism in Latin America." *Journal of Latin American Studies* 41(3): 553–75.

Schrank, Andrew. 2003. "Foreign Investors, 'Flying Geese,' and the Limits to Export-led Development in the Dominican Republic." *Theory & Society* 32: 415–43.

Schrank, Andrew. 2005. "Conquering, Comprador, or Competitive? The National Bourgeoisie in the Developing World," in Frederick Buttel and Philip McMichael (eds), *Research in Rural Sociology and Development Volume 11: New Directions in the Sociology of Global Development*. Amsterdam: JAI/ Elsevier Science, pp. 91–120.

Schrank, Andrew. 2007. "Asian Industrialization in Latin American Perspective: The Limits to Institutional Analysis." *Latin American Politics & Society* 49(2): 183–200.

Schrank, Andrew. 2009. "Professionalization and Probity in a Patrimonial State: Labor Inspection in the Dominican Republic." *Latin American Politics and Society* 51(2): 91–115.

Schrank, Andrew. 2015. "Toward a New Economic Sociology of Development." *Sociology of Development* 1(2): 233–58.

References

Schrank, Andrew. 2017. "The Political Economy of Performance Standards: Automotive Industrial Policy in Comparative Historical Perspective." *Journal of Development Studies* 53(12): 2029–49.

Schrank, Andrew. 2019. "Cross-Class Coalitions and Collective Goods: The *Farmacias del Pueblo* in the Dominican Republic." *Comparative Politics* 51(2): 259–74.

Schrank, Andrew. 2020. "Mobile Professionals and Metropolitan Models: The German Roots of Vocational Education in Latin America." *European Journal of Sociology* 61(2): 185–218.

Schrank, Andrew. 2021. "Regulators without Borders? Labor Inspectors in Latin America and Beyond." *Global Networks* 21(4): 723–48.

Schrank, Andrew and Kurtz, Marcus. 2005. "Credit Where Credit Is Due: Open Economy Industrial Policy and Export Diversification in Latin America and the Caribbean." *Politics & Society* 33(4): 671–702.

Schrank, Andrew and Whitford, Josh. 2011. "Anatomy of Network Failure." *Sociological Theory* 29(3): 151–77.

Schuurman, Frans. 2003. "Social Capital: The Politico-Emancipatory Potential of a Disputed Concept." *Third World Quarterly* 24(6): 991–1010.

Schuyler, Robert Livingston. 1964. "History and Historical Criticism: Recent Work of Richardson and Sayles." *Journal of British Studies* 3(2): 1–23.

Schwartz, Herman. 2007. "Dependency or Institutions? Economic Geography, Causal Mechanisms, and Logic in the Understanding of Development." *Studies in Comparative International Development* 42: 115–35.

Schwinn, Thomas. 2012. "Globalisation and Regional Variety: Problems of Theorization." *Comparative Education* 48(4): 525–43.

Scott, James. 1998. *Seeing Like a State: How Certain Schemes to Improve the Human Condition Have Failed*. New Haven: Yale University Press.

Scott, James. 2009. *The Art of Not Being Governed: An Anarchist History of Upland Southeast Asia*. New Haven: Yale University Press.

Seers, Dudley. 1963. "The Limitations of the Special Case." *Bulletin of the Oxford University Institute of Economics & Statistics* 25(2): 77–98.

Selznick, Philip. 1952. *The Organizational Weapon*. Santa Monica: Rand Corporation.

Sen, Amartya. 1979. "Equality of What?" The Tanner Lecture on Human Values, delivered at Stanford University, May 22.

Sen, Amartya. 1981. "Public Action and the Quality of Life in Developing Countries." *Oxford Bulletin of Economics and Statistics* 43(4): 287–319.

Sen, Amartya. 1988. "Freedom of Choice: Concept and Content." *European Economic Review* 32: 269–94.

Sen, Amartya. 1999. *Development as Freedom*. New York: Alfred A. Knopf.

Seth, Michael. 2013. "An Unpromising Recovery: South Korea's Post-Korean War Economic Development: 1953–1961." *Education about Asia* 18(3): 42–5.

Shadlen, Kenneth C. 2008. "Globalization, Power, and Integration: The Political

Economy of Regional and Bilateral Trade Agreements in the Americas." *Journal of Development Studies* 44(1): 1–20.

Shadlen, Kenneth, Schrank, Andrew, and Kurtz, Marcus J. 2005. "The Political Economy of Intellectual Property Protection: The Case of Software." *International Studies Quarterly* 49(1): 45–71.

Shandra, John, Leckband, Christopher, and London, Bruce. 2009. "Ecologically Unequal Exchange and Deforestation: A Cross-National Analysis of Forestry Export Flows." *Organization & Environment* 22(3): 293–310.

Shaw, D. John. 2002. *Sir Hans Singer: The Life and Work of a Development Economist*. New York: Palgrave Macmillan.

Shaw-Taylor, Leigh. 2020. "An Introduction to the History of Infectious Diseases, Epidemics and the Early Phases of the Long-run Decline in Mortality." *Economic History Review* 73(3): E1–E19.

Shin, Gi-Wook. 1998. "Agrarian Conflict and the Origins of Korean Capitalism." *American Journal of Sociology* 103(5): 1309–51.

Shin, Gi-Wook. 2006. "Neither 'Sprouts' nor 'Offspring': The Agrarian Roots of Korean Capitalism," in Chang Yun-Shik and Steven Hugh Lee (eds), *Transformations in Twentieth-Century Korea*. London: Routledge, pp. 33–63.

Shin, Gi-Wook and Hytrek, Gary. 2002. "Social Conflict and Regime Formation: A Comparative Study of South Korea and Costa Rica." *International Sociology* 17(4): 459–80.

Sicat, Gerardo. 2014. "The Bangsamoro's Labor Market Policies: How to Promote More Employment and Eradicate Poverty." *Philippine Star*, September 24.

Siegel, Matt. 2013. "Australia Adopts Tough Measures to Curb Asylum Seekers." *New York Times*, July 19.

Silva, Eduardo. 1993. "Capitalist Coalitions, the State, and Neoliberal Economic Restructuring: Chile, 1973–88." *World Politics* 45(4): 526–59.

Silver, Beverly. 2019. "Afterword: Reflections on 'Capitalist Development in Hostile Environments.'" *Journal of Agrarian Change* 19(3): 569–76.

Simmons, Beth, Dobbin, Frank, and Garrett, Geoffrey. 2006. "Introduction: The International Diffusion of Liberalism." *International Organization* 60(4): 781–810.

Simmons, Erica. 2014. "Grievances Do Matter in Mobilization." *Theory & Society* 43(5): 513–46.

Singer, Hans. 1961. "Trends in Economic Thought on Underdevelopment." *Social Research* 28(4): 387–414.

Sjoberg, Gideon. 1955. "The Preindustrial City." *American Journal of Sociology* 60(5): 438–45.

Skocpol, Theda. 1977. "Wallerstein's World Capitalist System: A Theoretical and Historical Critique." *American Journal of Sociology* 82(5): 1075–90.

Smart, Alan. 2008. "Social Capital." *Anthropologica* 50(2): 409–16.

Smelser, Neil and Swedberg, Richard. 2005. *The Handbook of Economic Sociology*, 2nd edn. Princeton: Princeton University Press.

References

Smith, Jackie. 2001. "Globalizing Resistance: The Battle of Seattle and the Future of Social Movements." *Mobilization* 6: 1–20.

Smith, Tony. 1979. "The Underdevelopment of Development Literature: The Case of Dependency Theory." *World Politics* 31(2): 247–88.

Solow, Robert. 1980. "On Theories of Unemployment." *American Economic Review* 70(1): 1–11.

Solow, Robert. 2001. "Applying Growth Theory across Countries." *World Bank Economic Review* 15(2): 283–88.

Somers, Kay. 2007. "Exploring the United Nations' Human Development Index." *Mathematics Teacher* 101(3): 214–24.

Sorensen, Clark W. 1994. "Success and Education in South Korea." *Comparative Education Review* 38(1): 10–35.

Sorj, Bernardo and Fausto, Sergio. 2011. "The Sociologist and the Politician: An Interview with Fernando Henrique Cardoso." *Latin American Perspectives* 38(3): 169–93.

Spillman, Lyn and Strand, Michael. 2013. "Interest-Oriented Action." *Annual Review of Sociology* 39: 85–104.

Stark, David. 1996. "Recombinant Property in East European Capitalism." *American Journal of Sociology* 101(4): 993–1027.

Stevenson, Jonathan. 2017. "The Cold Warrior Who Never Apologized." *New York Times*, September 8.

Stinchcombe, Arthur. 1965. "Social Structure and Organizations," in James March (ed.), *Handbook of Organizations*. Chicago: Rand McNally, pp. 142–93.

Stinchcombe, Arthur. 1968. *Constructing Social Theories*. New York: Harcourt, Brace, & World.

Stinchcombe, Arthur. 1974. *Creating Efficient Industrial Administrations*. New York: Academic Press.

Stinchcombe, Arthur. 1986. "Reason and Rationality." *Sociological Theory* 4(2): 151–66.

Stinchcombe, Arthur. 1997. "On the Virtues of the Old Institutionalism." *Annual Review of Sociology* 23: 1–18.

Stinchcombe, Arthur. 1999. "Ending Revolutions and Building New Governments." *Annual Review of Political Science* 2: 49–73.

Stinchcombe, Arthur. 2003. "The Preconditions of World Capitalism: Weber Updated." *Journal of Political Philosophy* 11(4): 411–36.

Storm, Servaas. 2015. "Structural Change." *Development & Change* 46(4): 666–99.

Subramanian, Arvind. 2014. "Keynote Speech by Dr Arvind Subramanian, Peterson Institute for International Economics." NSE-NYU Indian Financial Markets Conference, Mumbai, August 4.

Sung-Chan, Hong. 2013. "Land Reform and Large Landlords in South Korea's Modernization Project." *Seoul Journal of Korean Studies* 26(1): 23–45.

References

Surowiecki, James. 2015. "Why the Rich Are So Much Richer." *New York Review of Books*, September 24.

Swedberg, Richard. 1997. "New Economic Sociology: What Has Been Accomplished, What Is Ahead?" *Acta Sociologica* 40(2): 161–82.

Swedberg, Richard. 2005. "Towards an Economic Sociology of Capitalism." *L'Année sociologique* 55(2): 419–49.

Szelényi, Iván. 1978. "Social Inequalities in State Socialist Redistributive Economies." *International Journal of Comparative Sociology* 19(1/2): 63–87.

Szreter, Simon. 2018. "Marx on Population: A Bicentenary Celebration." *Population and Development Review* 44(4): 745–69.

Taiwan Review. 1964. "Free Enterprise for Prosperity," June 1. Available at https://taiwantoday.tw/news.php?unit=4&post=7127

Takeuchi, Shinichi. 2019. "Development and Developmentalism in Post-genocide Rwanda," in Yusuke Takagi, Veerayooth Kanchoochat, and Tetsushi Sonobe (eds), *Developmental State Building: The Politics of Emerging Economies*. Singapore: Springer, pp. 121–34.

Tannenberg, Marcus. 2014. "On the Road to Better Governance: The 'Middle Class Particularism' and Quality of Government." MA thesis, University of Gothenburg.

Tawney, R. H. 1929. *Equality*. New York: Barnes & Noble.

Taylor, Matthew. 2020. "Fossil Fuel Pollution behind 4m Premature Deaths a Year." *Guardian*, February 11.

Taylor, Scott. 2014. "Capitalism and African Business Cultures." WIDER Working Paper 2014/054. Helsinki: United Nations University World Institute for Development Economics Research.

Teckenberg, Wolfgang. 1989. "The Stability of Occupational Structures, Social Mobility, and Interest Formation: The USSR as an Estatist Society in Comparison with Class Societies." *International Journal of Sociology* 19(2): 28–75.

Telles, Edward. 1995. "Structural Sources of Socioeconomic Segregation in Brazilian Metropolitan Areas." *American Journal of Sociology* 100(5): 1199–223.

Telles, Edward. 2014. *Pigmentocracies: Ethnicity, Race, and Color in Latin America*. Chapel Hill: University of North Carolina Press.

Telles, Edward, Flores, René D., and Urrea, Fernando. 2015. "Pigmentocracies: Educational Iinequality, Skin Color and Census Ethnoracial Identification in Eight Latin American Countries." *Research in Social Stratification and Mobility* 40: 39–58.

Tendler, Judith. 2002. "Fear of Education." Background paper for *Inequality and the State in Latin America and the Caribbean*. Washington: World Bank.

Therborn, Göran. 2012. "Class in the 21st Century." *New Left Review* 78 (November/December): 5–29.

References

Therborn, Göran. 2014. "New Masses: Social Bases of Resistance." *New Left Review* 85 (January/February): 7–16.

Thoene, Ulf. 2019. "Easing the Tension between the State and the Market? Developing Social Protection and Labour Law during Latin American Industrialization." *Cogent Social Sciences* 5(1): 1–17.

Thomas, Alfred. 1965. "Latin American Nationalism and the United States." *Journal of Inter-American Studies* 7(1): 5–13.

Thornton, Arland. 2001. "The Developmental Paradigm, Reading History Sideways, and Family Change." *Demography* 38(4): 449–65.

Tomaskovic-Devey, Donald and Avent-Holt, Dustin. 2019. *Relational Inequalities: An Organizational Approach.* Oxford: Oxford University Press.

Torche, Florencia. 2005. "Unequal but Fluid: Social Mobility in Chile in Comparative Perspective." *American Sociological Review* 70(3): 422–50.

Torche, Florencia. 2010a. "Economic Crisis and Inequality of Educational Opportunity in Latin America." *Sociology of Education* 83(2): 85–110.

Torche, Florencia. 2010b. "Educational Assortative Mating and Inequality: A Comparative Analysis of Three Latin American Countries." *Demography* 47(2): 481–502.

Torche, Florencia. 2014. "Intergenerational Mobility and Economic Inequality: The Latin American Case." *Annual Review of Sociology* 40: 619–42.

Toye, John. 2009. "Solow in the Tropics." *History of Political Economy* 41 (suppl.): 221–40.

Troianovski, Anton. 2021. "'You Can't Trust Anyone': Russia's Hidden Covid Toll Is an Open Secret." *New York Times*, October 18.

UBS. 2006. *A Comparison of Purchasing Power around the World.* Zürich: UBS.

UNCTAD (United Nations Conference on Trade and Development). 2018. *World Investment Report 2018: Investment and New Industrial Policies.* Geneva: UNCTAD.

UNDP (United Nations Development Programme). 2007. "Case Evidence on 'Ethics and Values in Civil Service Reforms.'" A UNDP Capacity Development Resource. New York: UNDP Capacity Development Group.

UNDP (United Nations Development Programme). 2019. "*Human Development Report 2019:* Beyond Income, Beyond Averages, Beyond Today: Inequalities in Human Development in the 21st Century." Technical notes. New York: UNDP.

UNESCO (United Nations Educational, Scientific, and Cultural Organization). 2017. *Reading the Past, Writing the Future: Fifty Years of Promoting Literacy.* Paris: UNESCO.

University of California Press. 2021. *Sociology of Development* website. Available at https://online.ucpress.edu/socdev/pages/About

USDOC (United States Department of Commerce). 1980. "Survey of Automotive Trade Restrictions Maintained by Selected Nations." Washington: Government Printing Office.

USDOC (United States Department of Commerce). 1985. *US Direct Investment*

References

Abroad: 1982 Benchmark Survey Data. December. Washington: Government Printing Office.

Valenzuela, J. Samuel and Valenzuela, Antonio. 1978. "Modernization and Dependency: Alternative Perspectives in the Study of Latin American Underdevelopment." *Comparative Politics* 10(4): 535–57.

Van Gunten, Tod. 2015. "Cycles of Polarization and Settlement: Diffusion and Transformation in the Macroeconomic Policy Field." *Theory & Society* 44: 321–54.

Varga, Mahai. 2021. "The Return of Economic Nationalism to East Central Europe: Right-wing Intellectual Milieus and Anti-liberal Resentment." *Nations & Nationalism* 27: 206–22.

Vasconcellos, Eduardo. 1997. "The Demand for Cars in Developing Countries." *Transportation Research A* 31(3): 245–58.

Velthuis, Olav. 2006. "Inside a World of Spin: Four Days at the World Trade Organization." *Ethnography* 7(1): 125–50.

Villarreal, Andrés. 2010. "Stratification by Skin Color in Contemporary Mexico." *American Sociological Review* 75(5): 652–78.

Viterna, Jocelyn and Robertson, Cassandra. 2015. "New Directions for the Sociology of Development." *Annual Review of Sociology* 41: 243–69.

Vodopivec, Milan. 1990. *The Labor Market and the Transition of Socialist Economies.* Washington: World Bank.

Wachs, Diego. 2021. "The Politics of Demography in Unequal Societies: Argentina and Brazil Compared," in Achim Goerres and Pierre Vanhuysse (eds), *Global Political Demography: The Politics of Population Change.* Cham: Palgrave Macmillan, pp. 303–24.

Wackernagel, Mathis, Monfreda, Chad, Erb, Karl-Heinz, Haberl, Helmut, and Schulz, Niels. 2004. "Ecological Footprint Time Series of Austria, the Philippines, and South Korea for 1961–1999: Comparing the Conventional Approach to an 'Actual Land Area' Approach." *Land Use Policy* 21(3): 261–9.

Wade, Robert. 1990. *Governing the Market: Economic Theory and the Role of Government in East Asian Industrialization.* Princeton: Princeton University Press.

Wade, Robert. 1992. "East Asia's Economic Success: Conflicting Perspectives, Partial Insights, Shaky Evidence." *World Politics* 44(2): 270–320.

Wade, Robert. 1993. "Managing Trade: Taiwan and South Korea as Challenges to Economics and Political Science." *Comparative Politics* 25(2): 147–67.

Wade, Robert. 1996. "Japan, the World Bank, and the Art of Paradigm Maintenance: the *East Asian Miracle* in Political Perspective." *New Left Review* 217 (May/June): 3–36.

Wade, Robert. 2002. "Bridging the Digital Divide: New Route to Development or New Form of Dependency?" *Global Governance* 8(4): 443–66.

Wade, Robert. 2004. "Is Globalization Reducing Poverty and Inequality?" *International Journal of Health Services* 34(3): 381–414.

References

Wade, Robert. 2012. "The Politics behind World Bank Statistics: The Case of China's Income." *Economic and Political Weekly* 47(25): 17–18.

Wallerstein, Immanuel. 1974a. "Dependence in an Interdependent World: The Limited Possibilities of Transformation within the Capitalist World Economy." *African Studies Review* 17(1): 1–26.

Wallerstein, Immanuel. 1974b. "The Rise and Future Demise of the World Capitalist System: Concepts for Comparative Analysis." *Comparative Studies in Society and History* 16(4): 387–415.

Wallerstein, Immanuel. 1976. "Semi-Peripheral Countries and the Contemporary World Crisis." *Theory & Society* 3(4): 463–82.

Wallerstein, Immanuel. 1981-2. "The USA in Today's World." *Contemporary Marxism* 4 (Winter): 11–17.

Wallerstein, Immanuel. 1988. "Development: Lodestar or Illusion?" *Economic and Political Weekly* 23(39): 2017–23.

Wallerstein, Immanuel. 1997a. "Eurocentrism and Its Avatars: The Dilemmas of Social Science." *Sociological Bulletin* 46(1): 21–39.

Wallerstein, Immanuel. 1997b. "Social Science and the Communist Interlude, or Interpretations of Contemporary History." *Polish Sociological Review* 117: 3–12.

Wallerstein, Immanuel. 2004. "The Ecology and the Economy: What Is Rational?" *Review* 27(4): 273–83.

Watkins, Mel. 1978. "The Economics of Nationalism and the Nationality of Economics: A Critique of Neoclassical Theorizing." *Canadian Journal of Economics* 11(suppl.): S87–S120.

Webber, Jude. 2013. "IMF Acts over Flawed Argentine Economic Data." *Financial Times*, February 1.

Weber, Max. 1930. *The Protestant Ethic and the Spirit of Capitalism*. London: Routledge.

Wei, Yung. 1976 "Modernization Process in Taiwan: An Allocative Analysis." *Asian Survey* 16(3): 249–69.

Weisbrot, Mark. 1999. *Globalization: A Primer*. Washington: Center for Economics and Policy Research.

Weiss, Linda. 1998. *The Myth of the Powerless State*. Ithaca: Cornell University Press.

Weitz, Eric. 2019. *A World Divide: The Global Struggle for Human Rights in the Age of Nation-States*. Princeton: Princeton University Press.

Welzel, Christian and Inglehart, Ronald. 2001. "Human Development and the 'Explosion' of Democracy: Variations of Regime Change across 60 Societies." Discussion Paper FS III 01-202. Wissenschaftszentrum Berlin für Sozialforschung (WZB).

White, Ben. 2007. "Clifford Geertz: Singular Genius of Interpretive Anthropology." *Development & Change* 38(6): 1127–208.

Whittaker, D. Hugh. 2001. "Introduction," in D. Hugh Whittaker (ed.), *Social

References

Evolution, Economic Development and Culture: What It Means to Take Japan Seriously. Cheltenham: Edward Elgar, pp. 1–34.

Williamson, John. 1990. "What Washington Means by Policy Reform," in John Williamson (ed.), *Latin American Adjustment: How Much Has Happened?* Washington: Petersen Institute for International Economics, ch. 2.

Williamson, John. 2000. "What Should the World Bank Think about the Washington Consensus?" *World Bank Research Observer* 15(2): 251–64.

Williamson, John. 2003. "The Washington Consensus and Beyond." *Economic and Political Weekly* 38(15): 1475–81.

Williamson, John. 2009. "A Short History of the Washington Consensus." *Law and Business Review of the Americas* 15(1): 7–24.

Winthrop, Rebecca and McGivney, Eileen. 2015. "Why Wait 100 Years? Bridging the Gap in Global Education." Brookings Institution, June 10.

Wisman. Jon. 1986. "The Methodology of W. Arthur Lewis's Development Economics: Economics as Pedagogy." *World Development* 14(2): 165–80.

Wolf, Naomi. 2010. "The High Cost of Cheap Fashion." *The Globe and Mail,* July 5.

Wolfers, Justin. 2015. "How Economists Came to Dominate the Conversation." *New York Times,* January 23.

Wong, Kandy. 2022. "New bureaus to Drive SOEs' Green Goals." *South China Morning* Post, March 20.

Woo, Dae-Hyung and Kahm, Howard. 2017. "Road to School: Primary School Participation in Korea, 1911–1960." *Journal of American-East Asian Relations* 24: 184–208.

Woolcock, Michael. 1998. "Social Capital and Economic Development: Toward a Theoretical Synthesis and Policy Framework." *Theory & Society* 27(2): 151–208.

Woolcock, Michael. 2011. "Development Practitioners: Technocrats, Missionaries or Diplomats?" June 2. Available at https://amudu-gowripalan. blogspot.com/2011/06/development-practitioners-technocrats.html

World Bank. 1993. *The East Asian Miracle: Economic Growth and Public Policy.* Oxford: Oxford University Press.

World Bank. 2011. "Rwanda – Governance & Competitiveness TA Project." Project Information Document: Appraisal Stage. Report No. AB6794.

World Bank. 2019. *World Development Report 2019: The Changing Nature of Work.* Washington: World Bank.

World Bank. 2020. *World Development Indicators.* Available at https://data bank.worldbank.org/source/world-development-indicators

World Bank. 2021. *World Development Indicators.* Available at https://data bank.worldbank.org/source/world-development-indicators

World Bank. 2022. *World Development Indicators.* Available at https://data bank.worldbank.org/source/world-development-indicators

World Trade Organization. 2021. *WTO in Brief.* Geneva: WTO.

References

Wright, Erik Olin. 1974–5. "To Control or to Smash Bureaucracy: Weber and Lenin on Politics, the State, and Bureaucracy." *Berkeley Journal of Sociology* 19: 69–108.

Wright, Erik Olin. 1979. *Class Structure and Income Determination.* New York: Academic Press.

Wright, Erik Olin. 1980. "Class and Occupation." *Theory & Society* 9(1): 177–214.

Wright, Erik Olin. 1996. "Review of *Embedded Autonomy: States and Industrial Transformation*, by Peter Evans." *Contemporary Sociology* 25(2): 176–9.

Wright, Mike, Wood, Geoffrey, Musacchio, Aldo, Okhmatovskiy, Ilya, Grosman, Anna, and Doh, Jonathan. 2021. "The Return of State Capitalism? How the Covid-19 Pandemic Put the Liberal Market Economies to the Test." London: London School of Economics.

Wu, Mark. 2016. "The 'China Inc.' Challenge to Global Trade Governance." *Harvard International Law Journal* 57(2): 261–324.

Yellen, Janet. 1998. "The Continuing Importance of Trade Liberalization." *Business Economics* 33(1): 23–6.

Yenkey, Christopher. 2015. "Mobilizing a Market: Ethnic Segmentation and Investor Recruitment into the Nairobi Securities Exchange." *Administrative Science Quarterly* 60(4): 561–95.

Zapata, Francisco. 1990. "Towards a Latin American Sociology of Labour." *Journal of Latin American Studies* 22(2): 375–402.

Zelizer, Viviana. 1985. *Pricing the Priceless Child: The Changing Social Value of Children.* New York: Basic Books.

Zettelmeyer, Jeromin. 2006. "Growth and Reforms in Latin America: A Survey of Facts and Arguments." IMF Working Paper WP/06/210. Washington: International Monetary Fund.

Zhao, Ding-xin and Hall, John A. 1994. "State Power and Patterns of Late Development: Resolving the Crisis of the Sociology of Development." *Sociology* 28(1): 211–29.

Ziai, Aram. 2013. "The Discourse of 'Development' and Why the Concept Should Be Abandoned." *Development in Practice* 23(1): 123–46.

Zucker, Lynne. 1983. "Organizations as Institutions," in Samuel Bacharach (ed.), *Research in the Sociology of Organizations, Vol. 2.* Greenwich: JAI Press, pp. 1–47.

Zuckerman, Ezra. 2010. "What If We had Been in Charge? The Sociologist as Builder of Rational Institutions," in Michael Lounsbury and Paul M. Hirsch (eds), *Markets on Trial: The Economic Sociology of the US Financial Crisis: Part B.* Bingley: Emerald Group Publishing Limited, pp. 359–78.

Zuckerman, Ezra. 2012. "Construction, Concentration, and (Dis)Continuities in Social Valuations." *Annual Review of Sociology* 38: 223–45.

Index

Index

Index

Index

Index

Index